Genealogical Abstracts from Tennessee Newspapers

Volume 2
1803–1812

Compiled by
Sherida K. Eddlemon

HERITAGE BOOKS
2010

HERITAGE BOOKS
AN IMPRINT OF HERITAGE BOOKS, INC.

Books, CDs, and more—Worldwide

For our listing of thousands of titles see our website
at
www.HeritageBooks.com

Published 2010 by
HERITAGE BOOKS, INC.
Publishing Division
100 Railroad Ave. #104
Westminster, Maryland 21157

International Standard Book Numbers
Paperbound: 978-1-55613-215-5
Clothbound: 978-0-7884-8393-6

ACKNOWLEDGMENTS

I want to thank my parents, Amelia and Nelson Eddlemon, for their encouragement on this endeavor; and my great grandparents, Eugene Pike and Ollie Wilson Pike, who sparked my interest in the "good ol' days." I am most grateful to Dr. James Johnson's staff at the Memphis Shelby County Public Library.

PREFACE

There is not a complete census available for Tennessee until 1830; however Tennessee became a state in 1796. The missing census records create a void that these old papers help to fill, since they pinpoint people at a specific place and at a particular time.

When reading these newspapers, you are aware of the meaning of "freedom of the press." People were not afraid to voice their opinions on anything, such as politics, or the character of an individual. They fought to settle this land and bring civilization to the wilderness. These newpapers are a portrait of their struggle to establish a new country.

Orginal spelling, punctuation, and wording are used to retain the spirit of the times and of the people. The title of offices such as those after a clerk's or sheriff's name were often abbreviated. For example: c. l. c. The initials stand for "clerk of Lincoln County." The word "deceased" is often abbreviated as "dec."

There are many variations in spelling of surnames and words. For example: GAORE, GOOR, GOORE, GORE. Spelling could be different even in the same article.

Notices were often repeated. In those cases, the notice is only picked up once unless additional genealogical data is in a subsequent reprinting.

Notices or news were often reprinted from other newpapers. It was by this method that information crossed the frontier. However, usually only the name of the town was given and often the name of the orginal source of the information is missing.

I want to wish you good luck in finding your lost ancestor. Hopefully, you may find him in these pages.

T A B L E   O F   C O N T E N T S

The Carthage Gazette and Friend of the People
Published by William Moore

January 26, 1809, Vol. 1, No. 7

The following is a list of letters remaining at the post office in Carthage on January 1, 1809, per T. MCNUTT, p. m.: Thomas ALLEN, James HENDERSON, Theron BROWNFIELD, Sally ALLEN, William BALDRIDGE, Richard BRITTON, Benjamin BENNIT, Chesley BRIDGEWATER, Oliver BADGER, Nathaniel COWLEY, John CAMPBELL, Joshua CONGER, Geo. CROWDER, Joseph COMMONS, James DOHERTY, jun., Thomas DILLON, John H. DAVIS, John DOHERTY, Thomas FIZZLE, Elijah FULKS, James FOSTER, George GERMAN, James GREEN, John GYSTEN, David HANKS, James CASTER, Radar HARROD, Sophia LYNCH, Henry LYON, Geo. W. MARTIN, Patrick MARTIN, Mathew MIETON, Eliza MORRAY, Benjamin MCNAVIN, John M'MANN, Joseph M'RAVIN, Archd. W. OVERTON, William PORTER, William ROBERTSON, David STILLWELL, William STILLWELL, John SHOEMAKER, William SMITH, Lee SULLIVAN, James SPAIN, Stephen SAMPSON, Obediah SPRADBURG, Peter TORIAN, Daniel TREDWELL, James VANCE, Lloyd VANHOOK, William VODEN, Morgan WILLIAMS, James WILSON, John WARE, Robert WARE.

On the fourth Saturday in February next in the town of Williamsburg, there will be a public sale directed by the court of Jackson County of 10 acres on the Roaring River which belongs to James M'NIGHT. The property was taken at the influence of Wm. GREY. Jas. COOK, sheriff, December, 1808.

On the fourth Saturday in February next, there will be a public sale directed by the court of Davidson County of 400 acres in Jackson County on Rock Spring Creek which belong to Thomas DILLON. The property being offered for sale includes the plantation where David PARKER now lives. The property was taken at the influence of Joseph DEMERON. Jas. COOK, sheriff, December, 1808.

The following persons have written letters to the editor: Wm. WALTON, Arthur S. HOGUN, Lee SULLIVAN.

On the four Saturday in February next in the town of Williamsburg, there will be a public sale of one town lot which belongs to James BREADENS. The property was taken at the influence of Sherwood Parish TATE. Jas. COOK, sheriff.

On the fourth Saturday in February next, there will be a public sale directed by the court of the Winchester District of 200 acres on Martin's Creek which belongs to Wm. COOK. The property was taken at the influence of Edward Hogan TATE. Jas. COOK, sheriff, December, 1808.

The Kentucky route post rider will leave Carthage by way of Dixon Springs and pass by Samuel GARRISON on Trammel Creek, Mr. MITCHEL, South Precinct, Warren County, and Mr. MONROE's. The return route will pass by Col. BROWN's, south precinct, Capt. KARUTH's on Puncheon Camp Creek, Mr. RHODES' Cotton Machine, and Capt. WITCHER's on the ridge.

Washington City, December 20th. William WELLS, Indian agent, arrived from Fort Wayne with LITTLE TURTLE, a Miami Chief.

January 30, 1809, Vol. 1, No. 8

Mrs. Sally ANDERSON died in the town of Liberty on the 21st. She was the consort of Mathias ANDERSON of that town.

The following persons will receive money for the purpose of establishing a Cotton Mill: Michail NOURSE, Andrew WAY, Thomas CARPENTER, John GARDINAR, Thomas HERTY, George ANDREWS, Robert ELLIOT, C. H. VARDEN, Henry INGLE, Charles MINSITS, Joseph CASSIN, David DOBBIN.

Febraury 6, 1809, Vol. 1, No. 9

The following is a list of letters remaining at the post office in Liberty on January 1, 1809, per A. DALE, M.: John HARPER, Daniel ALLEN, Nathaniel MOORS, John JETT, Alexander OWENS, William PHILLIPS, James TOWNSEND, Isaac TAYLOR, William WILSON, clerk of White County.

The Indian Queen is open for business in the town of Carthage. John HARMAN.

February 11, 1809, Vol. 1, No. 10

There will be a public Lottery. Simon BUFORD.

Died on Thursday evening, February 2nd, Isaac JOHNS. He was 32 years old and a citizen of Smith County.

For sale, 1000 acres. H. TOOLEY, Smith County.

On the 14th a brown bay horse strayed from H. MOORE's plantation. There is a reward offered for its return. W. P. LAWRENCE, Janaury 23th.

The following persons reported estrays in Smith County, per Basil SHAW, ranger:

(1) Frederick DEBO, two miles from Dixon Springs, has taken up a chesnut sorrel mare. The appraised value was given at $30 on September 13, 1808.

(2) Levy GRAHAM, on Caney Fork near McGarrah's Ferry, has taken up a chesnut sorrel mare. The mare was appraised at $50 on September 15, 1808.

The following persons have reported estrays in White County, per Daniel ALEXANDER, ranger:

(1) James BOUND, on Hutchin's Creek, has taken up a white mare. The appraised value is $15.

(2) Jesse MAINER, on Cane Creek, has taken up a roan strawberry mare. The appraised value is $35.

(3) Harrel SUGG, on Caney Fork, has taken up a bright sorrel mare. The appraised value is $22.

(4) David NICHOLS, in Hickory Valley, has taken up a

a sorrel horse. The appraised value was $20.

The following persons have reported estrays in White County, per Wm. GLENN, dep. ranger:

(1) William STEWARD, on Falling Water, has taken up a bay mare. On October 9, 1808, the mare was given an appraised value of $8.

(2) Joseph ROBERTSON, on Calf Killer Fork, has taken up a sorrel horse. On November 8, 1808, the horse was appraised at a value of $60.

(3) James WALLING has taken up a sorrel horse. The horse was appraised on November 14, 1808 at $25.

(4) John MOSS, four miles on Gum Spring, has taken up a sorrel horse. On October 3, 1808, the horse was appraised at the sum of $40.

(5) Caleb FRAILEY, at Port Republic, has taken up a dark sorrel mare. On December 22, 1808, the horse was appraised at the sum of $19.

Sanders M'MAHAN, on Barren Fork, Warren County, has taken up a sorrel filly. The value was appraised at the sum of $20. Richard BURKS, ranger.

For sale, salt petre. T. DICKSON, MILLER & Co., Glasgow, Barren County, Kentucky.

Young Celah will stand this season at my plantation on Goose Creek. James WARE.

February --, 1809, Vol. 1, No. 11

For sale, Mann's Lick salt. Basil SHAW.

March --, 1809, Vol. 1, No. 12

My wife Susannah WAGGONER has eloped from my bed without just cause. I will not pay her debts. My son Daniel and my daughter Caty are acting for themselves. I will not be responsible for their debts. Cornelius WAGGONER.

I lost three notes in Overton County December last. One note is on William GIBSON in said County for $150 bearing a date of July 30, 1809. The second note was on George CHRISTAIN in said county bearing a date of October, 1809. The third note was in the name of John LOVE of Rhea County bearing a date of August, 1809. William LEE.

March 13, 1809, Vol. 1, No. 13

The following persons have reported estrays in Warren County, per Richard BURKS, ranger:

(1) Gavin JOHNSON, on Hickory Creek, has taken up a dark chestnut sorrel mare.

(2) Godfrey ISBELL, on Hickory Creek, has taken up a grey horse.

New York, Feb. 16th. A man from St. Thomas brought the news that John MANNOT, carpenter and native of New York, was impressed at said city by a British Man of War.

Maj. Alexander ROGERS of the 27th Regiment was appointed as a collector of the Baltimore embargo laws.

The following persons have reported estrays in Jackson County, per James D. HENDLEY, ranger:

(1) Robert RICHMOND has taken up a bay mare. The mare was appraised on January 20, 1808 at $20.
(2) Andrew BLACKWOOD has taken up a black filly.
(3) James D. HENDLEY has taken up a sorrel mare. On December 29, 1808, the mare was valued at $13.50.
(4) Joseph CHAFFIN has taken up an iron gray horse. On December 29, 1808, the horse was appraised at $20.
(5) Richard CLARK, on Indian Creek, has taken up a bay mare. The mare was appraised at $35.

April 3, 1809, Vol. 1, No. 17

White County, Tennessee, February Sessions, 1808. Robert ARMSTRONG, collector, reports that the following tracts of property still have unpaid taxes for the year 1807. William PHILLIPS, s. w. c.

Reputed Owners	Acres	Situation
Robert ALLEN	2500	Caney Fork
George MATLOCK	500	Caney Fork
Jesse WITT	1280	Calf Killer Fork
Charles WITT	640	Calf Killer Fork
Robert SURSEY and		
William BLACK	2500	Cherry Creek
Andrew WADE	5000	Adj. Elijah CHISUM
Henry MIDDLETON and		
John RITLEDGE	19814	Elk River
William T. LEWIS	2500	Caney Fork
Alfred CARTER, heir of		
Landid CARTER, dec.	----	12 tracts Elk Riv.
Eliza WILLIAMS	640	Calf Killer Fork
John JENKINS	100	Calf Killer Fork

The following tracts of land are liable for a double tax:

Reputed Owners	Acres	Situation
Stephen COPELAND	5000	G. 325, Dec. 12,1796
John BOYD	640	W. 3444
Capt. Kedar BALLARD	3840	
Martin ARMSTRONG and		
Stokley DONELSON	4480	Path to Chicamonga
Nathan GOODWIN	1920	
James GLASGOW	5264	Calf Killer Fork
Willoughby WILLIAMS	4480	
Col. John SHEPARD	3840	Adj. James GLASGOW
Maj. Reading BLOUNT	3920	
Gen. Richard CASWELL	4456	

(Continued on following page)

(White County delinquent tax list continued)

Robert KING	5264	Caney Fork
John GARDNER	640	Caney Fork
Joshua HADLEY	640	Caney Fork
William HOGG	640	Caney Fork
Campbell PHILLIPS	640	
John RHEA and William TYRELL	640	
James CAMAN	100	
Thomas WADE	5000	G. 320, W. 1718
Stokley DONELSON	640	Gr. held by James EASTON

Jackson County, Tennessee, February Sessions, 1809. James COOK, sheriff, reports that the following tracts of land still have unpaid taxes for 1808. John BOWEN, c. j. c.

Reputed Owners	Acres	Situation
Henry WEST	228	Hamilton Rd., 1807
Thomas HICKMON	640	Cumberland Ri., 1807
John MILLER	50	Roaring River
Jason THOMPSON	440	Adj. Lt. WILLIAMS
Jason THOMPSON	220	Where Thomas COBBINS now lives
Isaac MOSES' heirs by his agent Isaac WALTER	2764	War Trace, 1807
William WILSON and John DIXON	440	War Trace
James PURSELL	100	Jennings' Creek
Lovel VENTRESS	640	Cumberland River
Spilsby COLEMAN	640	Obeds River
Joshua HADLEY	274	Cumberland River
Philip BRITTON	428	
William CLASBY	150	
Peter MORGAN	1360	Roaring River
John ELM's heirs	640	Proctor's Creek
John PAYTON	140	Jennings' Cr., 1807
James GILLESPIE	640	Barren, 1806, 1807
Edward HARRIS	320	Russel's Mill, 1807
Charles SAUNDERS	640	Roaring River, 1807
Joshua GOARE	150	Barren, 1807
John WHITE	500	Salt Lick Creek conveyed by Thomas HARVEY.
Jacob MEREM, agent for the heirs of Silby HARVEY	2250	1807
Martin JOHNSTON	320	Caney Fork
Arthur PARKER	196	Indian Creek
James CHERRY	500	
James TAYLOR	1360	1807

(Continued on following page)

5

(Jackson County delinquent tax list continued)

Daniel JONES	1237	Ky Line, 1807
Robert FENNER	640	Cumberland River
William CHRISTMAS	456	Where BLACKBURN lives.
Levy SANDERLIN	100	Walton Road
Armstead STUBBLEFIELD	200	1807
Daniel WILBOURN	100	Indian Creek
John FORD	640	Where Jonathan PRYOR now lives.
John MCOTAY	320	Jenning's Creek
William HILL	640	Indian Creek
John IRWIN	640	Barren
John MARTIN	640	Barren
William SANDERS' heirs	640	Barren
John HAYWOOD	5760	Camp Creek
Louson NURCE	200	Sampson Creek
Benjamin JOHNSON, assignee of John GADDY	2250	Obed's River
John P. WIGGIN	640	Doe Creek
Edward MALASKET	252	Cumberland River
Edward JINNINGS (sic)	140	Jennings' Creek
Micajah THOMAS	803	Lick Creek
Howel TATUM	25	Walton Road

The following persons have reported estrays in Warren County, per Isaac W. SULLIVAN, for Richard BURKE, ranger:

(1) Wm. HALL, on the Stones River, has taken up a roan horse, that was appraised at a value of $6.
(2) Henry M'KEE, on Charles Creek, has taken up a bay horse, that was appraised at a value of $20.
(3) Wm. CHISOLM, on Hickory Creek, has taken up a bay horse, that was valued at $20.
(4) Garr JOHNSTON has taken up a chestnut sorrel horse.
(5) Godfrey SHELL, on Hickory Creek, has taken up a gray horse, that was appraised at $20.

April 10, 1809, Vol. 1, No. 18

The following is a list of letters remaining at the post office at Dixon Springs on April 1, 1809, per Tilmon DIXON, p. m.: John and Robert ALLEN, William ALEXANDER, Samuel BAINS, Jesse BEESLEY, John BREVARD, Benjamin H. BROWN, Wilson CAGE, Thomas COTRELL, Joel DYER, jun., Stephen DEBOW, Burchet DOUGLASS, Charles DONOHO, Ruebin DICE, Jacob DICE, Walter DEVINGTON, Will EWELL, Nimraud FARRIS, Henry FARBY, John MORGAN, Josiah MARTIN, John L. MARTIN, Henry M'WHERTER, William MOORE, John MOORE, James NOWLEN, William SIMPSON, Dr. R. L. SAVERN, Thomas R. SHORT, William SHEPARD, Waren WALKER, Col. WALTON, Sherwood WILLIS, Dr. YANDLE.

For sale, a negro woman. Robert W. ROBERTS, liberty.

The following is a list of letters remaining at the post office in Lebanon on April 1, 1809, per Joseph JOHNSON, p. m.: John ALLCORN, Fredrick AUST, Henry BROOKS, Thomas BOUNER, Richard BANDY, James BOND, James CORNELIUS, William COPLE, Josiah or Royland CHANDLER, Jacob CRISMAN, Henry CARSON, Ruthy DREWRY, Robert EDWARDS, Duncan JOHNSON, Robert JOHNSTON, Sterling JONES, John LASLY, Zephaniah NEAL, John OZIAS, Robert O'NEAL, Tolivar RAGLAND, Anthony SEAL, Ralph SMITH, Moore STEPHENSON, James TAYLOR, Brittain WHITLEY, Hiram WILLIAMS, Thomas C. WILLIAMS, Jacob WINFORD, Thomas WOODS, Benjamin WILSON, Robert WHITAN.

I will apply to the Commissioner of West Tennessee on May next for a certificate on Grant No. 306 issued by North Carolina on May 7, 1796 to James GAINES for 1000 acres. James GAINES, sen., by his agent I. TAYLOR, jun.

May 11, 1809, Vol. 1, No. 22

I want to endorse Dr. NEWMAN of Nashville. Oliver BADGER.

Capt. TATEM from St. Croix arrived in Boston bringing the news, that the insurrection at Guadaloupe was in favor of the British.

Brier MARTIN is a candidate for a seat in the House of Representatives for Smith County.

For sale, tickets for a public lottery. James WRIGHT.

New York, March 2nd. The Society of Useful Arts gave an award for the best woolen cloth to George BOOTH, Poughkeepsie. Also winning awards were Samuel BASON, Balston; and Christopher SNYDER, Marbletown.

For sale, land in Jackson County. Pleasant KEARBY, William PATE, and Nicholas TEAL.

May 25, 1809, Vol. 1, No. 24

The following persons have reported estrays in Warren County, per Isaac W. SULLIVAN, deputy ranger, for Richard BURKER, ranger:

(1) Archibald NUNLY has taken up a brown mare.
(2) James THOMAS has taken up a sorrel mare.
(3) Nathaniel COULEY has taken up a bay horse.
(4) Daniel BOON has taken up a black horse.
(5) William MADDIN has taken up a black mare.
(6) John BAILEY has taken up a black horse.
(7) Elijah HARBOUR has taken up a sorrel mare.
(8) Thomas LOWERY has taken up a sorrel mare.

There will be tickets sold for a Paper Mill Lottery. The lottery will be under the direction of Maj. Joseph COLVILLE, Robert W. ROBERTS, and Isham PERKINS. William MOORE.

My wife Mary CALHOUN has left my bed without just cause. I will not pay her debts. William CALHOUN, Jackson County.

7

Wanted, good salt petre. William MILLER, Glasgow, Barren County, Kentucky, or Glenn MERHCT, White County.

The following persons have reported estrays in Smith County, per Basil SHAW, r. s. c.:

(1) William LANCASTER, on Smith's Fork, has taken up a bay mare. On May 13, 1809, the mare was appraised at a value of $20.

(2) Jeremiah WRIGHT, on Sullivan's Ferry, has taken up a sorrel mare. The mare appraised value is $60.

(3) Daniel CHAPMAN, on Hickman's Creek, has taken up a sorrel horse. On May 11, 1809, the mare was valued at the sum of $15.

May 13, 1809, Vol. 1, No. 25

Archibald LEE was appointed as messenger to carry dispatches to England.

I will apply to the Commissioner of West Tennessee on the first Monday in June next for a certificate on Grant No. 2459 for 640 acres, that was issued to John SMITH on the 13th of December, 1793. Elijah CHISUM.

June 9, 1809, Vol. 1, No. 26

The following persons have reported estrays in Jackson County, per James D. HENLEY, d. r. :

(1) William JARET, on Indian Creek on Caney Fork, has taken up a bay horse. On March 16, 1809, the horse was appraised at the value of $15.

(2) William WALLIS, on Rock Spring Creek, has taken up a brown horse. On March 26, 1809, the horse was appraised at the value of $8.

(3) David HERBET, on Indian Creek, has taken up a sorrel mare. The appraised value of the mare was given at $50 on April 28, 1809.

(4) James JONES, on Doe Creek, has taken up a bay mare.

(5) Alexander MARTIN, on Richmond's Ferry, has taken up a brown bay horse. On May 17, 1809, the horse was appraised at sum of $30.

(6) James VANCE, on Indian Creek on Caney Fork, has taken up a roan horse. On May 26, 1809, the horse appraised at the sum of $30.

(7) James BEDFORD, on the Roaring River, has taken up a bay horse. On May 5, 1809, the horse was given an appraised value of $40.

(8) Thomas NICHOLS has taken up a sorrel horse. The mare was appraised at $15 on April 19, 1809.

(9) Horatio WALKER, on the Cumberland River, has taken up a bay horse. On May 20, 1809, the horse was appraised at a value of $30.

(10) Sylvanus FOWELER has taken up a black mare.

8

(11) Stephen HANEY has taken up a black horse. The value of the horse was $20 on on May 20, 1809.

(12) Abraham SHANKLE, on Doe Creek, has taken up a bay yellow mare. On May 23, 1809, the mare was given an appraised value $8.

(13) John PETERSON, on Robertson Ferry, has taken up a sorrel mare.

(14) John BROOK, on Doe Creek, has taken up a bay filly. On May 23, 1809, the mare was appraised at $10.

(15) Nicholas HULE, on Doe Creek, has taken up a horse. On May 23, 1809, the mare was appraised at $8.

(16) James JONES, on Doe Creek, has taken up a bay filly. On May 23, 1809, the filly's value was $13.

(17) John RAYBURN, on Walton's Road, has taken up a bay mare. On May 19, 1809, the appraised value of the mare was given at $60.

(18) John ROSE, on Locks Ferry, has taken up a horse. On May 23, 1809, the horse was valued at $10.

(19) Stephen HANEY, on Walton's Road, has taken up a black mare. On May 13, 1809, the mare was valued at the sum of $30.

(20) Mark YOUNG, on Indian Creek of the Caney Fork, has taken up a bay mare. The appraised value of the mare was given at $19.15 on May 2, 1809.

Greene County, Bennington, Vermont, May 1st. Isaac OAKELY was born in Westchester, New York and went to sea at age 23 on the American ship Indostain. He served as a sailor until the spring of 1804. Then, on April 17th, he was impressed from the ship Ripley by the British ship the Prince of Wales. He refused to sign the ship's roll and received 550 lashes. He later escaped in Liverpool and returned to New York on the ship Hiram on December the 25th last. He is now at his brother's home in the Catskills. He has a mother, three brothers, and three sisters. They are all in this state. This account was told by Isaac OAKLEY and sworn before John BLANCHARD, j. p.

The following persons have reported estrays in Overton County, per B. TOTTEN, d. r. o. c.:

(1) John SEAHORN, on the Standing Stone, has taken up a bay mare. On May 8, 1809, the mare was given an appraised value of $30.

(2) William MARCHBANK, on Fort Blount Road, has taken up a horse. On May 16, 1809, the horse was given an appraised value of $10.

June 15, 1809, Vol. 1, No. 27

The following persons have written letters to the editor: Moses HODGE, Henry BOWEN, Richard COATS, Rial JINNINGS, Meredith COFFEE, John WILLIAMS, Henry HIPSHER, John DANIEL

9

Isaac CAMPBELL, Semore YORK, Abraham PRUETT, Andrew COFMAN, James BOWMAN, John KITCHEN, and Samuel MACBEE.

The following persons have reported estrays in Smith County, per Basil SHAW, ranger:

(1) Benjamin PARROT, on Mulherrin Creek, has taken up a sorrel mare. On May 1, 1809, the mare was given an appraised value of $40.

(2) Josiah STRANGE, on Caney fork, has taken up a sorrel mare. On May 29, 1809, the mare was given an appraised value of $25.

(3) James A. WHITESIDES has taken up a dark bay mare. On June 5, 1809, the mare was appraised at $3.

(4) Thomas LANCASTER, on Smith Fork, has taken up a bay horse. On June 9, 1809, the horse's value was $25.

(5) Bryant WARD, on Douglass Bent, has taken up a stud colt. On June 5, 1809, the colt's value was $10.

(6) Thomas ARMSTRONG, on Dixon Lick Creek, has taken up a sorrel horse. On June 10, 1809, the horse given an appraised value of $15.

(7) Steward PIPKIN, on the Barren River, has taken up a bay filly. On May 23, 1809. the filly was given an appraised value of $30.

(8) John BAKER, near Carthage, has taken up a bay filly. The appraised value of the filly was given at $20 on May 23, 1809.

(9) Rebecca HOGG, on Goose Creek, has taken up a bay mare. On June 9, 1809, the mare's value was $7.

June 29, 1809, Vol. 1, No. 29

Died in New York, Thomas PAINE.

The following persons have reported estrays in jackson County, per J. ROULSTON, j. p.:

(1) Jesse DEES has taken up a roan mare.

(2) William BUDWELL has taken up a sorrel colt.

(3) Sampson WILLIAMS has taken up a bay horse.

(4) Samuel ROULSTON, on Walton Road, has taken up a sorrel horse.

August 17, 1809, Vol. 1, No. 32

The following is a list of letters remaining at Blackburn Springs on June 1, 1809, per Benjamin BLACKBURN, p. m.: John JETT, Robert AUSTAN, Joseph COX, William GIBSON, William HAMILTON, Peter HULERT, Samuel HUFF, John ROBESON, Benjamin WATKINS, John STUART, William SUTTON, Charles TERRELL, E. WALLACE.

The following is a list of letters remaining at the post office in Carthage, per T. M'NUTT, p. m.: Robert ALLEN, Dan. ALEXANDER, Philip BURROW, Hardy BROWS, Robert BAKER, Charles BOULTON, John BOYD, Polly BLAIR, David BUNDY, William TRIGG,

Sampson BETHEL, Walter BEAN, Matthew BREWER, Henry COCKRUM, Nathaniel CAWLEY, John CALDWELL, Sarah DREW, Francis DOUGHERTY, David DICKSON, James EWING, John GREER, Frederick GRAY, William GLEN, Thomas GRARY, Barbary GREEN, Richard HANCOCK, Harman A. HAYS, Ruebin HAMPTON, William HANEY, Thomas T. HAYS, William JENKINS, Phillip JOHNSON, George JACKSON, Willis MACKLIN, Hezekiah M'KINNEY, John W. MANN, Stephen MONTGOMERY, Thos. MUSREY, Freeman MODGLIN, Rebeckah M'KABE, William PLUNKET, Francis PUTERFIELD, Joseph PAYNE, Joseph REASONOVER, G. W. RUTHERFORD, Bird SMITH, Timothy SHAW, Lee SULLIVAN, Maken SMITH, Mills STALLIONS, Peter SCHROEDER, Neil THOMPSON, Larkin THATCHER, James VENTERS, John WARD, Edward WALKER, Silas M. WILLIAMS, Waller WOOD, Horacio WALKER, Sarah WILLIAMS, Nat. W. WILLIAMS.

The following is a list of letters remaining at the post office in Dixon Spring on July 1, 1809, per Tilmon DIXON, p. m.: Stephen ANDERSON, Jessee BEESLY, Benj. BROCKET, Thomas CREWS, Charles DAUGHTEN, William EWELL, James GIVEN, George GORMAN, Jonathan D. GOODALL, John HARVEY, Joel HUNLEY, Adam HUNESMAN, Josiah HOWARD, George HARPOLE, Capt. HEART, Thos. KELLBREW, George LEWIS, Willis MACLIN, Seth MABRY, Alexander M. NELSON, Mary OWENS, Edward PALMER, Steward PIPKIN, George POWELL, John PATTERSON, Griffith W. RUTHERFORD, Philip SITTON, John STAFFORD, John SMITH, jr., Colonel William SANDERS, Betsey WILLIAMS, James WILSON, William WHITE, Col. WINN.

The following is a list of letters remaining at the post office in White Plains on June 30, 1809, per Daniel ALEXANDER, p. m.: Zachariah BECKOM, John BOWLES, Joshua BADGER, John CURREN, Robert CARUTHERS, Francis CHONEY, Thomas CLARK, Col. CHISSUM, John DEMENT, Anthony FLOWERS, John GORE, Thomas HENDRIX, Greenwood HARRISON, Maj. William HUBBETT, Ruebin HAMPTON, William JONES, John HARRISON, Henry KELSOE, Jacob MARTIN, James M'ADAMS, John M'IVER or Robert KYLE, W. M'COY, Rosanna MALL or James MALL, Jeremiah PERRY, James PENDERGRASS, Jonathan PHARR, John H. PHARR, Isaac ROBBINS, James ROLSTON, James RUSSELL, James TURNER, William WESTON, Greenburn WILSON, Thomas WITCHER.

September 1, 1809, Vol. 1, No. 34

Knoxville, August 16th. The Revd. Samuel CARRICK was buried.

Bids are being taken for the building of a court house in Burkesville, Cumberland County, Ky. Comm. John E. KING.

I was married on the 4th of December to Jemina BURGESS, tha daughter of Thomas BURGESS of Warren County, Tennessee. After eight months of marriage, I have has nothing but trouble, distress and uneasiness of mind. I am no longer responsible for debts of her contracting. Thomas STUART.

11

The following is a list of persons reporting estrays in Warren County, per Richard BURKS, ranger, by his deputy Isaac W. SULLIVAN, d. r.:

(1) David HARPOOL, on the Duck River, has taken up a bay horse. On June 26, 1809, the horse was given an appraised value of $35.

(2) Elisha HARBOUR, on the east fork of the Stones River, has taken up a black mare. The value of the mare was given at $12 on July 12, 1809.

(3) Owen EVANS, on Little Hickory Creek, has taken up a black horse. On June 30, 1809, the horse's value was appraised at $65.

(4) John D. S. PAINE, on the Rocky River, has taken up a sorrel mare. On July 20, 1809, the mare's value was appraised at $20.

(5) Nathan CONLY, on the Rocky River, has taken up a bay horse. The horse's value was $25.

(6) William TRAVIS, on the Barren Fork, has taken up a squeball sorrel horse. The horse's value was $14.

(7) John BUNNELS, on the Barren Fork of the Duck River, has taken up a red roan mare.

(8) Craven BELSHER, on the east fork of the Stones River, has taken up a brown bay horse. The value of the horse was given at $8 on July 11, 1809.

(9) Elijah MILLER, on the Barren Fork, has taken up a white mare. On July 11, 1809, the mare was given an appraised value of $30.

(10) Philip KERBY, on Mountain Creek, has taken up a sorrel mare. On July 10, 1809, the mare was given an appraised value of $12.

(11) William CARTER has taken up a bay horse. The value of the horse was appraised at $15 on July 3, 1809.

I will apply to the Commissioner of West Tennessee on the 25th of September next for a certificate on Grant No. 2401, issued in the name of Solomon HOLLING with a bearing date of January 7, 1794. The grant was conveyed by deed to Robert HUNT and then from HUNT to me. John HARMON, August 28, 1808.

The following persons have reported estrays in Smith County, per Basil SHAW, r. s. c.:

(1) Lincoln HARPER, on Defeated Creek, has taken up a sorrel mare. On August 14, 1809, the mare's value was appraised at $9.

(2) William WALTON, near Carthage, has taken up a bay horse. On August 26, 1809, the horse was given an appraised value of $65.

The following persons have reported estrays in Overton County, per B. TOTTEN, d. r. o. c.:

(1) Stanix HORD, on the Obeds River, has taken up a bay

horse. On July 20, 1809, the horse was given an appraised value at the sum of $30.

(2) John FRANKLIN, on Indian Creek, has taken up a horse. On August 12, 1809, the horse was given an appraised value of $60.

(3) Joseph HARRIS has taken up a sorrel mare. The horse was appraised at $30 on August 5, 1809.

The following persons have reported estrays in White County, per William GLENN, d. r. w. c.:

(1) George SANDERS, on Caney Fork, has taken up a brown bay horse. On May 26, 1809, the horse was given an appraised value of $25.

(2) George RAYMAN, near Rock Island, has taken up a sorrel mare. On July 7, 1809, the mare was given an appraised value of $30.

(3) Joseph SMITH, on the south side of Caney Fork, has taken up a bay filly. On June 1, 1809, the filly was appraised at a value of $16.

(4) Robert ARMSTRONG, on Falling Water, has taken up a bay gelding. On June 28, 1809, the gelding was given an appraised value of $12.

(5) Jacob ORTNER has taken up a black mare.

(6) Bird SMITH, on Falling Water, has taken up a black mare. On June 18, 1809, the mare was appraised at the amount of $30.

(7) John WEVER, on Calf Killer Fork, has taken up a chesnut sorrel horse. On June 24, 1809, the horse was given an appraised value of $20.

(8) James COOPER, on Calf Killer Fork, has taken up a bay horse. On July 1, 1809, the horse was valued in the amount of $10.

(9) John MADWELL has taken up an iron grey filly. On June 16, 1809, the filly was valued at $16.

After a short illness, Thomas DARDIS died on Thursday.

September 16, 1809, Vol. 1, No. 36

The copartnership of C. FINLEY & Co. will expire April next. T. M'NUTT for C. FINDLEY & Co.

Daniel LAMBERT died in London at the age of 40. He weighed 739 pounds.

I will apply to the Commissioner of West Tennessee on the 20th of September for a certificate on 640 acres issued on North Carolina Grant No. 540, dated September 15, 1797 to Thomas SMITH. Thomas W. COSBY.

Dr. Charles F. MABIUS cured a negro boy who was blind in 1807. Josiah HOWELL.

Dr. Charles F. MABIUS cured the sore eyes of a 5 year old negro boy. Testified by James BRADLEY on September 9, 1809.

I will apply to the Commissioner of West Tennessee for a

for a certificate on Grant No. 2399 from North Carolina, dated January, 1797, issued to James REED. The tract was transferred by a deed of conveyance from John B. CROSS, sheriff of Overton County. Isaac TAYLOR, jun., for himself and agent for John BRAHAN, John M'DONALD, and Benjamin TOTTEN.

I have appointed Robert ALLEN, clerk of Smith County, to act as deputy registrar of said county. Daniel BUFORD, reg.

The following persons have reported estrays in White County, per Francis PORTERFIELD:

(1) Jacob HART has taken up a sorrel horse. The horse was appraised at $12 on July 6, 1809.

(2) Edward STONE, on Falling Water, has taken up a bay mare. On July 15, 1809, the mare was given an appraised value of $13.

(3) Abijah ROSS has taken up a sorrel mare. The mare was appraised at $30 on July 20, 1809.

(4) Moses DAVIS has taken up a yellow bay filly. On August 12, 1809, the filly was appraised at $12.

(5) Richard PORTERFIELD, on Falling Water, has taken up a sorrel mare. On August 1, 1809, the mare's value was appraised at $20.

(6) Joel MELTON has taken up a bay mare. The mare was valued at $20 on August 24, 1809.

(7) William DENNY, on Loss Creek, has taken up a colt. The colt's value was $6 on August 16, 1809.

(8) James ELSOD, on Falling Water, has taken up a bay horse. On August 23, 1809, the horse was given an appraised value of $20.

October 15, 1809, Vol. 1, No. 38

The following is a list of letters remaining at the post office at Carthage, per T. M'NUTT, p. m.: John ARMSTRONG, Burwell AKIN, James AKIN, Daniel ALEXANDER, John AMESTEN, Green BURROW, William BRADBERRY, Isaac BATES, John BINNON, John BRANSFORD, Edmund J. BAILEY, John CANNADAY, Benjamin CLARK, John CALLOWAY, John CAMPBELL, Nathaniel COSBY, Willie O. DAVIS, Thomas DUNHAM, John DAVIS, Aberton DRAKE, Richard DRAKE, James DUGHERTY, Jessee DEES, Peter ETHERAGE, James EWINGS, Zachary FORD, Thomas FIZZLE, Elijah FORMAN, Pleasant GRIFFISS (sic), Robert GILCREST, Harbet GRIFFIN, Thomas HAMILTON, John HARPOTT, Charles HAYS, Henry HATCHER, Johnson PHILIP, John JOHNSON, Roger LARKIN, Malachi LEGRAND, Edward LILLA, John LOONEY, James LEWIS, William W. LEGON, George LANCE, Shadrach MOORE, Joel MEADER, Mary MOSS, Thomas MELTON, John MARTIN, Daniel M'LEOD, Rederick M'LEOD, Wright OUTLAW, James PIPER, George POWELL, Thos. ROBINSON. Henry WRIGHT, Thos. RICHARDSON, Abraham SMITH, Jas. H. SHROPSHIRE, James STRICKING, Jessee SULLIVANT, John L. SHAW, Zachariah

TATE, Essex STANFORD, Thomas STEWARD, Wlliam TUBB, John VINING, John WISEMAN.

The following is a list of letters remaining at the post office in White Plains on September 30, 1809, per Daniel ALEXANDER, p. m.: Joseph ANTHONY, Elizabeth BROWN, Isaac BILYEY (sic), Martin BEARD, Maj. BRIANT, G. BARRINGTON, Col. Alexander LOWERY, Thomas BOUNDS, James CHELTON, James CLE, Josiah COPLAND, John COX, John CAMPBELL, Gabriel DILLARD, William ERWIN, Thomas ELI, William GLENN, James Y. GREEN, Colonel Leroy HAMONS, Aaron HIGGINBOTHAM, Henry HILL, John JETT, Kadon LEE, Benjamin LEVAN, Richard M'CARY, Maj. Isham RUSELL, John NUNLEY, George PARKER, Warren PHILPOTT, Daniel RAMSEY, Alexander THOMAS, George WHITE, sheriff.

The following is a list of letters remaining at the post office in Dixon Spring on October 1, 1809, per Tilmon DIXON, p. m.: Jessee BEAVER, Messrs. William BRANDON and William ALEXANDER, J. A. ERWIN, Fredrick UHLES, Msrs. Walter CARUTH and Steph. MONTGOMERY, Ruebin DICE, Hexy DICE, Henry FARLEY, William GRANDOE, Thomas GRAY, Stephen JACKSON, James LEWIS, John LEE, Mary MOSS, John PAGE, James PIPER, William VAUGH, Lee SULLIVAN, William BROCKET, William RAWLENS, Aaron VORHIS.

November 17, 1809, Vol. 1, No. 42

Two bay mares strayed or were stolen from the subscriber living on Goose Creek, Smith County. James PALMER.

The following persons have reported estrays in Franklin County, per J. YOUNG, r. f. c.:

(1) Robert MUSICK, on Waggoner's Creek, has taken up a bay mare. On August 12, 1809, the mare was given an appraised value of $40.

(2) Nathaniel HUNT has taken up a bay mare. The mare was appraised at $20 on September 5, 1809..

(3) Anthony BURRIS, on the Elk River, has taken up a sorrel horse. On September 25, 1809, the horse was given an appraised value of $20.

(4) Samuel M'CLUSKY, on Boiling Fork of the Elk River, has taken up a bay horse. On September 29, 1809, the mare was given an appraised value of $50.

(5) Thomas DAVIS, on the Upper Settlement on the Elk River, has taken up a bay mare.

All persons are cautioned against trading for a note passed to William FIVEASH of Smith County for a saddle which was valued at $18. Elijah HUMPHREY.

December 15, 1809, Vol. 1, No. 44

The copartnership of the blacksmith business is dissolved by mutual consent. Samuel EVETTS and William WILLIAMS.

Will all those indebted please come forward. W.O. DAVIS.

15

On the 11th, John SEAHORN of Overton County died. He leaves a wife and five children.

On the 10th in the town of Abington, Virginia, James KING died. He was the brother to William KING of that place. He leaves a wife and three small children.

January 2, 1810, Vol. 1, No. 46

The following is a list of letters remaining at the post office in Carthage on January 1, 1810, per Charles HERVEY, a. p. m.: Ransom ATKINS, John B. ARMSTRONG, Isaac BITTIC, William S. ALLEN, Henry BOHANNON, George BELL, Joseph BISHOP, Nathaniel BURDINE, William BUNDY, Benjamin BOWERS, Chesley BRIDGEWATER, Andrew J. CONNER, William CREESY, W. CARSIN, Charles CANNAWAY, Thomas CHANDLER, William CREELEY, Robert CHAPMAN, Nathaniel COSBY, William DILLARD, Daniel DRAPER, John DALE, Thomas DURHAM, Capt. Thomas DILLON, J. LONNEY, William GOODALL, William WALTERS, John GRISHAM, John GOORE, Samuel GIBSON, Thomas K. HARRIS, Kader HAMIL, Edmund HOWARD, Abel HEATSON, Daniel HAMMOCK, Jacob OVERALL, Thomas HOPKINS, Henry KIONS, H. LYONS, D. LOONEY, J. LYON, John LEE, William MOORS, Isaac MOORS, Micajah MIGET, Jesse MANN, Thomas MARSHAL, Joseph MILLEN, Daniel NORTON, William PUGH, Willoughby PUGH, John RISELL, Jesse SULLIVENT, Jerry WRIGHT, William SULLIVEN, Hardin SLOE, Simon STONE, Elijah TURMAN, Bryan WARD, Frederick TURNER, Neill THOMPSON, Luke WARD, John WILLIAMS.

Wanted, dry hides. William STEWART & Co.

On the 2nd of February in the town of Williamsburgh, there will be a public sale directed by the court of Jackson County, of one lot which belongs to John SMITH. The property was taken at the influence of Thomas DRAPER. J. COOK, sheriff.

There will be a public sale at the White County court house of 200 acres which belongs to Thomas M'DANIEL. The property was taken at the influence of Robert CARTRIGHT. William PHILLIPS, sheriff.

My wife Molly has absented herself from my bed without just cause. I will not pay her debts. William FITZGERALD.

The following persons have reported estrays in Smith County, per B. SHAW, r. s. w.:

(1) John FITE, on Smith's Fork, has taken up a mare.
(2) James ROYAL, on Buffaloe Creek, has taken up a roan horse.
(3) John PORTER, on Jackson's Branch, has taken up a mare.
(4) James WILSON, on east Goose Creek, has taken up a bay horse.

On the first Monday in February next in the town of Warren, there will be a public sale directed by the court of

Warren County of 200 acres which belongs to Armstead STUBBLEFIELD. The tract adjoins Joseph COLVILLE. The property was taken at the influence of John ROGERS. William C. SMART, s. w. c.

February 9, 1810, Vol. 1, No. 50
The following is a list of letters remaining at the post office at Dixon Spring on Janaury 1, 1810, per W. B. BENGE for Tilmon DIXON, p. m.: James ARMSTRONG, Thomas K. HARRIS, J. BRANSFORD, W. CROSS, Alexander CAMPBELL, John DICKSON, John DREW, Moses FISK, Bird GREGORY, Nelson GILLIESPIE, Josiah HOWARD, Peter A. HESSAN, James HOLT, William LIGGON, Roger LARKIN, Henry MERRICK, Willis MACLIN, Champ MADDEN, Williams MGEE, John MEASE, Richard NICKOLLS, James PALMER, Arthur PARKER, James WHITENEY, Joseph SULLIVENT.

The following is a list of letters remaining at Fort Blount alias Williamsburgh on January 1, 1810, per S. WILLIAMS, p. m.: Colonel James ARMSTRONG, Thomas ANDERSON, Isaac BILLEW, Margaret BADGER, Malcom BRICE, William CONNEL, Colonel CHISM, Sampson DAVID, Joseph GILLESS, Mr. HUFFMAN, Leonard HUFF, Abraham HUDDLESTON, Christopher HUFFMAN, John STAFFORD, Daniel HUFFMAN, Henry JOHNSON, Samuel KING, Norman NORTON, Gilmond POOL, Andrew ORR, Abraham SMITH, Elijah SANDERS, Samuel SUTHERLING, Charles SWEAZEA, John SHANKLE, James WARD, John WALKER, William WHITE, Andrew DAVIDSON, Dr. RIDLEY.

The following is a list of letters remaining at the post office at White Plains on January 1, 1810, Daniel ALEXANDER, p. m.: Thomas ANDERSON, Joseph ANTHONY, John BREWER, Joshua BADGER, William BRUCE, William BOYD, James BOATRIGHT, Joseph CUMMINGS, William C. SMART, Stephen FIELDS, Moses GISS, Amos GOODMAN, Wm. GLENN, Mr. HERRING, James HUSE, James ISAAC, John JETT, Reziah JARVIS, Washington LEDBERTON, Moses STEED, William LEWIS, Samuel LEWIS, John METCALF, George WHITEMAN, Abraham MOORE, George PARKER, Thomas PRICE, Samuel SMITH, Joseph SMITH, John SLOANE.

The following persons reported estrays in Smith County, per Basil SHAW, r. s. c.:
  (1) Solomon BLAIR, on Peyton's Creek, has taken up a sorrel mare, On January 1, 1810, the mare was given an appraised value of $5.
  (2) Edward BROWNFIELD, on Hickman's Creek, has taken up a horse. On January 12, 1810, the horse was valued at the sum of $30.
  (3) William PENDARVIS, on Turkey Creek, has taken up a bay mare. On January 12, 1810, the mare was given an appraised value of $16.
  (4) Richard SCOTT, on Dixon's Creek, has taken up a bay horse. On December 27, 1809, the value was $55.

(5) John PORTER has taken up a roan horse colt. The
     appraised value on January 9, 1810 was $2.50.
(6) John HARVEY, on Hickman's Creek, has taken up a
     chestnut sorrel mare. On January 3, 1810, the mare
     was appraised at $32.50.
(7) Nathaniel ROUNDTREE, on Plunket's Creek, has taken
     up a grey mare, On January 2, 1810, the mare was
     appraised at the sum of $40.
(8) Thomas CREWSON, on Smith's Fork, has taken up a
     chestnut sorrel mare. On January 6, 1810, the mare
     was appraised at the sum of $20.

March 23, 1810, Vol. 2, No. 53
    Overton County, Tennessee, November term, 1809. John B.
CROSS reports that the following tracts of land still have
unpaid taxes for the year 1809. The property will be sold
on the first Monday in April next at the court house. B.
TOTTEN, clerk.

Reputed Owners	Acres	Situation
Samuel SMITH	202	Big Cane creek
William SNOW	160	
Felps REED	2500	Lick Creek
Hardy MURPHY	477	Granted to Nancy SHEPPARD.
Benjamin TOTTEN	2280	by deed from the Jackson Co.,Shf.
Josiah COLLINS	2300	G. No. 307, W. 47. Dtd. Oct. 25, 1783
Capt. William LYTLE	4500	Cumberland River
William SCONCE	300	Obeds River
Stephenson MOOR	200	E. F. R. River
James HENDERSON	1300	
John KARR	58	
Charles MOORE	300	Obeds River
Samuel A. MARTIN	3500	Obeds River
Caleb WILLIS	100	W. Fork Caney
Josiah COLLLINS	1280	Bear Creek
		G. to John GADDY
Samuel HOPKINS	110	Eagle Creek
Thomas HOPKINS	3000	
David ROSS	2500	
James BROOKS and		
James WOODS	640	G. 257
Andrew ALEXANDER	1000	G. 393
Thomas HOUSTON	640	G. 209
Ephraim DUNLAP	640	G. 260
William MCRARY	200	G. 253
Landon CARTER's heirs	260	Brimstone Creek

(Continued on following page)

18

(Overton County delinquent tax list continued)

JAMES DANDER	640	Spring Creek
Micajah THOMAS	1000	Obeds River
Stockley DONEL	1000	G. 2729
Robert ANDERSON	188	
Richard H. LOVE	1280	G. 302
Isaac MCUMMIN	357	Langdon Cr., G. 8352

Jackson County, Tennesseee. The following is a list of persons who still have unpaid taxes for the year 1809. The property will be sold on the first Monday in April next. John BOWEN,

Reputed Owner	Acres	Situation
John ELLUM's heirs	690	Proctor's Creek
Francis GRAVES	3127	Salt Lick
Nancy SHEPARD	640	
Hardy MURFREE	1530	
Jason TOMPSON	640	
Matthew BROOKS	1560	Cumberland River
William WALTON	640	
Joshua HADLEY	274	
Daniel CHERRY	274	Walton Road
Heirs of William SANDERS	300	
Samuel HUNTER	100	
Nancy STEEL	640	
James MERCER	920	
Daniel ANDERSON	640	1807, 1808, 1809
James GALASPEY	640	1807, 1808, 1809
Patton ANDERSON	5000	1807
William LITTLE	1000	Walton's Rd., 1807
Elizabeth STEEL	640	Conveyed by Robert JOHNSON, 1807
Howel TATUM	250	
John IRWIN	640	Barren River, 1807
John BLACKMORE	640	Where Widow PATE lives, 1807
Francis BOSS	640	Occ.by Joseph PROIR
John WHITE	500	Salt Lick
Martin JOHNSON	320	Caney Fork
Arthur BARKER	196	Indian Creek
James CHERRY	500	
Levy SANDERLIN	100	
John MCAULEY	320	
John P. WIGGINS	640	Doe Creek

For sale, dry goods and groceries. Edward FOSTER.

I wish to forwarn the public against trading or taking assignments against two notes of hand held by Eprhaim THOMAS dated August, 1808. I will not pay said notes unless compelled by law. John TELL.

A runaway negro by the name of JACK was committed to the

19

jail of Smith County. He says that he is 22 years old and is the property of Mathew JOHNSTON who lives on Little Harpeth Williamson County. John HARMON, jailor.

The following persons have reported estrays in Warren County, per (no ranger given):

(1) William GOSUT, on Hickory Creek, has taken up a black mare. On November 8, 1809, the mare was given an appraised value of $20.

(2) A. BAYES, on Hickory Creek, has taken up a grey filly. The filly was given an appraised value of $11 on November 20, 1809.

(3) George LANE, on Hickory Creek, has taken up a horse. The horse was valued at $25.

(4) James THOMAS, on the Rocky River, has take up a brown horse. The horse was valued at $30.

(5) James CLARK, on the Rocky River, has taken up a sorrel mare. The mare was valued at $25.

The Nashville Whig
Published by M. and J. Nowell

September 2, 1812, Vol. 1, No. 2

Duncan M'ARTHUR, above the fortress at Detroit, sent a letter to Capt. H. BRUSH in which he mentioned Col. MILLER with the Ohio militia.

Wanted, an apprentice and one or two journeyman for the painting business. John ROGERS, Nashville, Aug. 12, 1812.

For sell, two hogshead of tobacco. W. W. COOKE.

Reward $10. On the 22nd, the arm of my still and a brass cock with 20 pounds of lead was stolen from my still house. James CAMPBELL, August 29, 1812.

On the 23rd of September next, I shall apply to the Commissioner of west Tennessee for a certificate for 600 acres on Sulpher Creek, Robertson County. The tract was granted, by virtue of military warrant no. 1115, in the name of Andrew BREAKY, assignee of John SMITH. Henry AYRES, August 26, 1812.

September -, 1812, Vol. 1, No. 3

For sale, the 363 acres on which I now live about ten miles from Nashville on Mill Creek. Thos. WILLIAMSON.

I have purchased the library of the late Dr. Thomas Ryon BUTLER. E. T. PAINE, Springfield, August 6, 1812.

James G. HICKS, cabinet maker, has commenced business in the town of Nashville in the house formerly occuppied by John and Thomas DEATHERAGE.

The Bell Tavern is open for business in Nashville. Thomas CHILDRESS.

Open for business, a private boarding house at the sign of the Square and Compass. James CONDON.

September 16, 1812, Vol.1, No. 4

Will all those indebted to the subscriber, please come forward and settle as one of the partners will possibly set out for Philadelphia on the 15th of next month. CANTRELL & READ, Nashville, September 7, 1812.

For rent, the premises where Clayton TALBOT lately lived which adjoins the town of Nashville.

September 23, 1812, Vol. 1, No. 5

Isaac HULL has made an offical statement concerning the conflict between the Consitution and the British frigate Guerriere.

John B. HOGG has been elected principal surveyor of the Second District in place of Col. P. ANDERSON, resigned.

William WALLACE wishes to inform the public that he has received a fresh supply of leather from Philadelphia.

For sale, my possessions in the town of Franklin, Williamson County. Richard ORTON.

September 30, 1812, Vol. 1, No. 6

Died in this town on his way home from New Orleans on Saturday evening last, Wm. P. MEEKER of Philadelphia.

Edmund and Geo. HEWLETT wish to inform the public, that they are open for the saddle business.

I shall apply to the Commissioner of West Tennessee on the behalf of Thomas OVERTON, on the 14th of October next, for a certificate on 640 acres issued by North Carolina on Grant No. 3265, dated December 22, 1797 to John MANN. Thomas OVERTON claims the property by a deed from John MANN. Jessee BLACKSAN, attorney in fact for Thos. OVERTON.

October 7, 1812, Vol. 1, No. 7

Lt. Isaac PAXTON of this town died on thursday morning last after a lingering illness. He was 26 years old and a native of Rockbridge County, Virginia. He was a member of the Nashville Volunteer Company of Infantry.

Will all those indebted to the firm of WARD & PAXTON come forward and make payment to the surviving partner. Joseph WARD, Nashville, October 7, 1812.

October 14, 1812, Vol. 1, No. 8

For sale, pepper, tinware, coffee and other goods, PATTON & ERWIN.

Reward $10. On the 28th, William JOINER deserted form the Cantonment near Nashville. He is 23 years old, with a dark complexion and hair, brown eyes, and was born in Nash County, North Carolina. He is a shoemaker by trade and is fond of drink. A. GRAY, Capt. 24th Reg. U. S. Army.

The following persons were mentioned in a report by Brig. Gen. W. HULL at Detroit on August 13, 1812: Lt. Colonel MILLER, Captain BRUSH, Capt. GILCHRIST, Capt. ULLERY, Capt. BARRSLER, Capt. M'CALLOUGH of the spies, Lt. PEATZ, Ensign ROBBY, Ensign ALLISON, Major VAN HOORN, Major BAKER, Capt. BAKER of the 1st U. S. Reg., Captain BREVORT, Lt. WHISTLER, Capt. BURTON and Capt. FuLLER of the Ohio Volunteers, Capt. DELANDER of the Michigan Volunters, and Major MUIR of the 41st British.

October 21, 1812, Vol. 1, No. 9

There will be races at Harbet HARWELL's near Springfield, Tennessee.

John H. BOWEN, of Sumner County, is a candidate for the Third District.

On the 29th of October next, the house and property of Henry HYDE, dec'd., on White Creek, is for sell at auction.

John WHITE, attorney at law in Columbia, was married to Miss Abigail DICKERSON, of this town, by the Rev. Gideon BLACKBURN.

For sale, an assortment of goods. James HANNA.

Reward $10. On the 18th, John SMITH deserted. He was born in Lancaster County, Pennsylvania of Dutch parents. He speaks broken English, has a dark complexion and eyes, is about 30 years old and is 5 ft., 9 in. tall. Alex. A. WHITE, 1st Lt. 7th Reg. U. S. Infantry.

October 28, 1812, Vol. 1, No. 10

For sale, land in Robertson County. Robert B. MITCHELL

Married on Thursday evening last by Rev. CRAIGHEAD, Nicholas WILSON, merchant of St. Genevieve, to Miss Eliza ERWIN, daughter of Capt. Joseph ERWIN of this ounty.

Reward $20. Strayed or stolen from the subscriber on the Sulpher Fork of the Red River, Robertson County, a brown mare. Tho. B. TUNSTALL.

In this town on Friday last, Captain Benjamin GRAY, from Salem, Massachuetts, died on his way home from New Orleans. He was the nephew of the Hon. Wm. GARY, Lt. Gov. of Mass.

Reward $50. On the 22nd a negro man called JIM, ranaway from the subscriber's plantation seven miles east of Nashville. He is about 19 or 20 years old, and 5 ft., 6 or 7 inches tall. He is believed to have been stolen by James SMITHFIELD, who was convicted of horse stealing September term last in the Davidson Circuit Court. Felix GRUNDY.

Will all those indebted to Thomas PORTER come forward and settle their accounts.

The following persons were mentioned in Acts passed at the Second Session of the General Assembly of Tennessee: William NASH, Moses FISK, Elijah HUMPHREYS, Robert SELLERS, John C. M'LEMORE, Nathan EWING, George EVANS, Bennett SEARCY, Isham SIMMS, Thomas INGRAM, Joseph BROWN, Solomon COTTON, Peter GILL, Alexander M'CAULY, Charles C. EVANS, Theopilus WILLIAMS, John M'CULLY, James PURSLY, John O. M'LEMORE.

November 4, 1812, Vol. 1, No. 11

Will all those indebted to the estate of Thomas MASTERSON, dec., come forward and make payment. A. POTTER,

The following persons were mentioned in letters with war news: Major M. D. HARDEN, Capt. CHEPINS of Bufflaoe (sic), Maj. SCHUYLER, and Major DODGE.

Vincennes, October, 20th. On Friday morning, Indians killed the son of Thomas HOLLINGSWORTH.

November 18, 1812, Vol. 1, No. 13

I will leave this place in ten or fifteen days. Will all

those indebted please come forward and make payment to Thomas CRUTCHER. Eleanor WINN.

Those persons wishing a subscription to "The Reporter" printed in Lexington, Kentucky by William W. WORLSEY, please apply to Wilkins TANNEHILL.

November 25, 1812, Vol. 1, No. 14

On Sunday evening last on the 8th by J. E. TURNER, William S. BRADBURN, merchant of Springfield, to Miss Nancy PLUMMER, daughter of the late William PLUMMER.

Oliver BUSH, private in Capt. WALLIS' company of valunteers was convicted of desertion.

On the 7th of Janaury next, we shall apply to the Commissioner of west Tennessee for a certificate on Grant No. 1263, dated December 10, 1790, by North Carolina John M'NEESE for 640 acres. We hold claim by a deed from the sheriff of Stewart County. Bennett SEARCY, Robert COOPER, Jno. C. M'LEMORE.

December 2, 1812, Vol.1, No. 15

I shall apply to the Commissioner of west Tennessee on the 25th of December next for a certificate on Grant No. 1774, dated May 20, 1793, for 357 acres from North Carolina to David ALLISON. Asa SHUTE.

The following persons were mentioned in the Battle of Queenstown: Colonel VAN RENSSELAER, Lt. Col. CHRISTIE, Lt. VALLEAU, Captain ARMSTRONG, Captain MALCOM, Capt. WOOD, Lt. HUGININ, Lt. GANSEVOORT, Lt. RANDOLPH, Lt. CARR, Lt. LUSH, Capt. GIBSON, Capt. MACKESNEY, Capt. LAWERENCE, Col. ALLEN, Col. MEAD, Col. STRAHON, Lt. COl. SCOTT.

I will not be responsible for any debts other than those by my written order. J. WHITESIDE.

A bay horse has strayed from the subscriber from the plantation of Jenkin WHITESIDE on Mill Creek. Wm. Randolph HESS.

December 9, 1812, Vol. 1, No. 16

For sale, several tracts of land in Stewart County, Montgomery County, and Hickman County in Tenn. Will those interested see Charles WILLIAMS, on Elk Creek, John SUTTON near Clarksville or Captain James ALLSTON near Vernon. William HART.

For rent, several plantations. John STUMP or C. STUMP.

Archibald DEWEL will you please pay to Colin S. HOBBS two dollars on this day of June 22, 1812. Wm. DEW.

December 16, 1812, Vol. 1, No. 17

On the first of January next of the estate of Thos. MASTERSON, dec. Chapman WHITE and Thos. WASHINGTON.

The United States Herald
Published by Theoderick F. Bradford

August 11, 1810, Vol. 1, No. 5

The following is a list of letters remaining at the post office in Dover which if not taken out will be sent to the General Post Office as dead letters, per James RUSSELL, p. m.: Peter BLACKON, Gilbert BARRY, Daniel BUCHANNIN, Ephraim R. DAVIDSON, Isaac LANIER, Burwell LANIER, Rebekah M'RINNY, Daniel M'MILLAN, John MANIN, Enoch MASHBURN, Wm. M'GUNDY, Jacob M'CARTY, William PRYOR, Abner PEARCE, Mark RUSHING, Thomas SMITH, John Scale STOLE, Benjamin SPENCER, Elizabeth WATSON.

For sale, salt. James WILLIAMS.

A new store is opening in the town of Clarksville on Water Street in the house formerly occuppied by Mr. CARRAWAY. Owen REILLY.

Dr. Maxwell SHARP has returned to Clarksville and is open for business.

The following persons have reported estrays in Roberson County, per Levi NOYSE, r. r. c.:
  (1) A bay mare was taken up by John ALLPIN. The mare appraised at a value of $12.
  (2) Garland HALL, on the middle fork of the Red River, has taken up a sorrel horse, The horse was given an appraised value of $40.
  (3) Levi NOYES, living in Springfield, has taken up a sorrel mare. The mare was appraised at $53.
  (4) John COULS has taken up a bay horse, The horse was given an appraised value of $70.
  (5) Plummer WILLIS, in Springfield, has taken up a bay mare. The mare's value was appraised at $35.

For sale at the town of Clarksville, an assortment of dry goods, hardware, groceries, wines, bar iron, shot, whiskey and gun powder. Geo. SIMPSON, attorney for Wm. TRIGG, surviving executor of Wm. KING, dec.

We learned from Virginia, that James PERRY, post rider from Fredericsburgh to Fauquier court house, has been apprehended for the robbery of the mail.

Gen. Wade HAMPTON arrived in Columbia on the 20th of June from the west.

On the 22nd of October next, bids will be taken for the building of a court house at Shelbyville, Bedford County. Commissioners: John AKINSON, William WOOD, Bartlett MARSTIN, Howel DAWDRY, Benjamin BRADFORD, Daniel M'KISSIC.

For sale, 400 acres of which 100 is under fence and a dwelling house in Montgomery County. John STEWART.

On the 6th of September next, there will be a public sale directed by court of Davidson County of the interest of

Solomon KITTS to 5000 acres on Grant No. 280, and 5000 acres on Grant No. 281. The property was taken at the influence of Martin HESS; John HENRY; John CONRAD; TOBER, FREY & PESTALOZZI. John ALLEN, s. s. c.

The following persons have reported estrays in Dickson County, per Francis S. ELLIS, deputy ranger:

(1) Edmund HOWARD, living on Town Creek one mile from Charlotte, has taken up a bay mare. The mare was appraised at the value of $40.

(2) Wm. MORRISS, living near Griffin's Mill, has taken up an iron grey mare. The mare was appraised at the sum of $45 on June 7, 1810.

(3) Thomas MARTIN, on Jones' Creek near Maj. STRONG's, has taken up a sorrel horse. On May 14, 1808, the horse was appraised at the value of $15.

The following persons have reported estrays in Montgomery County, per James BUNTING, r. m. c.:

(1) William C. JAMISON has taken up a black horse. The horse was appraised at $5 on June 5, 1810.

(2) John COFFERY has taken up a bay horse. The horse was appraised at $8.

(3) Thomas SMITH has taken up a bay horse. The horse was appraised at a value of $7.50.

The following persons have reported estrays in Roberson County, per Levi NOYLES, r. r. c.:

(1) John ROBERTSON, on Spring Creek, has taken up a bay mare. On March 31, 1810, the mare was given a value of $20.

(2) Jacob PICKERING, in Springfield, has taken up a dun yellow filly. On April 24, 1810, the mare's value was appraised at $20.

(3) William FLETCHER, on the Red River, has taken up a bay mare. On April 12, 1810, the mare was given an appraised value of $18.

(4) Michael FISER, on Kerr's Creek, has taken up a bay filly. On April 23, 1810, the filly was given an appraised value of $20.

(5) James PIKE, for John PHILIPS, has taken up a dark grey colt. The colt was valued on May 10, 1810.

Wilson's Knoxville Gazette
Published by George Wilson

January 3, 1807, Vol. 3, No. 7

On the 14th of February next in the town of Kingston, there will be a public sale directed by the court of Roane County that belongs to James GORDON. The property was taken at the influence of William LUMKIN against James GORDON as security for John WADDLE. John BROWN, sheriff.

There is a reward offered for the return of Robert BEALL, apprentice, who absconded on the 25th of November last from the subscriber in Knoxville. Jacob FORMWALT.

The following land grant patents were left with me by Stokely DONELSON. Please apply to Mr. WILSON or myself. Geo. FARRAGOOD.

Persons	Acres	Grant	Date
Thomas CHAPMAN	200	753	1783
John NEELY	640	868	1790
Thomas JOHNSON	347	609	1784
John RUSSELL	300	753	1796
Samuel M'CLARY	500	202	1792
Stokley DONELSON	300	561	1794
Stokley DONELSON	300	19	1782
Seth JOHNSON	100	26	1782
James BROWN	200	306	1793
Robert POGUE	150	76	1782
John HERROD	100	206	1793
Robert REED	640	555	1794
Robert SMITH	200	1027	1791
James MITCHELL	200	1247	1793
James CANNADY	200	208	1795
John RING	1011	345	1790
Abner CHAPMAN	400	825	1790
Henry WHITE	640	1219	----
William HORD	150	608	1797
Stokley DONALDSON sold to			
Capt. MILLER	2000	314	1793

The trial of John DESKINS is for sale at Anthony M'GUIRE's store. John G. USTIC.

On the 7th of February next at the town of Kingston, there will be a public sale of 675 acres that belong to William SNODDY. The property was taken at the influence of John YOUNG and William CALLY. John BROWN.

On the 17th of January next, there will be a public sale directed by the court of Sevier County of 30 acres that belongs to John HAWK. The property was taken at the influence of Hugh BODKIN. Wm. MITCHELL.

On the 17th of January next, there will be a public sale directed by the court of Sevier County of a tract of land

27

which is the property of Mordicai GAST. The property was taken at the influence of John BRABSON and John KERR. Wm. MITCHELL.

On the 26th of August last, a bay horse was stolen from the subscriber by Joseph BRITT. Wm. HINNAT, sen., near Smithfield.

On the 23th of January next, there will be a public sale directed by the court of Washington County of 150 acres which belongs to Joseph BLACK. The property adjoins Abraham SNAPP, Nathan GANN and James GRAY. The land was taken at the influence of Ira GREEN. Joseph BROWN.

Reward $100. My negro man called PHILIP ranaway. He is 23 years of age. Deliver to me in Port Royal. John BAKER.

January 27, 1808, Vol. 4, No. 4

The following is a list of letters remaining at the post office in Knoxville on January 1, 1808, per J. ARMSTRONG, a. p.: Isaac ANDERSON, Benjamin BEALL, Robert BARR, Francis BOUNDS, James D. BENNET, Rev. John BROWDER, Mr. BUNN, Wm. O. BLOUNT, Joseph T. BELL, Wm. BOGAN, Richard BEARDEN, Jeremiah BROOKS, Mrs. Mary H. BOTTS, Hugh BRUFFY, W. BARCLAY, Thomas BREWER, Joseph CARTER, John CRAWFORD, Thomas CASEY, William CHRISTMAS, Robert CALVERT, Charles CARTER, John CHILDRESS, English CRAWFORD, Capt. Stephen W. CENTER, Mrs. Sally COBB, Mustoe CHAMBERS, Mr. CRAWFORD, Thomas DELAP, Robert DUNHAM, Hugh DUNLOP, Thomas DEAN, Mellieiah (sic) DAMEWOOD, Polly A. EPPS, Peter EPPERSON, Thomas EPPS, Jessee EVANS, Ezekeial ENGLAND, Mrs. FARAGOOD, Christain FOUST, John B. GILPIN, John GILBREATH, William GIBBS, Thomas GILLESPIE, William HANSFORD, Cornelies HICKEY, Stephen HARRIS, Elizabeth HUNTSMAN, Lewis HILL, Wm. HANNER, Robert HOLT, Edward HALEY, John HOGLIN, Wm. HAMBLETON, Abner JACKSON, Anthony INLONE, Frederick ICE, Rev. Wm. M'KENDREE, Hugh KENNEDY, WM. KELLY, Wm. LENTY, Mr. LIVINGSTON, William LILLARD, Caleb LOW, John LOWERY, Archy M'MILLAN, Andrew M'CALL, David MAXWELL, Rt. MASSEY, Rich. MIDLEY, Jas. MARTIN, Lieut. Wm. C. MEAD, John MAXWELL, Asher MOORE, John M'NUTT, Henry MINOR, Eliza MORRAY, William MILLOGAN, Dr. Charles MERIWEATHER, Daniel NORTON, Frederick NARIMOR, James ORE, Daniel OGG, William ODER, Col. Alexander OUTLAW, William PRATT, John PAUL, B. C. PARKER, Evans PHELAN, George ROBERTSON, Wm. ROAN, Moses REDDY, Isaac RUTHERFORD, John RUSSELL, Henry REED, Jesse SHARP, Mrs. Rosannah SLINBOUGH, Bird SMITH, Doct. Wm. SMITH, William STRANGER, John SEAR, Robert SEARCY, Col. John SAWYERS, Widow SMITH, Jessee SPIRES, James SCOTT, Edmund SWINN, Caleb and Rebecca SHOD, Thomas TODD, Joseph THOMPSON, John TOMLIN, Patrick VANCE, John VANBABBLER, Doct. Thomas VANDYKE, Robert WRIGHT, Simeon WILLET, Benjamin WILLIAMS, James WILLIAMS, Jinkin WHITESIDES, Mary WHITE, John WILKS,

John S. WILSON, James WALTON, Mathew WALKER, Jacob MARRICK, William WEBB, Martha WHITE.

On the 12th of March next in the town of Dandridge, there will be a public sale directed by the Roane County court of 520 acres, No. 1100, that is the property of William SNODDY. The property was entered in the name of William T. LEWIS and William SNODDY in what was once Greene County. The property was taken at the influence of John YOUNG and William CALLY. James BRADFORD, sheriff of Jefferson County.

The following is a list of letters remaining at the post office at Greenville, per W. DICKSON, p. m.: John VANSANT, Daniel M'CLELLAND, John WEAMJAM, Henry LANG, Joshua BRUNSEN, Richard GLOVER, Thomas LOVE, William PRATT, Francis HULL, Elijah THOMPSON, Benjamin VANPELT, James HISE, Benjamin HARRISON, John ALEXANDER, William WOOLSEY, William CLARK, John MOORE, John RYAN, Saunders REDDEN, Mrs. Fanny SHAW, James SHIELDS, Stephen PERKINS, Ephraim PRICHETT, James HAYS, John COPELAND, William KILGORE, Col. KINCHELOE, sen., Andrew SMILEY, David BIDOLE, William ALEXANDER, John HAYS.

I shall apply to the Commissioner of East Tennessee in the town of Knoxville for a certificate for North Carolina Grants No. 1142 for 3590 acres, No. 1143 for 5660 acres, and No. 1145 for 7730 acres to John SEVIER, jun. The grants were dated September 10, 1794. Heirs of Andrew GREER, dec.

On the 10th of March in place of holding court in Campbell County, at the house of John YENT, there will be a public sale directed by the Hamilton District Court of 200 acres on Big Walnut Cove that is the property of Micajah CROSS. The property was attached by the State. It is part of a tract formerly owned by Charles I. LOVE. Michael HUFFAKER, sheriff of Campbell County.

On the 20th of March next at the town of Maryville, there will be a public sale directed by the Blount County Court of a tract owned and formerly occuppied by George MONTGOMERY. The property was taken at the influence of WHITE & HENDERSON. Saml. COWAN.

On the 6th of February next in the town of Elizabethton, there will be a public sale directed by the court of Carter County of 200 acres on Indian Creek, including a saw mill, grist mill and ironworks, that is the property of Charles WHITSON. The property was taken at the influence of William PUGH. Archibald WILLIAMS, sheriff of Carter County.

On the 12th of March next at the town of Rutledge, there will be a public sale directed by the Hamilton District Court of a small tract that is the property of Ambrose YANCEY. The property was taken by Isakiah MIDKISS against Ambrose YANCEY, Robert YANCEY, Martin ASHBURN and Charles WADDLE, James CONN, sheriff of Grainger County.

On the 20th of February next in the town of Rogersville,

there will be a public sale directed by the Hawkins County Court of 200 acres that belong to Peter EDWARDS on Big War Creek. The property was taken at the influence of William COCKE. A. LOONEY, sheriff.

I have given a bond of security for lands south of the French Broad and Holston Rivers and I am ready to receive it. Thos. MCORRY.

Hamilton District, September term, 1807. Rebekiah LOVELACE, by her father, John BERRY vs. William LOVELACE. William LOVELACE is ordered to appear in court and answer the petiton for divorce on the 4th Monday in March next. F. A. RAMSEY, clerk.

Reward $20. On the 12th of March last, a negro man called JOHN ranaway from the subscriber. He appears to be about 50 years old. He was with another fellow of mine who was taken up in Jefferson. He is headed form Gloucester County, Virginia. John FARMER.

I have authorized George WILSON to attend to my office of Clerk & Master. Joseph GREENE.

I have a cotton machine. John WITT.

On the 30th of January 30th in the town of Blountsville, there will be a public sale directed by the court of Sullivan County of 490 acres, that is the property of Conrad SHARETS, sen. The property was taken at the influence of David OWENS. James PHAGEN, sheriff of Sullivan County.

On the 6th of February next in the town of Elizabethton, there will be a public sale directed by the Carter County Court of a moity of land that is the property of William PARKISON. The property was taken at the influence of Flud (sic) FORTNER. Archibald WILLIAMS, sheriff of Carter Co.,

On the 6th of February next, I shall apply to the Commissioner of East Tennessee for a certificate on Grant No. 218, dated September 20, 1787, for 2000 acres which was issued to James COZBY and Samuel GIVENS. James COZBY and Samuel GIVENS.

On the 20th of February next in the town of Maryville, there will be a public sale of a tract that is the property of James SLOAN. The tract is occuppied by Henry FERGUSON. Saml. COWAN, sheriff of Blount County.

At the September session of the Anderson County Court, I shall petition for a division of 1000 acres on the north side of the Clinch River near Pilot Knob. The land was issued on Grant No. 1887 to Martin ARMSTRONG and George DOHERTY. John UNDERWOOD, Knoxville.

February 3, 1808, Vol. 4, No. 5

Williamson County, Tennessee, January Sessions, 1808. Stephen CHILDRESS, sheriff and collector, reports that the following tracts of property sill have unpaid taxes for the

year 1807. The property is to be sold on the first Monday
in July next in the town of Franklin. N. P. HARDIMAN.

Reputed Owners	Acres	Situation
Eleazer ALEXANDER	600	
ANDERSON & GRACEY	5000	
Matthew ALEXANDER	1000	
Daniel ANDERSON	640	West Harpeth
James BROWN	160	Big Harpeth
Moses BUCHANON	1800	
Robert BUCHANAN	1280	
John Branom BRANAR	5000	
John BRYAN's heirs	100	Little Harpeth
Jehu DAVIE	320	1 white poll
James DOHERTY	320	M'Crory's Creek
John DAVIDSON	500	Tombigby, 1 black
Ephraim DAVIDSON	1500	
George DOHERTY's heirs	4800	West Harpeth
John ECHOLS	192	West Harpeth
Andrew EWING	284	
John EATON	2680	Hay's Creek
John EDMISTON	1350	
Thomas EDMISTON	1600	
Wm. EWING	284	Spencer's Creek
Stewart FAMBROUGH	120	
Charles GILMORE's heirs	660	West Harpeth
Edward HARRIS	750	Duck River
John HENDERSON	700	Elk River
Robert HENDERSON	567	Richland Creek
Welcom HODGE	160	Nelson Creek
Samuel JACKSON	1262	Big Harpeth
John KIRKPATRICK	800	Duck River
William LITTLE	640	
James LEWIS	228	
William LYTLE	1000	
Joel LEWIS	1000	Leiper's Fork
Abram MAURY	160	
William MOCRY (sic)	190	1 white poll
William M'GEE	1000	West Harpeth, 1 white poll
Jessee MURRELL	146	1 white poll, 1 black poll
James MAYFIELD	753	Duck River
James M'CUSTON	426	Duck River
James MUHERN	320	Mill Creek
John M'CRAKEN	1500	Elk River
John M'NAIRY	11000	
John MORRAL	740	West Harpeth
George M'CLAINE, jun.	1000	

(Continued on following page)

31

Alexander NELSON	5000	
Robert NELSON	5905	
William ORTON's heirs	200	Mill Creek
James OWENS	5000	Globe Creek
James H. PATTERSON	200	Duck River
John PARKER	1280	Leiper's Fork
Thomas PARKER	120	
Noble STOCKETT's heirs	248	Big Harpeth
David SLOAN	640	Big Harpeth
Benjamin SMITH's heirs	1500	
Michael GILCHRIST	1000	
James HOUSE	200	
Washington L. HANNUN	1000	Globe Creek
James HUGGINS	1000	
David JUSTICE	2000	
Hugh LEIPER	1017	
William MACLIN	1000	
G. W. RUTHEROFRD	5000	
John REED and others	2500	
Sterling ROBERTSON	1000	
Eldridge ROBERTSON	1000	
James ROBERTSON, jun.	1000	
William SHEPPARD	3500	
John WALKER	240	
John WATTS	1200	
Daniel WHEATON, dec.	1000	
Thomas TALBOT	2000	Flat Creek
John THOMPSON	640	
James A. WILSON	1200	
Sampson WILLIAMS	1494	
Daniel ANDERSON	5000	
James ARMSTRONG	5000	
David BUCHANAN	190	Spencer's Creek
John BROWN	5000	
John CLENDENING	2560	M'Crory's Creek
Archibald CRATCH	600	
Alfred M. CARTER	4000	
John CHILDRESS, sen.	1000	
William GREENLEE	800	
Elijah REDSHAW	242	
William BRANDON	1280	Wilson's Valley

The following tracts are liable for a double tax:

Reputed Owners	Acres	Situation
Sarah ALLEN	640	
Martin ARMSTRONG	20000	
John ARMSTRONG	5000	Richland Creek
Edward ARMSTRONG	500	Duck River

(Continued on following page)

32

(Williamson County delinquent tax list continued)

Name		Amount	Location
Thomas BUNCOMB's heirs		5000	
Micajah BARROW		200	Murfree's Fork
Joseph BLITHE		3520	Rutherford Creek
Amos BALCH		1000	Duck River
Thomas CLARK		7400	Richland Creek
Thomas B. CRAIGHEAD		1280	Little River
John DICKSON		1000	Tombigby
Simon ELCOTT		1000	Duck River
Robert FENNER		4030	Richland Creek
William GILBERT		5000	
John GORDON		lot	
James GILLESPIE		3030	E. F. Big Tombigby
William HILL		1500	
Robert HAYS		5000	Richland Creek
John HAYWOOD		5000	W. Richland Creek
Joshua HADLEY		3840	Duck River
Andrew HUNT		5000	E. F. Big Tombigby
Joseph HINES		5000	Duck River
Levi HINES, jun.		466	Duck River
Levi HINES		300	Duck River
Tignal JONES		2100	Duck River
Robert IRVEN		3200	Richland Creek
Michael KIRKPATRICK		1000	No. side Elk River
William LOGGINS		640	
John LOCK		2000	Duck River
James M. LEWIS		4000	Richland Creek
Robert LANIER		640	Martin's Creek
John M'CORKLE		640	
John MARR		1000	
Henry MUNFORD		5000	
William MORSE		5000	W. F. Cain Creek
Benjamin M'CULLOCH		1240	
Mark MITCHELL		5000	
John NELSON		15000	
John PATTON		320	Little Harpeth
Rees PORTER, sen.		1180	So. side Duck River
Elijah PATTON		1000	Knob Creek
Elijah ROBERTSON		10000	Richland Creek
William RAINEY		4000	
Daniel SMITH		1000	Duck River
Gatlib SHOBER		1000	So. side Elk River
John SEVIER		2115	Richland Creek
Robert SMITH		5000	Sugar Creek
Michael SWEATMAN		640	M'Crory Creek
Edward THURSBY		10000	
Caleb TAIT		5000	Richland Creek
Robert W. SMITH		2500	Rock Creek

(Continued on following page)

33

(Williamson County delinquent tax list continued)

David VANCE	620	Swann Creek
James WATSON	7081	
Isaac WRIGHT	500	Big Harpeth
Thomas THOMPSON	700	Duck River
David ROBERTSON	310	Duck River
James WHITE	70	Harpeth

Reward $10. Sometimes July last, a negro man by the name of VERGIL, about 22 or 23 years old, ranaway from the subscriber. He calls himself HAMBLETON. Quin Morton BURWELL.

On Monday last, Benjamin WHITE, jun. was apprehended on suspicion of robbery.

Reward $10. Thomas HUTCHINS is wanted by the subscriber in Stuart (sic) County on business not to his advantage. Those with information, please write Jesse DONSON, p. m., Dover, Stewart, c. h. t. Jessee DONSON and John CHAMBERS.

February 10, 1808, Vol. 4, No. 6

On the 19th of April next in the town of Knoxville, there will be a public sale directed by the Knox County Court of one lot in said town that is the property of John H. WETZEL. The property was taken at the influence of Richard G. WATERHOUSE. Joseph LOVE, sheriff of Knox County, by his deputy James C. LUTTREL.

On the 19th of March next in the town of Dandridge, there will be a public sale directed by the court of Jefferson County of 200 acres on Long Creek, that is the property of Elisha ESTIS. The property was formerly occuppied by Benjamin BRADFORD. The property was taken at the influence of James BRADFORD, assignee of Benjamin BRADFORD. Jas. DOHERTY, coroner of Jefferson County.

I will not pay any debts other than those by my written order. Thomas RIPLY.

On the 19th of March next in the town of Maryville, there will be a public sale directed by the Roane County Court of a claim of land in Blount County on the Holston River, that is the property of John TRIMBLE. The tract adjoins John RANKIN. The property was taken at the influence of Archibald LACKY. Saml. COWAN, sheriff of Blount County.

The Registrar's Office is open for business. Edw. SCOTT.

For sale, cut nails, spikes, and nail rods. Andrew and Thomas ELLICOTT, Baltimore.

February 17, 1808, Vol. 4, No. 7

In Campbell County on Walnut Creek, there is 60 acres in lots being offered for sale in order to establish a town called Jacksborough. Commissioners: Sampson DAVID, John INGLISH, John YOUNT, John NEWMAN.

February 24, 1808, Vol. 4, No. 8

The partnership of Josiah and John NICHOL is dissolved by mutual consent at the firm in Maryville. Will all those indebted pay John NICHOL at Kingston or Abram K. SHAFER. Josiah NICHOL and John NICHOL.

On the 10th of March next at the house of John YENT, in place of holding court in Campbell County, there will be a public sale directed by the Hamilton District Court of 200 acres on Big Walnut Cove which was formerly owned by Charles I. LOVE. Michael HUFFTAKER, sheriff of Campbell County by his deputy Wm. HANCOCK.

March 2, 1808, Vol. 4, No. 9

I have opened a house of private entertainment on the Cumberland Road near Hurricane Branch. William GIBSON.

A sorrel horse was taken up by David WILLIAMS on the Chucky River six miles from Greeneville, Greene County. Thomas MURPHY, ranger.

March 9, 1808, Vol. 4, No. 10

Philadelphia, February 11th. Capt. WILLIAMS of the Sea Nymph arrived at New York from St. Croix brought information about the blockade at Martinque.

March 16, 1808, Vol. 4, No. 11

Reward $20. A mulatto boy called JOHN, age 20, 5 ft., 5 or 6 inches tall, ranaway from the subscriber. He will try for Ohio and will pass as John WARD or John MATCHER. Robt. CKOCKETT (sic), Wythe County, Virginia.

Reward $10. Ranaway from the subscriber on the Wolf River, Stockden's Valley, Overton County, near the Kentucky line, a negro man called STEELE. He is about 30 years old and 5 ft., 8 inches tall. In order to receive the reward, please deliver said negro to Matthew CAMPBELL, Grainger County. John BEATY.

March 23, 1808, Vol. 4, No. 12

Wanted, a well digger. A. B. ARMSTEAD, Captain U. S. Artillerists, Highwassee Garrison.

The partnership of Samuel MARTIN & Co. of Kingston, Roane County is dissolved by mutual consent. Samuel MARTIN and William KING.

March 30, 1808, Vol. 4, No. 3

Mr. GARDENIER was shot by Mr. CAMPBELL.

On the 16th of April next at the town of Dandridge, there will be a public sale directed by the court of Jefferson County of 213 acres, that is the property of Daniel JACKSON. The property was taken at the influence of William JOHNSTON against Daniel JACKSON and Jessee RIGGS. James BRADFORD, sheriff of Jefferson County.

Miss Charlotte ROULSTON, age 11, died. She was the daughter of George ROULSTONE, dec.

On Friday evening last, the house of Col. John MCCLELLAN of Roane County burned.

On the 21st of May next at the town of Marysville, there will be a public sale directed by the court of Blount County of a tract, that is the property of Jacob HUNTER and John REID. The property was taken at the influence of John BOYD. Saml. COWAN, sheriff of Roane County.

On the 7th of May next in the town of Sevierville, there will be a public sale directed by the court of Sevier County of 2 acres and 9 poles on Middle Creek, that was surveyed for Benjamin PEARSON and transferred to John GILLIHAN. The property was seized by James P. H. PORTER, Wm. MILLER, and Pleasant M. MILLER. Wm. MITCHELL, sheriff of Sevier County.

On the 7th of May next in the town of Sevierville, there will be a public sale of two tracts on Millicken Creek, that is the property of John HATCHER. The property was taken at the influence of John CLABAUGH. Wm. MITCHELL, sheriff.

On the 7th of May next in the town of Sevierville, there will be a public sale directed by the Sevier County Court of 47-3/4 acres on Knobb Creek, that was surveyed in the name of John GUIN and transferred to James HAMBLETON. The tract was attached by John HAUCK. Wm. MITCHELL, sheriff.

On the 21st of May next in the town of Maryville, there will be a public sale directed by the Roane County Court of a tract of land in Blount County, that is the property of John TRIMBLE. The land adjoins John RANKIN. The tract was taken at the interest of Archibald LACKEY. Saml COWAN, sheriff of Blount County.

April 6, 1808, Vol. 4, No. 14
Roane County, Tennessee, December Sessions, 1807. The following tracts of land will be sold in the town of Kingston on the first Monday in July next to satisfy the unpaid taxes for the year 1807. John BROWN, s. r. c.

Reputed Owners	Acres	Situation
Stockley DONELSON	---	Grant No. 223
Landon CARTER's heirs	1000	Adj. William BUCK
David PATTON or		
George GORDON	1000	
Guyon LEIPER's heirs	400	Grant No. 1254
Robert BURTON	3000	White Oak Springs

The following persons are signers to a letter to the editors: Joseph CLAY, Abram TRIGG, John RUSSELL, Josiah MASTERS, George CLINTON, jun., Gurdon S. MUNFORD, Samuel SMITH, John THOMPSON, Peter SWART, Edwin GRAY, John HARRIS,

W. HOGE, Samuel SMITH, Daniel MONTGOMERY, Samuel MACLAY, David R. WILLIAMS, James M. GARNETT, John RANDOLPH.

New York, March. On the 26th of January, Capt. SPINK from Cadiz was boarded by the gunship Dragon off Madeira.

On the 14th of May in the town of Blountsville, there will be a public sale directed by the court of Sullivan County of a tract of land, that is the property of John JENNINGS. The property was taken at the interest of William WALLACE. James PHEGAN, sheriff of Sullivan County.

On the 10th of May next in the town of Elizabethton, there will be a public sale directed by the court of the Superior Court of the Washington District of 200 acres on Indian Creek and ironworks, that is the property of Michael SWINGLE. The property was taken at the influence of George REINICKER against Michael SWINGLE and Leonard SWINGLE. A. WILLIAMS, sheriff.

Hickman County, Tennessee, January term, 1808. William PHILLIPS, collector, reports that the following tracts of land still have unpaid taxes for the year 1808 and are liable for a double tax. William STONE, c. m. c.

Reputed Owners	Acres	Situation
Levi DAWSON	1225	Duck River
Michael BUTLER	640	Hurricane Creek
John GWIN	640	Hurricane Creek
Alexander MARTIN	640	Hurricane Creek
Jonathan E. ROBERTSON	80	Greys Bend
Joel LEWIS and		
Aaron PARKER	100	Duck River
David ROBERTSON	100	Mill Creek
George MARTIN	60	Bear Creek
James ALSTON	80	Beaver Creek
Benjamin EVANS	45	Baron Fork
Richard WHITE	320	Hurricane Creek
Thomas PARSONS	228	Beaver Creek
John KING	457	Lick Creek
Elizabeth RBERTSON	640	Beaver Creek
William MOORE	640	Duck River
William POLK	640	Duck River
Robert BRADLEY	640	Hurricane Creek
Hancock NICOLS	640	Hurricane Creek
John GILLS	358	
Ann GREER	640	Little Piney
John ALLEN	1120	Duck River
Robert & John ROWLAND	428	Hurricane Creek
Solomon PARKER	753	Lick Creek
James RICHARD	357	Lick Creek
Ruebin GRANT	640	Lick Creek
Thomas PARSONS' heirs	640	Adj. Joshua HADLY

(Continued on following page)

37

(Hickman County delinquent tax list continued)
    Humphrey HARELY   240   Military Line
    William BRYAN   274   Leatherwood
    Richard BRITAIN   398   Pine River
    Philip COKE   640   Hurricane Creek

The following is a list of letters remaining at the post office at Rogersville on April 1, 1808, per F. DALZELL, p. m.: James AMIS, James ARMSTRONG, Ephraim ANDREWS, Joseph ANDERSON, John ARMSTRONG, William BRADLEY, Ruebin BARNETT, William BAILEY, Moses BALL, William BRICE, Thomas BROOKS, John BRIANT, James CHARLES, Benjamin CLOUD, Joseph CLIPPER, Ballard COLDWELL, James COOPER, Tabitha COX, Margaret CAMPBELL, Jessee DAY, John ELLIS, James FORGERY, Doct. FINLAY, Bazet GRISSEL, Jacob GROVES, Pilomel GREEN, Thomas GIBBONS, Richard GRAMEIN, John GIBBONS, Hezekiah HAMBLTON, William HOWELL, Nathl. HENDERSON, Drury HOLT, Mary HUMMEL, John HINSON, James HAGOOD, James HAGON, Amase HOWELL, James HORNBACK, Xpher (sic) HAYNES, James JOHNSTON, Thomas JOHNSTON, Abraham JAGO, John JOHNSTON, Thomas INGRAM, Pleasant JOHNSTON, Randal LAWRENCE, James LAUPER, William LYON, Richard MCCARMACK, George MAXWELL, Martin MENES, Christain MALOBY, Samuel MCPETERS, Alexander MCCANSE, Jacob MILLER, Gabriel MCCRAW.

April 12, 1808, Vol. 4, No. 15
The following is a list of letters remaining at the post office at Knoxville on April 1, 1808, per John ARMSTRONG, a. p. m.: Thomas BROWN, Minor BELL, Willie BLOUNT, Mrs. Barbery BARRINGER, Ebenezer BYRAN, William BELL, Joseph BALL, Samuel BRON, James and John BRUCE, Iashel CHAPMAN, Thomas V. CHAPMAN, Samuel CRAIG, Alexander CAMPBELL, Joel CANNON, Andrew CAMPBELL, John CAMPBELL, William CUNNINGHAM, William CLARK, William COSSINEL, Samuel CUNNINGHAM, James CHEEK, Francis DOWLER, John DOUGLE, Wm. DAVENPORT, Miss Lucy FRANKLIN, Jessee DELOZENIR, James FINLEY, Cristian FOUST, Reade S. FLOYD, Thomas GOLAHER, John GIBSON, Francis B. HAYNES, Luke HENDRICK, Thomas HALL, Joseph HAMBLETON, Jacob HAM, William HENFORD, Col. David HENLY, William HORD, Miss NANCY HERRIN, Samuel HENDERSON, Michael KARNES, Josiah KINDRED, William LEUTY, Charles LITTLETON, Francis MAYBERRY, Robert MILLER, Quin MORTON, John MCIVER, John MILLER, James MCNEAR, James MCCOWN, Rev. William MCCAMPBELL, David NORTON, Doct. John NEWMAN, Mrs. Margaret NEWMAN, Danl. OSBORN, Peter PARSONS, Jacob PATTON, John PEYTON, Edward PEARSE, Benj. PRICE, James C. PATTON, Thomas PATTERSON, George ROWLAND, Lieut. Gilbert C. RUSSELL, James RUSSELL, John SMITHFIELD William REEDER, Absolem RUTHERFORD, Miss Fanny REDMAN, Col. William RAMSEY, Thomas ROBINSIN, Valentine ROBERTSON, Isaac RUTHERFORD, Andrew RUSSELL, John RUTHERFORD, William WHITE,

William RONE, Rev. Saml. G. RAMSEY, Peter STUART, George THAUGHTER, Mrs. Margaret SWAN, Thomas B. SPAIN, George SHUTTER, Daniel STEWART, Williston TALBOT, Doct. Alfred THURSTON, Joseph THOMPSON, Thomas UPTON, William or John WHITEMAN, Reverend Thomas WILKINSON James WOOD, Benjamin WATKINS, Jesse WITT, James WILSON, William WHITE, John WATSON, William WHITEMAN.

The following is a list of letters remaining at the post office at Greeneville on April 1, 1808, per Wm. DICKSON, p. m.: George GORDON, William MOTT, David BIDDLE, Robert M'CALL, James JONES, Robert DICKSON, Zachariah KINNEMAN, James LANDRUM, Morris MORRIS, jun., Ezekial FRAZIER, John GAMBLE, Harman COSSMAN, Jacob STEGLE, Lewis BALL, William KELLY, James PATTERSON, Abraham DOUGHERTY, Henry ERNEST, Morris MORRIS, sen., Samuel HENDERSON, jun., Andrew ENGLISH, jun., Michael BRIGHT, Robert WILSON, George FEEGARDER, John PITTWAY, William HARPER, Messers. William and Iree BRADFORD, George WOLF, Jacob LONGE, Benjamin VANPELT, Gravner MARSH, John TURNER, Edward BRANSCOM, Nathan BARNS, Lydia or William JONES, Rev. George WELLS, Daniel DUN, Henry MILLER, Kernal, CONUAIN, Cornelius NEWMAN, Andrew M'PHARLAND, Isaac WALKER, Robert GRAGG, David COPELAND, Daniel COSSMAN.

Grainger County, Tennessee, November term, 1808. James CONN, collector, reports that the following tracts of land still have unpaid taxes for the year 1806. Ambrose YANCEY.

Reputed Owners	Acres
James COOPER	400
John ADAIR	600
Godfrey CARRIGER	500
William HUNT	200

Burke County, North Carolina, Court of Equity, March term, 1808. Alexander SINCLEAR vs. James BRYSON, William BRYSON, and John DAWES. John DAWES is not a resident of the state of North Carolina. He is ordered to appear in court on the fourth Monday in September next and answer the bill of complaint. A. L. ERWIN, c. m. e.

Diomed will stand this season at Stephen HAYNES' in Knoxville. John SNAPP.

I shall apply to the Commissioner of East Tennessee for a certificate on Grant No. 431, dated July 29, 1793, issued to Thomas KEY for 1000 acres in Hawkins County which is now called Grainger County. The property was conveyed to Francis MAYBERRY and assigned to Thomas GRAHAM, Nathl. GRAHAM, Mordica MENDINGEALL, Ryan SUMMONS.

May 11, 1808, Vol. 4, No. 19

On the 25th of June next in the town of Dandridge, there will be a public sale directed by the court of Jefferson County of 200 acres which is owned and occuppied by Joseph

DAMERON. The land adjoins Adam WEAVER and Chas. PORTER. The property was taken at the influence of Chas. T. PORTER. Jas. BRADFORD, s. j. c.

Campbell County, Tennessee, March term, 1808. Michael HUFFTAKER, sheriff, reports that the following tracts of land still have unpaid taxes for 1807. James GRANT, clerk.

Reputed Owners	Acres
Willie BLOUNT	1600
Britain RAGSDALE	135
Robert DELAP	200

Asa HAZEN, cabinet maker, opened a shop in Knoxville.

Charleston, April 12th. The schooner Citizen under the command of Capt. STURGES arrived with fifty-two marines commanded by Lt. Master PICKNEY.

Azekiah DOTY, on Lick Creek in Greene County, has taken up a chesnut sorrel mare. On April 5, 1808, the mare was appraised at a value of $50.

Hamilton District, In Equity, March term, 1808. Barclay MCGHEE vs. John MONTGOMERY and Edward LYNCH. Edward LYNCH is not an inhabitant of this state and he is ordered to appear in court on the second Monday September term next, Joseph GREER, by his deputy, G. WILSON.

Hamilton District, In Equity, March term, 1808. James DALES vs. Francis MAYBERRY and Leroy TAYLOR. Francis MAYBERRY is ordered to appear in court on the second Monday in September next term. Joseph GREER, by his deputy, G. WILSON.

May 18, 1808, Vol. 4, No. 20

On the 14th of May next in the town of Blountsville, there will be a public sale directed by the court of Sullivan County of a tract of land, that is the property of John JENNINGS. The property was taken at the influence of William WALLACE. James PHAGAN, s. s. c.

May 25, 1808, Vol. 4, No. 21

On the 14th of July next in the town of Dandridge, there will be a public sale directed by the Jefferson County Court of 100 acres acres on Muddy Creek, that is the property of Joseph COPLAND. The land adjoins Josiah DENTON. The property was taken at the influence of Thomas BRYAN. James BRADFORD, s. j. c.

On the 2nd of July next in the town of Dandridge, there will be a public sale direct by the Hamilton District Court of two tracts of land, that are the property of Joseph DAMERON. The land adjoins John M'DONALD. The property was taken at the influence of NINNY & GRAHAM. Parry TALBOT.

On the 2nd of July next in the town of Dandridge, there will be a public sale directed by the Jefferson County Court of 150 acres on Last Creek, that is the property of Joseph HODGIN. The property was formerly owned by Ebenezer JOHN. The property was taken at the influence of Ebenezer JOHN. Parry TALBOT, d. s. j. c.

On the 4th of July next in the town of Dandridge, there will be a public sale directed by the Jefferson County Court of 200 acres on Flat Creek, that was owned and occuppied by Samuel MOORE. The property was taken at the influence of Joseph DAMERON. James BRADFORD, sheriff of Jefferson County, by his deputy, Jas. DOHERTY.

On the 4th of July next in the town of Dandridge, there will be a public sale directed by the Jefferson County Court that was owned and occuppied by Antipart THOMAS. The property was taken at the influence of Henry WALKER against Antipart THOMAS, John MOORE and Samuel MOORE. James BRADFORD, sheriff of Jefferson County, by his deputy, Jas. DOHERTY.

On the 4th of July next in the town of Dandridge, there will be a public sale directed by the court of Jefferson County of 50 acres owned and occuppied by Jonathan HEARELD. The property was taken at the influence of John RHEA against Samuel MOORE. James BRADFORD, sheriff, by his deputy, Jas. DOHERTY.

June 1, 1808, Vol. 4, No. 22

James HOPKINS, taylor, commenced business in the house lately occuppied by James DARIS. Mrs. HOPKINS offers her services as a mantua-maker.

Reward $20. A negro man called PHILL, age 40, ranaway from the subscriber living in Cumberland County, Kentucky. He is headed for North Carolina. David JONES.

The following persons have reported estrays in Sevier County, per Benj. AMORRET:
- (1) Elizabeth WEBB, on the Cumberland Ridge, has taken a yellow sorrel mare. On May 28, 1808, the mare was appraised at $30.
- (2) William ROBINSON, on the east fork of the Pigeon River, has taken up a sorrel horse, The horse was appraised at $40 on May 28, 1808.

Robert SMITH, on the Little Chucky in Greene County, has taken up a stray horse, On May 21, 1808, the horse was given an appraised value of $20. Thomas MURPHY, ranger.

June 8, 1808, Vol. 4, No. 23

A rifle was found on the road from Oresville. James FORGY, Hawkins County.

All persons are forewarned from trading with the negroes of Joseph GREER. James CHARTER.

On the 4th of July next in the town of Dandridge, there

41

will be a public sale directed by the Jefferson County Court of 100 acres, that is the property of Joseph COPELAND. The land adjoins Josiah DENTON. The property was taken at the influence of Thomas BRYAN. James BRADFORD, s. j. c.

On the 16th of July next in the town of Dandridge, there will be a public sale directed by the court of Jefferson County of 150 acres, that is owned and occupied by Jacob PURKEY. The property was taken at the influence of Jacob LAYMAN against Christopher LAYMAN, Jacob LAYMAN and Jacob PURKEY. James BRADFORD, sheriff of Jefferson County.

On the 23rd of July next in the town of Jonesborough, there will be a public sale directed by the court of Washington County of 13 acres and a lot with a house, that was formerly occuppied and is currently owned by John IRWIN. The land adjoins James LONG. The property was taken at the influence of William M'KINSEY & Co. Joseph BROWN, s. w. c.

June 15, 1808, Vol. 4, No. 24

Reward $20. On the 6th of June a pregnant, negro, woman called RACHAEL ranaway from the subscriber. Joseph YOUNG, near Jonesborough, Washington County.

Nimrod PINDENGRASS, on Walding Creek, Sevier County, took up a bay horse. On June 7, 1808, the horse was appraised at a value of $10. Benjamin AMONNET.

Godfrey GRAINGER, jun., on the Watauga near Elizabethton, Carter County, took up a sorrel gelding. On June 6, 1808, the horse was appraised at $35. James JOHNSON, ranger.

Rueben BERRYMAN, in Blount County, has taken up a sorrel mare. On June 16, 1808, the mare was appraised at $40. John GARDINER, ranger.

June 22, 1808, Vol. 4, No. 25

For sale, assorted goods. Calvin and Gideon MORGAN.

On the 13th of August in the town of Rutledge, there will be a public sale directed by the court of Grainger County of 250 acres on Richland Creek, that is the property of Lewis EDWARDS. The land is occuppied by Richard DUMVILL. The property was taken at the influence of Adam LITTLE. James CONN, sheriff of Grainger County.

On the 14th of July next, I shall apply to the Commissioner of East Tennessee for a certificate on Grant No. 1205, dated November 27, 1792, issued to Jonathan LANGDON for 640 acres. Jonathan LANGDON.

Reward $20. On the 4th of May last, a negro called JOE, age 35, ranaway from the subscriber living in the Cherokee Nation. James ROGERS.

July 6, 1808, Vol. 4, No. 26

The following is a list of letters remaining at the post

office at Rogersville on July 1, 1808, per F. DAZELL, p. m.: Lincon AMIS, Thomas ARMSTRONG, William ARMSTRONG. Hains AMIS, Major ANDERSON, William BRICE, John BRIANT, Mordicai BEAN, Samuel BLACKWELL, Docher BRAGG, John BIGLEY, Hutchins BURTON, Doctr. John BALLUS, William BRADLEY, Thomas CONWAY, William R. COLE, Edward COX, John CARNS, Jacob COX, William COCK, Joseph CLIPPER, John COX, Jacob CRESS, Jesse DILLON, Archibald CORMER, Samuel COEN, Richard OLVILL, Jessee DAY, John ECKFERD, Dr. John ELLIS, Hough FORGEY, Thomas GALLION, Doctr. FINLEY, John FOSTER, Thomas GIBBONS, Fanny GILLESPY, James HADGES, William HOWELL, James HAGOOD, Christain HAINS, James HOLLINGWORTH, Amare HOWELL, Thomas JOHNSTON, Andrew INGRAM, Capt. KILE, Capt. KLINE, George KITE, William KING, Micajah LEE, JOHN LEE, Thomas LEE, John LAWSON, John LANE, Lemuel LANIER, Randolph LAWRENCE, Presley MCLOMEN, Joseph MCCULLOUGH, Eli MCVAY, Thomas MORRISON, John MAISBY, Daniel OWENS, John MORRISETT, George MORELACK, Enoch MORRISETT, Zadoe MOORE, William PHILIPS, John PROVINCE, Joseph PARKER, John RUTHERFORD, William RAYNOLDS, George ROBERTS, Henry W. RICHARDSON, John ROBERTS, Moses RHEA, Woodford RICHARDS, Philip SIMMERMAN, Lockley STUBBLEFIELD, Paris SIMS, John SHROPSHIRE, Samuel STUBBLEFIELD, John STAINS, John TATE, Theophilus TERMENT, ELijah TANCRA, James WEST, Joseph WETHERS, Samuel WILSON, Larkin WEBB, William YOUNG, John YOUNG, Francis YOUNG.

Reward $20. On the 27th, Henry HAYS deserted. He is 5 ft., 7-1/2 inches tall, has black hair, hazel eyes, and is 25 years old. He was born in Burlington County, New Jersey. He is by occupation a nailer. A. B. ARMISTEAD, Capt. U. S. Artillerists, Highwassee Garrison.

Adam FEAGELLY, on Boyd's Creek, Sevier County, has taken up a brown mare, On June 25, 1808, the mare was appraised at $25. Benjamin AMONNETT, ranger.

For sale, dry salt. William KING.

July 13, 1808, Vol. 4, No. 27

The following is a list of letters remaining at the post office in Knoxville on July 1, 1808, per J. ARMSTRONG, a. p. m.: Robert ARMSTRONG, William ARRONTON, James ASDILL, James BENNET, John BELL, Nicholas BOND, Thomas BROWN, Thomas BOYD, Peter BENNETT, John BROWN, Rice BUCKNER, John Harry BURTON, John BAREGER, Greeham CROWDER, Joseph CALLOWAY, William COO, Samuel CHAYNE, William COUPLAND, Peter CAN, Matthew COUNCIL, Judge CAMPBELL, James HAVEY, Edward CORMICK, John CARWELL, William CROW, William COPELAND, Mary CLIFT, Jessee CAMERON, Joseph CROUCH, Stephen CLARK, James B, COWELL, Peter DOSER, Daniel CALBIRTH, Col. Thomas DAVIS, Elijah DOWELL, Archibald DUNLOP, Henrry (sic) D. ENCLE, James EPPS, Peter EPPERSON, Richard ELAM, Thomas FIGURES, Pleasant FURGUSON, Christopher

LIGHTNER, George   GROVE, Maj. James   GRANT, Francis   GION,
James   GULLY, Alex.   GASTON, Lewis   HILL, Dennis   HENLY, John
HUCKABY, Thomas   HUDEBURK, James   HUCHESON, Henry   HANKER,
Ricahard HUMPHRIES, Thomas HOPE, Thomas HALL, John HACKETT,
Ambrose JONES, Jessee B. KEY, George KOOK, Peter KENER, Hugh
KENNEDY, John   KENNEDY, James   C, LUTTREL, William   LITTLE,
Robert LINDSAY, Acquilla LOW, John LOVE, James   LUTTREL,
Richard   H. LOVE, Charles   LUKES, John   K. LONDON, Moses
LOONEY, Luke LEAS, Samuel LOVE, Jacob LONIS, William M'LIN,
James   MOORE, John   MOTTIS, James M'NAIR, Quin MORTON, Nancy
M'CLURE, Theoderick MASCEY, Thomas M'KNIGHT, David MITCHELL,
Samuel   MONTGOMERY, Starks   MOORE, Mrs. Alce MURPHY, Edward
M'COLLEY, John   M'DONALD, Alex. M'CLINTOCK, James and Thomas
M'CONNEL, Capt. Enos NOWLAND, William T. NORTHERN, William
PRATT, Col. Alexander OUTLAW, William PINN, Joseph PAYNE,
Benjamin   PRIDE, Thomas   RYLAND, Absolem   ROWLAND, George
ROWLAND, James ROBINSON, Charles REAGAN, Joseph RANEY, Isaac
RUTHEROFRD, Hannah SAWYERS, Jessee SULLIVAN, William SHOOK,
Benjamin   SAUNDERS, Layton SMITH, Abel STAFFORD, Archibald
TRIMBLE, William   TATE, William TALBOT, Michael TABLER, Jas.
WICKS, Richard THOMPSON, Tomas (sic)   UMPHRIES, Elizabeth
VANCE, Thomas WRIGHT, Benjamin WHEELER, Buckner WILSON, Mrs.
M. WHITE, William WILLIAMS, John WITT, Jenkin WHITESIDES.
     On the 13th of August next in the town of Rutledge, there
will be a public sale directed by the court of Grainger
County of 80 acres on Skin Creek, that is the property of
Lewis EDWARD. The property was taken at the influence of
Gilbert VANDIGRIFF. James CONN, sheriff of Grainger County,
by his deputy, Isaac CAMPBELL.
     The copartnership of ALLEN & ALLISON is dissolved by
mutual   consent. John   ALLEN, William   ALLEN, and   John
ALLISON.

July 20, 1808, Vol. 4, No. 28
     The following is a list of letters remaining at the post
office in Greenville on July 1, 1808, per Robert DICKSON:
Martial AYERS, Col. Ewen ALLISON, Soolmon (sic) BEALS, David
BIDDWELL, Rhudulpus (sic) BOS, Raneld (sic) CARTER, James
CALLINGHAM, Nicholas   DRACE, Daniel DUGGER, William HOUSTON,
Philip HOWELL, Francis HUGHES, Isaac HONE, Walter HARRIS,
John   KENNEDY, James LAND, Christopher LOTSPICK, Henry
MCLAUGLIN, Grayner MARSH, Cornelius NEWMAN, Thomas RODGERS,
John   REYNOLDS, John   RADER, Susanna   ROANS, Capt. George
RINHER, Samuel ROBINSON, Robert SMITH, Benjamin SEVERTAKE,
Major TEMPLE, William WEST.
     On the 27th of August next in the town of Kingston, there
will be a public sale of a tract of land, that is the
property of Thomas SHYES. The property adjoins William
GARDENDENSHIRE. The land was taken at the influence of James

GALAHER against Thomas SHYES and Samuel RUTHERFORD. John BROWN, s. r. c.

On the 27th of August next in the town of Kingston, there will be a public sale directed by the Roane County Court of 99 acres on Cow Spring Creek, that is the property of William WALKER. The tract is occuppied by Dancy DRINCARD. The property was taken at the influence of Michael GOZA, John BROWN, s. r. c.

On the 27th of August next in the town of Kingston, there will be a public sale directed by the court of Roane County of 130 acres on White Oak Creek, that is the property of William JONES. JONES resided on the tract last summer. The property was taken at the influence of Samuel C. MOORE. John BROWN, s. r. c.

The following is a list of invalid pensioners mentioned in Congress on April 25, 1808.

Names	Amount	Date		
Thomas Lamar DAVIS	$ 2.50	December	29,	1807
Albert CHAPMAN	10.00	October	17,	1807
Ambrose HOMAN	2.50	December	15,	1806
Richard SCOTT	2.50	October	5,	1807
Francis BLOOD	5.00	December	16,	1806
Jonas GREEN	5.00	October	8,	1807
William GREEN	8.00	February	7,	1807
Seth WEED	6.00	October	7,	1807
Peter SMITH	4.00	July	16,	1806
Samuel LATHROP	5.00	September	22,	1807
William JOHNSON	2.50	April	1,	1807
James HOUSTON	15.00	July	13,	1807
Jedediah HYDE	15.00	August	3,	1807
Samuel NESBIT	5.00	October	18,	1807
Sheperd PACKARD	3.00	February	7,	1807
Richard KISBY	4.00	March	24,	1807
Jonathan WILKINS	2.50	March	26,	1807
Waterman BLADWIN	5.00	October	25,	1807
John CLARK	8.00	December	15,	1807
John VENUS	2.50	December	11,	1807
John HOLCOMBE	15.00	December	1,	1807
Richard STEADS	4.00	December	9,	1807
Alexander JONES	3.33	June	19,	1794
Benjamin SADDLER	3.00	January	1,	1803
Benjamin JENKINS	2.50	September	16,	1807
William SCOTT	25.00	March	12,	1807
James BRUFF	20.00	August	17,	1807
Nathan TAYLOR	10.00	February	19,	1808
Aaron STEVENS	10.00	February	24,	1808
Simon MORGAN	20.00	March	2,	1808
Jonathan PATCH	5.00	July	11,	1806

(Continued on following page)

(List of invalid pensioners continued)

Name	Amount	Date
Ebenezer ROWE	5.00	January 16, 1807
Benjamin KENDRICK	3.33	January 1, 1806
Nicholas LOTT	2.50	January 23, 1808
Nicholas HOFF	5.00	February 22, 1808
Samuel SHAW	8.00	February 13, 1808
Humphries BECKET	2.50	January 8, 1808
Silas PAIROTT	6.00	February 10, 1808
Jared HINKLEY, jun.	2.50	January 19, 1808
Francis DAVIDSON	4.00	January 16, 1808
Andrew WAGGONER	20.00	November 2, 1807
George RICHARDSON	4.00	February 10, 1808
William WALLACE	8.00	January 16, 1808
Joseph BIRD	4.00	January 29, 1808
John St. JOHN	5.00	January 29, 1808
Abner SNOW	3.75	January 27, 1808
Aaron CRANE	2.50	November 3, 1807
James HAWKLEY	5.00	January 6, 1808
Jon VAN ANGLEN	15.00	November 3, 1807
James BUDEN	2.50	March 28, 1808
Isaac BURNHAM	4.00	January 1, 1803
Benjamin HILLAMN	10.00	March 14, 1808
Silas PIERCE	10.00	March 17, 1808
Randel M'ALISTER	5.00	March 7, 1808
John DURNAL	3.00	April 17, 1808
Jabez CHURCH	2.50	February 22, 1808
Thomas MACHIN	10.00	March 19, 1808
David RICHEY	2.50	April 2, 1808
James CAMPBELL	4.00	September 25, 1807
John BEARDSLEY, jun.	5.00	November 13, 1807
Thomas BRISTOL	5.00	October 22, 1807
Josiah SMITH	5.00	December 29, 1807
Joseph WACE	5.00	December 29, 1807
Daniel BUCK	5.00	December 17, 1808
Lemuel KING	5.00	December 23, 1807
William WALLACE	5.00	November 17, 1807
Joseph SAUNDERS	5.00	February 7, 1807
William HASTINGS	5.00	February 11, 1807
Joshua LOVEJOY	5.00	June 5, 1807
Isaac HIGGINS	3.33	September 29, 1807
Rueben DOW	15.00	February 19, 1807
Joseph HARRYS	5.00	September 15, 1807
David RANNEY	5.00	November 5, 1807
John WHITEHORN	5.00	September 30, 1807
Richard SHERMAN	5.00	October 8, 1807
Noah SINCLAIR	3.75	October 8, 1807
Nathaniel CHURCH	5.00	October 8, 1807
Gershorn CLARK	5.00	January 1, 1808

(Continued on following page)

(List of invalid pensioners continued)

John M'KINSTREY	12.00	December	7, 1807
Ebenezar PERKINS	5.00	September	15, 1808
Henry TEN EYCK	15.00	November	21, 1807
Thomas SIMPSON	13.33	December	24, 1806
John RYBECKER	4.00	April	18, 1807
Lemuel DEAN	5.00	October	8, 1807
Thomas JOHNSTON	5.00	April	17, 1807
Levi CUBBECK	3.75	June	20, 1808
Samuel ROSSETTER	5.00	January	30, 1808
Jeremiah PRITCHARD	13.33	January	6, 1808
Abner GAGE	5.00	January	6, 1808
John DEVOE	5.00	January	30, 1808
Nathaniel BRADLEY	5.00	January	26, 1808
Thaddeous SEELY	2.50	January	9, 1808
John HERRON	2.50	January	26, 1808
Peter NEVUIS	4.00	February	17, 1808
John HAMPTON	6.00	February	17, 1808
Roswell WOODWORTH	5.00	March	23, 1808
David HULLBELL	5.00	March	19, 1808
John M'COY	5.00	March	15, 1808
Caleb HUNT	5.00	March	5, 1808
Henry GATES	5.00	March	9, 1808
David HALL	5.00	February	12, 1808
Jonah COOK	5.00	April	4, 1808
William NELSON	5.00	January	22, 1808

August 17, 1808, Vol. 4, No. 33

On the 24th of September next in the town of Knoxville, there will be a public sale directed by the court of Knox County of 200 acres, that is the property of John SMITH. The tract adjoins Joseph HIPPENSTALL. The property was taken at the influence of John HUNTSMAN. Joseph Love, sheriff of Knox County.

On the 17th of September in the town of Dandridge, there will be a public sale directed by the court of Jefferson County of 150 acres, that is the property of Joseph DOGINS. The tract adjoins Aaron NEWMAN and William CODWELL. The property was taken at the influence of Austin ELMORE and Joseph NEWMAN. James BRADFORD, sheriff of Jefferson County.

My wife Ann DAVIS has eloped from my bed without just cause. I will not pay her debts. John DAVIS.

My wife Nancy has found herself repugnant to the duties of a wife. I will no longer live with her or pay her debts. Mordicai MICHELL, Blount County.

Robert FARNSWORTH, on the Chucky River, has taken up a sorrel horse. The horse was valued on August 3, 1808 at the sum of $30. Thomas MURPHY, ranger, Greene County.

Edwin E. BOOTH wrote a letter to the editor.

A chesnut sorrel mare strayed or was stolen from the subscriber near the head of the Sequatchee. Mathias BRILES and Jonathan WARREN.

John COSBY on Thursday, the 11th, was married by Rev. Isaac ANDERSON to Miss Abigail MCBEE. Both are of this county.

On the 27th of September next in the town of Maryville, there will be a public sale directed by the District Court of East Tennessee of several town lots, that are the property of John LOWERY. The property was taken influence of Alexander FULTON and James FULTON. Charles T. PORTER, marshall of the District of East Tennessee, by his deputy, William SMITH.

The following persons were appointed trustees of East Tennessee College: Richard MITCHELL, Hawkins County; Andrew GALBREATH, Hawkins County; John RHEA, Sullivan County; James KEY, Sullivan County; Augustine P. FORE, Greene County; John GASS, Greene County; Mathew STEPHENSON, Washington County; John KENNEDY, Washington County; David DEADERICK, Washington County; George DUFFIELD, Carter County; Francis A. RAMSEY, Knox County; James RICE, Jefferson County; Joseph HAMILTON, Jefferson County; Geo. DOHERTY, Jefferson County; Alexander SMITH, Cocke County; Hopkins LACY, Seveir County; John COCKE, Grainger; Maj. LEA, Grainger County; John CROZIER, Knox County; Joseph B. LAPSSAY, Blount County; Robert GANT, Blount County; John LOWREY, Blount County; William GRAHAM, Claiborne County; Arthur CROZIER, Anderson County; George W. CAMPBELL, Knox County; Thomas I. VANDYKE, Roane County; John SEVIER, Knox County; Thomas EMMERSON, Knox County; John WLLIMS, Knox County; Archabald ROANE, Knox County; Francis A. RAMSEY, Knox County.

Daniel MARTIN, on Walnut Cove, Campbell County, has taken up a bay mare. On August 17, 1808, the mare was appraised at the sum of $30. Thomas CAMPBELL, ranger, by his deputy, Even WALLACE.

On the 26th of September next in the town of Knoxville, there will be a public sale directed by the Knox County Court of 150 acres on Bull Run, that is the property of John MITCHELL. The property was taken at the influence of Walter ALVES. Jos. LOVE, sheriff, by his deputy, David LOVE.

On the 1st of October in the town of Knoxville, there will be a public sale directed by the Knox County Court of lot no. 13, that is the property of William MACLIN. The property was taken at the suit of Alfred M. CARTER for the use of James AIKEN, plaintiff. Joseph LOVE, s. k. c.

Doublehead, a Cherokee chief, dec., in his will stated that Thomas N. CLARK, John D. CHISOLM, and Return MEIGS would take care of his children and dipose of his estate.

There was a letter to the editor from G. SHALL.

Josiah NICHOLS examined the accounts of the firm of PRITCHETT & SHALL and the account books of Francis DOWLER. Francis DOWLER gave a bill of sale on July 24, 1808 for a tract of property to Joseph C. STRONG, William I. SMITH, John BROWN, and Pat CAMPBELL.

August 24, 1808, Vol. 4, No. 34

On the 8th of October next in the town of Knoxville, there will be a public sale directed by the Knox County Court of 201 acres on the south side of the Holston and French Broad Rivers, that is owned and occupied by James MOORE. The property adjoins Edward MASON. The property was taken at the influence of Thomas LYTLE. Joseph LOVE, sheriff of Knox County, by his deputy, David LOVE.

There was an Act passed for the relief of George HUNTER of Philadelphia.

September 7, 1808, Vol. 4, No. 36

I am empowered to make applications for the following persons for their warrants, which were entered at CARTER's office. Nathl. TAYLOR.

Claimant	Acres	Warr. No.	Location
Wm. WHITSON	100	2443	Cocke County
John BEAN	100	2673	Bedford County
Joseph TIPTON	---	1700	Carter County
John DAVIS in behalf of Ezekial BEARD	640	1689	Ash County, NC
John ADAMS	300	1819	North Carolina
David HUGHS	600	269	Sullivan County
Joseph BULLARD's heirs	100	2318	Bedford County
Jessee BOUNDS	200	2441	Mockeson Gap, Va
Daniel HARRISON	31	2743	Flint River
William DAVIS	440	762	Lick Creek
Wm. BEAN's heirs	250	589	Hawkins County
Jonathan TIPTON	150	1133	Buncomb C., Nc
Jessee BOUNDS	100	206	Mockeson Gap, Va
Robert KING, by him transferred to Stockley DONELSON then to John KEITH	200	428	
Entered by John ROBINSON, claimed by John KEITH	200	1320	South Carolina

The following was entered at ARMSTRONG's office:

Claimant	Acres	Warr. No.	Location
Joseph TIPTON	200	1427	Carter County

On the 15th of October in the town of Dandridge, there will be a public sale, directed by the Jefferson County Court of 100 acres that is owned and occupied by Samuel MOORE. The property was attached by Joseph DAMERON. James BRADFORD, s. j. c., by his deputy Parry TALBOT.

Reward $1. A bound boy named Burton P. SHIVERS absconded from the subcriber on the west fork of the Little Pigeon. He is 16 years old and has a fair complexion and hair. Anthony LAWSON.

For sale, saddle trees. John M. TELFORD.

My husband Henry SNIDER has left without just cause. Jane SNIDER, Sullivan County. Witness John TREDWAY and Warham EASLEY.

On the 17th of September in the town of Dandridge, there will be a public sale directed by the court of Jefferson County of 120 acres, that is the property of John CARSON. The tract adjoins Alexander KELSO. The property was taken at the influence of CAMPBELL, MARTIN & Co. James BRADFORD.

September 1808, Vol. 4, No. 37

I will not pay my wife's contracts. Dudley COX.

There is a $10 reward for the return of a chestnut sorrel mare, that strayed or was stolen from the subscriber. Jacob GROVES, Hawkins County.

October 5, 1808, Vol. 4, No. 40

The following is a list of letters remaining at the post office in Knoxville on October 1, 1808, per John ARMSTRONG, a. p. m.: David AIVES, John BRAZELTON, Shadrick BRIDGET, James BRYLZE, Mrs. Patsy BALLARD, Francis BOUNDS, Miss JANE BAYE, Michael CHILDERS, John CLARK, William COE, Jefferson CAMPBELL, Joseph CALLEWAY, Berryman S. CLARY, Francis CARDS, Alexr. CAUNS, Thomas CRANK, David CUNNINGHAM, Samuel DAVIS, Robert CHILDERS, Isaac CHARLES, Jonathan DOUGLASS, Nathaniel DAVIS, Rueben DUNNINGHAM, Jacob DICKENSON, Archibald DUNLOP, Binns DURRIN, John DOHERTY, Thomas DUGGIN, Deverix GILHAM, Solomon FUDY, William FLETCHER, Elias DRIGGS, Eleven HITCH, Joshua EPPS, Moses BROOKS and Samuel FLEMING, Jacob HAM, Thomas GILLESPIE, William GRAYSON, Richard HUMPHRIES, Thomas ELLICOTT, Edward HARRIS, Spencer HARTLEY, Thomas HALL, John HARRIS, William HUGHS, Richard JEARDIN, Lewis JONES, Charles KIRKPATRICK, Hugh KENNEDY, Jacob KENNEDY, Samuel KERR, Moses LOONEY, Wigton KING, Rev. James KINNADAY, Wm. LONG, Clemment LANIER, Richard LLOYD, George LAWES, Wm. LEUTY, Samuel MAY, John MCMAHON, Elevin MOORE, James MITCHELL, Jos. MCMILLAN, Henry MILLER, John MCINTIRE, John MILLER, Robert MOORE, Wm. MOORE, Moses MORDICA, Quin MORTON, Rueben MONDAY, Mitchell MCFARLAND, George MARTIN, James MCKIDDY, Andrew NEILY, David NIMMO, Thomas NEWLAND, William NORTHERAER, Thomas NANCE, Peter PARSONS, Thomas PRATT, Thos. POTTERS, William PRATT, Wm. PURRIS, Frederick PEETERS, Isaac RUTHERFORD, William READERS, Bartlett REAMS, Joseph ROBINSON, David SEVERS, Wm. VANCE, Isaac STOUGHT, James SHEPPARD, Abraham SMITH, Walter SIMS, Rev. Frederick STEER, Mark SWADLEY, Vinian STEEL, Jas.

WILSON, James THOMPSON, William VANCE, Jacob VARNER, West WALKER, Susannah WAGGONER, Martha WHITE, Isaac WRIGHT, John WADDLE, William WILSON, Mrs. Ann WHITE, Mrs. Mary WHITE, Mathew WALKER.

I have opened for the business of boot and shoemaking in the house formerly occuppied by John H. WETZEL, that is next to Wm. I. SMITH. William HEATH.

I want to forewarn the public against trading or taking assignments on four notes given to Edom DIXON at $100 each and payable June, 1808. Said DIXON failed to comply with his written contract and I will not pay the notes. Jacob COOK.

The following is a list of letters remaining from the post office at Greenville on October 1, 1808, per Robert DICKSON, a. p. m.: James ANDERSON, Michael BURGLAR, Claudius BUSTARD, Samuel Y. BALCH, Michael BRIGHT, John BINNET, John BACON, Joseph BROWN, Hezekiah COPLAND, Peter CRUMB, Daniel M'CLELLAND, Enoch CONISON, Thomas CHAMBERS, Richard ELLIS, John EVANS, Jonathan EVANS, William GRANT, Jacob GRAY, John GREGG, Finsley HEATH, John M. A. HAMBLETON, William HOUSTON, Joseph HOLT, Isaac JUSTIC, Christopher KIRBY, Mrs. Ann LOVE, William MYERS, John MOORE, Samuel MALBASH, John REDDER, John RIEV, Susannah ROWAN, Mrs. Jane RUSSELL, Benjamin SANDS, Robert SMILEY, Wm. SMEDLY, William WEST.

The following is a list of letters remaining at the post office at Rogersville on October 1, 1808, F. DALZELL, p. m.: George ARGINBRIGHT, John BRAND, Wm. BRIGHT, William BRADLEY, Thomas CALDWELL, George COX, William COX, Abrahan COLEVIN, John CARMACK, Thomas DOGGETT, Thomas DODSON, Michael DEEKER, Townshead S. DUKE, John FOLKES, John FORD, John GILLAM, Jacob HECKNEY, John HAWKINS, Samuel HELTON, Jonathan LONG, Elijah KINCHOLE, William HORD, James HAGOOD, John LANE, John POINDEXTER, Christian PEARSON, William NOEL, Isham MILLS, David MARTIN, Enoch MORRISET, Samuel M'PHETERS, William ROWAN, William RIGHT, Henry W. RICHARDSON, Stephen RICHARDS, Wm. STUBBLEFIELD, Christain SIMMONS, John TATE, John TIBS, Herman C. VEID, John VAUGH, Aaron WELLS, David WEER, Martin WHELISS.

My wife Sarah has taken to bad practices and has absented herself from my home. I will not pay her debts. John AYERS.

I have in my possession a bay mare which was supposed to be stolen from Grainger County. Jacob SHAWMAN.

William ISABEL, on Hob Creek, Sevier County, has taken up a bay mare. On October 5, 1808, the mare was appraised at $13. Benj. AMONNETT, ranger.

A gentleman, who arrived from Vermont, stated that Capt. MORR was found guilty of murder.

On the 22nd of October next in the town in Jonesborough, there will be a public sale at the direction of the court of

Washington County of 33-3/4 acres, that is the property of Massey TANNER. The tract adjoins Joseph BRITTON. The property was taken at the influence of David G. VANCE. Joseph BROWN, sheriff of Washington County.

Wanted, a drummer and fifer. G. W. SEVIER, Capt. U. S. Regiment, Knoxville.

A negro called BOB was committed to jail. He says that he ranaway from Joseph MCCRAVENS near Nashville. Charles DONOHOO, jailor, Maryville.

November 2, 1808, Vol. 4, No. 44

Hamilton District, In Equity, September term, 1808. Christian RHOADS vs. Stephen DUNCAN. Stephen DUNCAN is not an inhabitant of of this state. He is ordered to appear in court during next term and answer the bill of complaint. Joseph GREER, clerk & master, by his deputy, G. WILSON.

Robert CARR, on the French Broad, Sevier County, has taken up a bay mare. On October 20, 1808, the mare was appraised at $40. Benj. AMONNETT, ranger.

On the 26th of November next in the town of Kingston, there will be a public sale directed by the Roane County court, that is owned and occuppied by Leonard BAWERMAN. The property was taken at the influence of SHALL & PRITCHETT. John BROWN, sheriff of Roane County, by his deputy, Thos. BROWN.

Reward $10. Ranaway from the subscriber a negro man named PETER. He is 50 years old and is part of the estate of Col. Thomas KING, dec. He is heading for South West Point. Nancy KING, admtrx., Jos. MCMINN, Hawkins County.

On the 19th of November next in the town of Rutledge, there will be a public sale directed by the court of Grainger County of 100 acres, that is owned and occuppied by John NEWMAN. The property was taken at the influence of NEAL & SIMPSON, James CONN, sheriff of Grainger County.

On the 26th of November next in the town of Kingston, there will be a public sale of town lot no. 56, that is the property of Adam FORMWALT. The property was taken at the influence of Enoch WILLETT. John BROWN, sheriff of Roane County, by his deputy, Tho. BROWN.

For sale, household furniture, cattle, and horses. Wm. MOORE.

All persons are forewarned against trading or taking assignments for two notes given on December 31, 1806 to William DAWSON, Lenoir County, North Carolina, for $240 and $250, that are payable on December 31, 1808. William DAWSON absconded without giving me a title. He sometimes goes by the name of Henry Williams LAWSON. Henry WOOLARD.

Maury County, September term, 1808. David ROSS, by his agent Thomas HARNEY, will apply for a certificate issued in the name of William BROWN for 640 acres. Joseph B. PORTER.

November 9, 1808, Vol. 4, No. 45
I shall apply to the Commissioner of East Tennessee for a certificate on Grant No. 739 issued on September 10, 1795 to Robert YOUNG for 5000 acres. The land was then in Hawkins County. Micajah CROSS claims the land by virtue of a sale of execution.

David WHITE, on White Creek, Blount County, has taken up a bay mare. On November 9, 1808, the mare was appraised at $35. John GARDINER, ranger.

On the 19th of December next in the town of Kingston, there will be a public sale directed the Roane County Court of a 1/5 part of Thomas SHOY's right to 400 acres on Caney Creek. The property was granted by North Carolina to Guyon LIEPER on July 12, 1790. The property was taken by James GALLIHER against Samuel RUTHERFORD and Thomas SHOY. John BROWN, sheriff of Roane County.

On the 3rd of December next in the town of Jonesborough, there will be a public sale directed by the court of the Washington District of 970 in Washington County, that is the proeprty of John HAMPTON. The property adjoins Christr. TAYLOR. The property was taken at the influence of John MCGINNESS. Joseph BROWN, sheriff of Washington County.

In the town of Rogersville, there will be a public sale directed by the Hawkins County Court of 320 acres, that is the property of Lawrence YOUNCE. The tract is occuppied by David LINKAID and adjoins Samuel GIMMEL. Also being sold is 140 acres, that adjoins Thomas HOPKINS. The property was taken at the influence of Jeremiah BURNET. A. LOONEY, shff.

In Rogersville, there will be a public sale directed by the Hawkins County Court of 100 acres, that is the property of Absalom ROSEBERRY. The tract adjoins John COCKERHAM. The property was taken at the influence of William MORRIS, A. LOONEY, s. h. c.

I shall apply to the Commissioner of East Tennessee on the behalf of the heirs of William WARD, deceased, for a certificate for 640 acres, that was issued by North Carolina on November 10, 1784 on Grant No. 560 to William WARD.

November 16, 1808, Vol. 4, No. 46
On Thursday evening last, Rev. Samuel CARRICK married James TRIMBLE, attorney of this town, to Miss Leletia CLARK, daughter of Thomas N. CLARK of South West Point.

On the 13th of December next in the town of Jefferson, there will be a public sale directed by the Jefferson County Court of 100 acres on the south side of the French Broad, that is the property of Joseph SWELLY. The property was taken at the influence of Hannah WILSON, executrix of Daniel

WILSON, dec. James BRADFORD, sheriff of Jefferson County. On the 9th, a note for $130 was lost on the road between Knoxville and Mr. MEREDITH's. John BROWN. Open, a turnpike. William COCK.

December 14, 1808, Vol. 4, No. 5

On the 21st of January, there will be a public sale directed the Blount County Court of of a tract, that is the property of William GREENE. The property adjoins Mary LACKEY. The property was taken at the influence of Samuel LOVE & Co. Samuel COWAN, sheriff of Blount County, by his deputy, Andrew COWAN.

On the 14th of January next in the town of Dandridge, there will be a public sale, directed by the Jefferson County Court of a tract, that is owned and occuppied by Solomon BOHART. The property was taken at the influence of Silas HALL and Hamilton BRADFORD. James BRADFORD, sheriff of Jefferson County, by his deputy, Jacob HARMON.

On the 14th of January next in the town of Dandridge, there will be a public sale directed by the Jefferson County Court of 100 acres, that is the property of William B. SEWELL and George SEWELL. The property adjoins Wm. ROULSTON. The tract was taken at the influence of Jesse MOORE. James BRADFORD, sheriff of Jefferson County, by his deputy, Jacob HARMON.

December 21, 1808, Vol. 4, No. 51

For sale, some negroes and four stud horses. William P. CHESTER.

Thomas MCCULLOUGH, on the Little River, Blount County, has taken up a sorrel mare. John GARDINER, ranger.

In the town of Jonesborough, there will be a public sale directed by the court of Washington County of two lots, that belong to Andrew BELFOUR. The property was taken at the influence of David DEADERICK. Joseph BROWN, sheriff.

On Saturday last, a jury impanneled (sic) to try the indictment of Richard BERRY of Washington County. They brought back a verdict of guilty of robbing the mail.

January 17, 1809, Vol. 5, No. 3

The following is a list of letters remaining at the post office at Greeneville on January 13, 1808, per John R. RENTPHRO.: John A. AKEN, James ANDERSON, John BENNETT, Michael BRIGHT, Stephen BROOKS, Jacob BRUNER, Levi CARTER, Michael BROILS, James CREELEY, George GORDON, Jacob GRAY, Catey GREGGORY, Joseph HOLT, James HAYS, Epraim HICKSON, Aron HOPTON, Edmund HEATH, Joseph HENDERSON, Wm. HAWKINS, Thomas JONES, A. KENNEDY, Zachariah KIMERMON, Aron LIP--, Wm. MYERS, Joseph MCANDREW, James MURNEY, Scolafield MADOX,

Mr. PATTERSON, Joseph   REYNOLDS, Margaret   ROGERS, John
REDDER, Jas. SCOTT, Robert   SMITH, Thomas   TEMPLE, William
WEST, Henry TEEZEER, Thos. TITSWORTH, Ephraim WILSON.
Norfolk, December 5th. Capt. COLLINS from Jamaica spoke
on the 9th with the British sloop Henry. Capt. LONGSHIELD
informed him about the war in Europe.
In an article regarding seamen and marines, the following
persons were mentioned: Mr. NELSON, Mr. STORY, Mr. NEWTON,
Mr. PITKINSON, Mr. VARNUM, Mr. HOLLAND, D. R. WILLIAMS.

January 25, 1809, Vol. 5, No. 4
Abraham COLLINS, acknowledged counterfeiter of bank
notes, arrived in Knoxville with Mr. HENDERSON and another
man not known. He took the Cumberland Road early on Saturday
for New Orleans. Let everyone be on their guard.
The Rev. Lawner BLACKMAN, President elect of the
Methodist Episcopal Church, will preach at the court house
in Knoxville tommorrow.
On the 17th of March next in the town of Kingston, there
will be a public sale directed Roane County Court of 3500
acres, that was granted by North Carolina to LEWIS and
LENORE. The property was taken at the influence of James
GLASGOW and Robt. WHITE and his wife. John BROWN, sheriff.
The following persons have reported estrays in Blount
County, per John GARDINER, ranger:
    (1) Samuel MCCULLOUGH, jr., on the Little River, has
         taken up a bay horse.
    (2) James W. LACKEY, on Cloyd's Creek, has taken up a
         bay horse. The horse was valued at $15.
    (3) Samuel MCCULOUGH has taken up a sorrel mare.

February 1, 1809, Vol. 5, No. 5
Mrs. Catherine HAYNES, consort of Stephen HAYNES of this
town, died on Saturday morning last.
Application will be made Commissioner of East Tennessee on
the first of March next for a certificate on Grant No. 90,
dated November 14, 1790, by North Carolina to Thomas COLDWELL,
deceased.

February 8, 1809, Vol. 5, No. 6
Robertson County, Tennessee, January term, 1808. John B.
CHEATHAM, collector, reports that the following tracts of
land still have unpaid taxes for; the year 1807. Thos.
JOHNSON, c. r. c.

Reputed Owners	Acres	Situation
John BEARDING	420	Cabble's Creek
Thomas CLARK	246	
Daniel TURNER's heirs	640	Miller's Creek

(Continued on following page)

55

(Robertson County delinquent tax list continued)

Thomas HOPKINS	640	Holly's Lick
William JORDAN	640	
Richard CROSS	100	Cabble's Creek
Susannah HART	2560	Several tracts
Walter BROWN	640	

Williamson County, Tennessee. Notice is hereby given to the owners of the following tracts of land, that I shall on the first Monday in July next in the town of Franklin proceed to sell the property. S. CHILDRESS, sheriff.

Reputed Owners	Acres	Situation
William LYTLE	640	Leiper's Fork
Isaac PRICE	3000	Rutherford's Creek
Robert PAGE	70	West Harpeth
Thomas PARKER	120	McCory's Creek
Clement WALL	33	Grove Creek
William POLK	5000	Harpeth
Richard PAGE	160	1 white poll
William PAGE	150	Hay's Creek
Capt. Wm. RICHARD	1280	West Harpeth
David SHELBY	1200	Arrington's Creek
John SMITH	100	Harpeth
William TUTON	190	Nelson's Creek
Robert NELSON	580	McCory's Creek

The following tracts are liable for a double tax:

Reputed Owners	Acres	Situation
John ANDERSON	286	Late prop. of Robert HAYS. 1806, 1807,1808
William GALLAGHER	1500	Rutherford's Creek
Samuel BLAIR	160	Little Harpeth
James WINCHESTER	550	Part of Curtis IVY's tract. 1804,5,6,7,8.
James GALLOWAY	5000	Cedar Creek, 1807
Archibald CRATCH	550	1808

For the year 1808:

Reputed Owners	Acres	Situation
Daniel TURNER's heirs	640	Miller's Creek
Thomas HOPKINS	640	Holly's Lick
Susannah HART	2500	
John BEARDING	420	Caleb's Creek
Thomas DEADERICK	540	Red River
John NEVILLE	115	Caleb's Creek

For the year 1809:

Reputed Owners	Acres	Situation
Nathan TURPIN's heirs	640	Sychamore Creek
Alexander NELSON	274	Col. FORD's old place
Thomas BEATTY	1000	Battleground Creek
Andrew HAMPTON	640	Elk Fork
Armstead MILLER	640	Miller's Creek

56

Williamson County, Tennessee, January Sessions, 1809.
Stephen CHILDRESS, collector, reports that the the following
tracts of land still have unpaid taxes for the year 1808.

Reputed Owners	Acres	Situation
Alexander CRAWFORD	150	Murfree's Fork
ALLEN & BURTON	---	Two town lots
Benjamin H. COVINGTON	640	Big Harpeth
Robert B. CURRY	115	Harpeth
Peter EDWARDS	1097	Big Harpeth
John B. EVANS	540	Arrington's Creek
Robert FENNER	4030	Richland Creek
Isaac GILLESPIE	748	Flat Creek
Robert HULME	124	Big Harpeth
John HAINS	150	
Elijah LINCOLN	---	Town lot
James M. LEWIS	228	Leiper's Fork

On the first day of April in the town of Knoxville, there
will be a public sale directed by the Circuit District Court
of East Tennessee of 575 acres on Hawk Creek, that is the
property of William COOKE. Charles T. PORTER, marshall, by
his deputy, Wm. SMITH.

On the 25th of March next in the town of Rogersville,
there will be a public sale directed by the Hamilton
District Supreme Court of 300 acres on the north side of the
Holston River, that is the property of Robert KING. The
property was taken at the influence of Peter TANNER against
John CHISHOLM, Alexander CARMICHAEL, and Robert KING. A.
LOONEY, sheriff of Hawkins County.

The following persons have reported estrays in Roane
County, per M. NELSON, ranger:
(1) Thomas N. CLARK, living at South West Point, has
taken up a bay horse.
(2) Lewis KIRKPATRICK, on the Clinch River, has taken
up a sorrel horse.

February 22, 1809, Vol. 5, No. 10
There is a notice to SEVIER, that was signed by Wm.
LILLARD and I. THOMAS, jun.

HEWLETT & BARTHOLOMEW saddlers is open for business in
Knoxville. Edmund HEWELETT and Joseph BARTHOLMEW.

On the 15th of April next in the town of Knoxville, there
will be a public sale directed by the 7th District United
States Court of East Tennessee of 1000 acres, in Roane
County, that is the property of Alexander OUTLAW. The tract
is currently occupied by Edward SMITH. The property was
taken at the influence of John CAMPBELL, Gidion SMITH, Wm.
SMITH, Charles HODGES, and John TAYLOR. Charles T. PORTER,
marshal, by his deputy, Wm. SMITH.

On the 15th of April next in the town of Dandridge, there

will be a public sale directed by the court of Jefferson County of 100 acres on Long Creek, that is the property of Charles WILLIAMS. The tract adjoins George EDGAR and Benjamin BRADFORD. The property was taken at the influence of the state. James BRADFORD, sheriff of Jefferson County, by his deputy, Jacob HARMON.

Will persons indebted to the estate of Dennis MURPHY, dec., please come forward and settle their accounts. James CHARTER, admin.

On the 15th of April next in the town of Dandridge, there will be a public sale directed by the court of Jefferson County of 200 acres on Long Creek, that is the property of Wm. WILLIAMS. The tract adjoins Robert MCCLENHAN. The property was taken at the influence of the state. James BRADFORD, sheriff of Jefferson County, by his deputy Jacob HARMON.

William PHILLIPS has opened a house of private entertainment on the Wilderness Road about 35 miles east of Carthage.

On the 15th of April next in the town of Rutledge, there will be a public sale directed by the court of Grainger County of 350 acres on the south side of Richland Knob, that is the property of John BURDS. The property was taken to satisfy a judgement obtained by William MCNEIL. James CONN.

March 15, 1809, 5, No. 11

Reward $30. A dark chestnut sorrel horse was stolen from the subscriber on the first day of this month. Robert MANN, Roane County.

On the 10th of Setember term next, we will petition the Superior Court of the District of Hamilton for a partition of tract of land granted to Richard HENDERSON by North Carolina. Thomas HART and Joseph HART.

March 22, 1809, Vol. 5, No. 16

On Thursday the 16th in the 81st year of her life, Mrs. Margaret CHAPMAN died. She was the relict of Thomas CHAPMAN of Knox County.

Hickman County, Tennessee, Janaury term, 1809. William PHILLIPS, collector, reports that the following tracts of land still have unpaid taxes for the year 1808. William STONE, c. h. c.

Reputed Owners	Acres	Situation
Barton SCOGGINS	100	Indian Creek
Thomas PARSON	640	Pine River
Thomas POLK's heirs	2191	Defeated Creek
Henry JONES	640	Pine River
Oliver SMITH	640	Pine River

(Continued on following page)

58

(Hickman County delinquent tax list continued)

William MOORE	3840	Duck River
Daniel SHAW	2360	Duck River
Phillip TAYLOR	1755	Duck River
James COUNCIL	3840	Duck River
James BRENSON	320	
Daniel CHERRY	480	Duck River
Henry JONES	64	Garner's Creek
Edward HARRIS	274	Duck River
Nicholas LONG's heirs	1000	Military line
William MCGEE	50	Bear Creek
James NORRIS	100	Turnbull Creek
William, Joseph, David, and		
George BROWN	274	Pine River
Samuel SPRAGGINS	768	Duck River.
John DAVIS	474	Lick Creek
Jessee WILLIAMS	274	Duck River
John DAVIS	220	Duck River

The partnership of James WHITE and John LYNCH is dissolved by mutual consent. Burrville, March 16, 1809.

March 29, 1809, Vol. 5, No. 13

Hickman County, Tennessee, January Session, 1809. William PHILLIPS, collector, reports that the following tracts of land still have unpaid taxes for the year 1808 and are liable for a double tax. William STONE, c. h. c.

Reputed Owners	Acres	Situation
Levi DAWSON	4225	Duck River
Michael BULLER	640	Hurricane Creek
John GWINN	640	Hurricane Creek
Alexander MARTIN	640	Hurricane Creek
Jonathan F. ROBERTSON	80	Duck River
Joel LEWIS and Aaron PARKER	100	Duck River
David ROBERTSON	100	Mill Creek
George MARTIN	50	Bear Creek
James ALSTON	80	Bear Creek
Benjamin EVANS	45	Sugar Creek
Richard WHITE	320	Hurricane Creek
Thomas PARSONS	228	Beaver Creek
John KING	457	Lick Creek
Elizabeth ROBERTSON	640	Pine River
Anthony HART	640	Beaver Creek
William MOORE	640	Duck River
William POLK	640	Duck River
Robert BRADLEY	640	Hurricane Creek
Hancock NICHOLS	640	Hurricane Creek
John GILES	350	Pine River
Ann GREER	640	Duck River

(Continued on following page)

(Hickman County delinquent tax list)

Jessse COBB	640	Little Piney
John ALLEN	1120	
Solomon PARKE	733	Lick Creek
Robert and John ROULARD	224	
James RICHARD	357	Lick Creek
Thomas PARSONS' heirs	228	Beaver
Humphrey HARDY	357	Military Line
William BRAYAN	274	Leatherwood
Richard BRITAIN	398	Pine River
John HARVEY	640	Tumbling Creek
Philip COLE	640	Hurricane Creek

On the 13th of May next in the town of Jacksborough, there will be a public sale directed by the court of Campbell County of 150 acres in Powell's Valley, that is the property of Littleberry CROWLEY. The tract is occuppied by Joseph BARRON. The property was taken at the influence of Sampson DAVIS, surviving partner of the firm of KING & DAVID. Thos. MOAD, sheriff of Campbell County.

On the 6th of May next, there will be a public sale directed by the Sevier County Court of 39-3/4 acres on Knob Creek, that is the property of Morton HAUCK. The tract adjoins John BRABSON. The property was taken in execution by Thomas STUART and James CHARTER. Wm. MITCHELL, sheriff of Sevier County.

On the 6th of May next in the town of Sevierville, there will be a public sale directed by the court of Sevier County of 235 acres on Middle Creek, that is the property of Jeremiah MATTHEWS. The tract adjoins John CLABAUGH, sen. The property was taken in execution by Alexander PRESTON & Co. Wm. MITCHELL, sheriff of Sevier County.

On the 6th of May next, there will be a public sale directed by the Sevier County Court of a tract on the north side of the French Broad, that is the property of William MERRIT. The tract adjoins Ralph CAMPBELL, Thomas MERRITT and others. The property was taken at the influence of Thomas WODKINS. Wm. MITCHELL, sheriff of Sevier County.

The Newspaper and Washington Advertiser
Published by George Wilson

November 5, 1803, Vol. 3, No. 108

Reward $10. Moses STOUT, between the age of 13 or 14, ranaway from the subscriber on the 20th of March. The subscriber is living in Washington County nine miles from Jonesboro in the neighborhood of ROSS' Ironworks. It is believed; he is headed to Virginia where his father lives. John M'ALISTER, sen. (September 24, 1803)

On the 5th of May last, I married Hannah SMITH, the daughter of Richard SMITH of Washington County. We have agreed to separate and live as before. I will no longer be responsible for her debts or contracts. Thomas BLAIR. (September 25, 1803)

On the 29th of December next, the personal estate of the Wm. EWING will be offered for sale. (September 25, 1803)

For sale in Leesburg, a tavern or store. William SMITH (September 23, 1803)

December 9, 1803, Vol. 3, No. 111

I forewarn all persons from trading or taking assignments on a note of hand for $40, that was given to Barney SHIELDS sometime in May, 1803. The note is payable on the 25th of December next. I have paid said note and given this public notice on October 22, 1803. Wm. HENRY.

I gave a note to George SHIELDS of Greene County for 240 bushels of corn, that was payable on November next. I will not pay said note unless SHIELDS makes good the title to a certain tract of land. David CAMPBELL (December 6, 1803)

On the 13th of September next I gave a note to William IRWIN of Russell County, Virginia in the amount of $116.66, that was payable on December the 25th next. The note was obtained fraudulently. Henry FARNSWORTH, Greene County (November 29, 1803)

All persons with deeds of conveyance in Tennessee are required to have them recorded in the Secretary of the United States' Office. Zach. COX. (November 29, 1803)

On the 4th of February next in the town of Jonesborough, there will be a public sale directed by the court of Sullivan County of 35 acres, that is the property of James REID. The land ajoins the property of Jacob SUMAN. The property was taken at the influence of John RICHAD. Joseph COUCH, sheriff of Washington County, by his deputy, Joseph BROWN. (December 6, 1803)

Dr. Solm. CASNER of Greene County is open for business.

For sale, dry salt, hardware, groceries, corn-fed pork. William KING, Saltville, Washington County, Virginia.

For sale, two likely negroes. Wm. HENRY.

Jackson ANDERSON, the son of James V. ANDERSON, died last night. He was three years old.

<u>February 1, 1804, Vol. 3, No. 113</u>

The commissioners appointed by the court of Sullivan County will meet at the house of the subscriber on the 20th of February next. Peter HICKMAN. (January 17, 1804)

Joseph GLASS has commenced the hatting business in the town of Leesburg. William GLASS, his father, is authorized handle his business. (January 31, 1804)

Will all those indebted come forward. T. STAURT.

Hawkins County, Tennessee, November Sessions, 1803. Alexander NELSON, reports that the following tracts of land still have taxes due for the year 1802. Richard MITCHELL.

Reputed Owners	Acres	Situation
Elisha WALLACE	300	
Thomas FLETCHER and		
Samuel HARRISON	640	Poor Valley
James HARRIS	180	Beach Creek

If Anthony BAYARD, who left his father Powel BAYARD of Rockingham County, Viginia about six or seven years ago to go to Tennessee or Kentucky, will apply to the subscriber in York County, Pennsylvania, he will receive a legacy that was left to him by his father. Henry BOWYER. (October 23, 1803)

Isaac HOUSE, a laborer, 6 ft. tall, slender made, broke jail. He was sentenced to 40 days on the 18th or 19th of September, 1804, in the jail of the town of Jonesborough. Joseph COUCH, Washington County, sheriff, sworn before me on January 2, 1804, George WILSON, justice of the peace.

William HILLARD, gold and silversmith is open for business in Jonesboro. (January 4, 1804)

On the 18th of February next, there will be a public sale of the property of John RICHARDS. It was taken as the property of Jacob WORK, heir of Robert WORK, dec. Thomas SHELBY, s. s. c., Blountsville. (December 14, 1803)

On the 18th of February next in the town of Blountsville, there will be a public sale directed by the Sullivan County Court of the property of John STONE. The property was taken at the influence of John SCOTT. Thomas SHELBY, sheriff, by his deputy James T. GAINES.

On the 11th of February next in the town of Elizabeton, there will be a public sale directed by the Carter County Court of 300 acres, that is the property of Samuel TULLIS. the tract is occuppied by Zachariah CAMPBELL. The property was attached by Moses HUMPHREY. A. BYLER, sheriff.

On the 4th of February next, there will be a sale in the town of Jonesborough of 320 acres, that is the property of Jacob SAPPINGTON. The land adjoins Clement and Nathan GANN The tract was taken by Mr. MOORE. Joseph COUCH, sheriff.

The Carthage Gazette
Published by William Moore

March 30, 1810, Vol. 2, No. 55

On the 16th of April next, there will be a public sale directed by the White County Court of 338 acres, that is owned and occuppied by William PHILLIPS. The property was attached by James PARROT. George WHITE, Coroner.

The subscriber wishes to employ a millwright, a joiner carpenter, and several laborers. William MOORE.

The following persons have reported estrays in White County, per J. A. LANCE, d. r. w. c.

(1) William BROWN, on Caney Fork, has taken up a dark brown horse. On March 17, 1810, the horse was appraised at $18.

(2) Robert JOHNSTON, living on the Turnpike Road, has taken up a bay filly. The filly was valued at $16.

(3) William GRIMES, on Caney Fork, has taken up a bay horse. On March 7, 1810, the horse was given an appraised value of $35.

(4) Alexander COOK, near Rocky Island, has taken up a dark bay mare. On March 12, 1810, the mare was appraised at $8.

(5) Levi BOXWORTH, on Falling Water, has taken up a brown bay mare. On March 19, 1810, the mare was given an appraised value of $16.

(6) Benjamin WEAVER, on Cherry Creek, has taken up a black horse. On March 2, 1810, the horse was given an appraised value of $8.

I want to forewarn the public against taking assignments for a note of hand given by me to Ephraim THOMAS, dated August 18, 1808. The notes are not just. John TEEL.

The following persons have reported estrays in Warren County, per (no ranger given):

(1) William GUSOT, on Hickory Creek, has taken up a black mare. On November 8, 1809, the mare's value was appraised at $20.

(2) A. BAYES, on Hickory Creek, has taken up a grey filly. On November 20, 1809, the mare was given an appraised value of $11.

(3) George LANE, on Hickory Creek, has taken up a bay mare. The mare was valued at $25.

(4) James THOMAS, on Rocky Road, has taken up a brown horse. The horse was valued at $50.

(5) James CLARK, on Rocky Creek, has taken up a sorrel mare. The mare was valued at $25.

May 4, 1810, Vol. 1, 59

On the 2nd of June next in the town of Gallatin, there

will be a public sale directed by the Sumner County Court
of 80 acres, that is the property of William LURRY. The
land is currently occuppied by Harvey R. WILLIS. The
property was taken at the influence of Bright HERRING. W.
H. DOUGLAS, Cotton Fields.

The following is a list of letters remaining at the post
office in Carthage on April 1, 1810, per Charles HERVEY, a.
p. m.: Major ARMSTRONG, James AKIN, Samuel BARNES, Benjamin
BENNET, John BAKER, Thomas BURMINGHAM, Daniel CAMBIAN, Nancy
CHEEK, James CANNAWAY, Henry CORNWELL, Joseph COOK, Abraham
DAVIS, John DAWSON, John Etheridge, Malachi EWIL, Stephen
FARMER, Mr. Wm. FERREL, Leonard FITE, John GORDON, Alexander
M'CALL, Abr. HUDDLESTON, John HARMON, John KIRK, Mary MOSS,
Roger LANKINS, John LEE, Patrick M'EACHRAN, John MATHUSON,
Daniel M'LEOD, John MILLER, Susan MACLIN, Moses MORE, Uzzi
PANKEY, Armstead MOORE, Jesse PATTY, John PATE, James PAIN,
John RUSSEL, David ROBERTSON, Mrs. A. RHODES, Jesse SIXTON,
Bird SMITH, William STEWART, Thomas SMITH, James C. ROLSTON,
Enoch RUST, Arthur TATE, Canelum TAYLOR, Frederick TURNER,
Arthur TURNER, William WHITE, Richard WOBACK, Robert WARD,
James WRIGHT.

On the 2nd of June next in the town of Gallatin, there
will be a public sale directed by the court of Sumner County
of 100 acres, that is the property of John LAFFERY. The
property was taken at the influence of James FORD, Thomas
MORSE, and Robert RUHEGH. W. H. DOUGLASS, Cotton Fields.

The following persons have reported estrays in Overton
County, per B. TOTTEN, d. r. o. c.:
   (1) John HUST, on the Wolf River, has taken up a grey
       horse. On April 19, 1810, the horse was given an
       appraised value of $60.
   (2) James OFFICER, near Standing Stone, have taken up a
       bay horse colt. On April 24, 1810, the colt was
       appraised at a value of $10.

The following persons have reported estrays in Smith
County, per Basil SHAW, r. s. c.:
   (1) William M'GINSON, on Caney Fork, has taken up a bay
       mare. On March 8, 1810, the mare was appraised at
       the sum of $15.
   (2) Susannah JOHN, on Mulherrin Creek, has taken up a
       black mare. On March 10, 1810, the mare was valued
       at the sum of $4.
   (3) Peter DAGNER, on Defeated Creek, has taken up a
       chesnut sorrel mare. The mare's value was given at
       the sum of $4 on February 10, 1810.
   (4) John KIRBY, on Goose Creek, has taken up a brown
       bay mare. On March 9, 1810, the mare was appraised
       the sum of $15.
   (5) Merlin YOUNG, on Jennings' Creek, has taken up a

64

black mare. On March 20, 1810, the mare was valued
at the sum of $10.
(6) R. P. LARKIN, on Sander's Bent, has taken up a
     sorrel mare. On March 23, 1810, the mare was given
     an appraised value of $12.
(7) Claiborne WRIGHT, on Sullivan Bent, has taken up a
     bay mare. The mare was valued at $30.
(8) Tancy K. WITCHER, on the Big Barren, has taken up a
     sorrel mare. The mare was valued at $22.
(9) Ellis BEASLY, in Bledsoesborough, has taken up a
     mare. On March 27, 1810, the mare was appraised at
     a value of $10.
(10) Lewis CORDER, on Beech Bent, has taken up a yellow
     bay mare. On March 21, 1810, the mare was given an
     appraised value of $10.
(11) Richard BRITTON, on Goose Creek, has taken up a
     sorrel mare. On February 10, 1810, the appraised
     value of the mare was given at $20.
(12) George BARNS, on Dry Fork, has taken up a sorrel
     horse. On February 10, 1810, the mare was given an
     appraised value of $20.
(13) Charles BOULTON, on Caney Fork, has taken up a bay
     horse. On March 1, 1810, the mare was appraised
     at the sum of $12.
(14) Benjamin SNOW, on Dry Fork, has taken up a sorrel
     mare. On March 28, 1810, the mare was given an
     appraised value of $12.50.
(15) Frederick TURNER on Tooley's Bent, has taken up a
     bay horse. On March 28, 1810, the horse was given
     an appraised value of $12.50.
(16) Joab HAIL, on Caney Fork, has taken up a mare.
Zebodiah STOCKSTILL, on Charles Creek, has taken up a
strawberry roan colt. T. H. EWEN.

May 25, 1810, Vol. 2, No. 62
The following is a list of letters remaining at the post
office at Fort Blount on April 1, 1810, per S. WILLIAMS:
Gasper BARGER, Marget BARGER, Thomas BILLINGSLEY, Noah
BENNET, Stewart DOSS, James HUSTON, John HUSTON, Erasmus
MAYS, John M'CARVER, William M'DOANLD, David M'CALLISTER,
Daniel NORTON.
On the 2nd of June next in the town of Carthage, there
will be a public sale of the plantation where Samuel
M'FERRIN lives. The property was taken at the influence of
John COOPER against Samuel M'FERRIN. George MATLOCK, shff.
On the 4th of June next in the town of Carthage, there
will be a public sale 640 acres, that is the property of
James BEVIN. The property adjoins Martin HYERS and Joel
SIMMONS. The land was attached by John GIVEN. G. MATLOCK.

Smith County, Tennessee, March Term, 1810. George MATLOCK, sheriff and collector of the public tax, for the year 1809 reports that the taxes still remain unpaid. Joseph W. ALLEN, clerk.

Reputed Owners	Acres	Situation
William HUGLET	100	
Francis SANDERS	200	
Griffith RUTHERFORD	620	1 white poll
Alexander BRADEN	640	
Charles CROUGHTON	1900	
James CROWTEN	50	
Edward GWIN	180	
Thomas HARDMAN	640	
John RUMBLER	50	
George WILSON	120	
William WHITE	355	
John LEE	120	1 white poll
James GLENN	100	1 white poll
Peter KING	100	1 white poll
Augustin CARTER	lot	Carthage
Thomas KING	640	
William HARRIS	172	
Richard CENTREL	100	1 white poll
James BLACKMORE	98	
John M'NAERY	900	
Daniel PRESS	283	
James WINCHESTER	502	
Gifferd DUDLEY	359	
Edwin HICMA's heirs	2148	
James HEMPHILL	640	
William SMITH	878	
Henry DICKENS	35	
Jesse NICKLES	244	1 white poll
Robt. HAMILTON	2000	
William HUGHLET	474	
Thos. JOHNSON	640	
Masenda MATHEWS	1000	
Plotomy POWEL	1000	
Jesse PARSINS	640	
Roger PARONS	640	
Michael ROBERTSON	640	
William TRIGG, jun.	640	
William TRIGG, sen.	1000	
Rueben WILKISON	2560	North side Cumberland
Robert DOUGLASS	2580	South side Cumberland
James SNELL	204	Round Lick
Andrew ARMSTRONG	274	Peyton's Creek
Samuel CUMMINGS	640	Warrent No. 2384

(Continued on following page)

66

(Smith County delinquent tax list continued)
     John and Ephraim DAVIDSON 168   Warrant No. 3251
     Edwin WILLOUGHBY   640   Warrant No. 4285
     Smith County, Tennessee, March Term, 1810. John GORSON,
late sheriff and collector of the taxes for the years 1807
and 1808, reports that the following tracts will be sold on
the first Monday in November next. Joseph W. ALLEN

Reputed Owners	Acres	Situation
Francis CHILD's heirs	2560	Cany Fork
John DAVIS	440	
Moses DOOLEY		For the stand of a stud horse
Thos. HAMILTON	1280	
John NEELEY's heirs	320	
Daniel WILBOURN	300	
Archibald CANNON	50	1 white poll
Abram ELLIS		1 white poll
William MORGAN	50	1 white poll
John HARVEY	200	Hickman's Creek
Robert DOUGLASS	2380	

     The following persons have reported estrays in Overton
County:
     (1) Polly SEAHORN, on the Cumberland River, has taken
          up a bay mare. On May 1, 1810, the mare was given
          an appraised value of $20.
     (2) Frederick DEEK, on Copeland Creek, has taken up a
          roan mare. On April 30, 1810, the mare was given
          an appraised value of $15.
     The following persons were mentioned in the list of laws
passed on the Second Session of the Eleventh Congress of the
United States: William RECTOR, Elias RECTOR, Levin JONES,
Jeremiah REYNOLDS, Harry CALDWELL, Amasa JACKSON, Tristen
HUSEY, William HAWKINS, John KERR.
     On the 14th of June next, I shall make application to the
Commissioner of West Tennessee for a duplicate of Warrant
No. 2750, that was part of a tract granted to John GADDY on
Grant No. 307 on March 7, 1796. The applicants received
their title by a sheriff's deed executed by Benjamin TOTTEN.
Wm. FLEMING for Jas. ARMSTRONG and Samuel HUDDLESTON.
     The partnership of C. FINLAY & Co. is dissolved by mutual
consent. C. FINLAY and T. M'NUTT.
     On the 2nd of June next in the town of Gallatin, there
will be a public sale directed by the Sumner County court of
100 acres on the Cumberland, that is the property of John
LAFFERY. The property was taken to satisfy three judgements
obtained by James FORD, Thomas MORSE and Robert RALIEGH. W.
H. DOUGLASS, d. s., Cotton Fields.
     In 1804 a note of hand was given to John HUGGENS for a
$52 debt, that was attached to my lands by Joseph LAND. I

forewarn all persons from purchasing said note from HUGGENS. Joseph Colville.

The following persons have reported estrays in Smith County, per B. SHAW, r. s. c.:
(1) Thomas LANCASTER, on Smith's Fork, has taken up an iron grey mare. On April 24, 1810, the mare was appraised at $25.
(2) Edward FARRIS, on Dixin's Creek, has taken up a black horse. On April 12, 1810, the horse's value was given at $16.
(3) William TAYLOR, on Indian Creek of the Caney Fork, has taken up a horse. On April 16, 1810, the horse was appraised at $12.
(4) Rebecca HOGG, on Goose Creek, has taken up a sorrel filly. On April 20, 1810, the filly was appraised at the sum of $12.
(5) John G. CARDWELL, on Defeated Creek, has taken up a brown bay mare. On April 12, 1810, the mare was given an appraised value of $16.
(6) Charles BOULTON, on Caney Fork, has taken up a bay mare. John L. MARTIN and Lent BOULTON appraised the mare at $25 on May 7, 1810.
(7) Morgan WILLIAMS, in Carthage, has taken up a sorrel horse. On May 7, 1810, the horse's value was $9.
(8) Josiah STRANGE, on Caney Fork, has taken up a dark iron grey horse. On May 7, 1810, the horse was appraised at $18.
(9) Ichabod THOMAS, on Caney Fork, has taken up a black horse. On May 7, 1810, the horse was appraised at a value of $20.
(10) John POE, on Round Lick, has taken up a bay mare. On April 27, 1810, the mare was valued at $5.
(11) Moses PENKSTON, on Round Lick, has taken up a white horse. On April 23, 1810, the horse was appraised at a value of $15.

The following persons have reported estrays in Overton County, per B. TOTTEN, d. r. o. c.:
(1) Joseph COPELAND, on the Roaring River, has taken up a sorrel mare. The mare was valued at $30.
(2) Benjamin WALKER, near Standing Stone, has taken up a bay stud colt. On February 7, 1810, the colt was appraised at $11.
(3) Isaac JOHN, on Mill Creek, has taken up a black mare. On February 8, 1810, the mare was appraised at the sum of $10.
(4) Samuel BROWN, on Spring Creek of the Roaring River, has taken up a horse. On February 13, 1810, the horse was valued at $13.50.
(5) Job CARLOCK has taken up a black mare.

The following persons have reported estrays in Warren County, per Francis PORTERFIELD, d. r. w. c.:
    (1) Richard JOHNSON, has taken up a bay mare. The mare was appraised at $60 on January 28, 1810.
    (2) Hazel JUGGS has taken up a sorrel mare. The mare was appraised at $2 on February 4, 1810.

The following persons have reported estrays in Smith County, per B. SHAW, r. s. c.:
    (1) Jessee PATTY, on Bluff Creek, has taken up a horse. On May 1, 1810, the horse was appraised at $2.50.
    (2) Moses EVITTS, on Defeated Creek, has taken up a sorrel mare. On May 7, 1810, the mare was given an appraised value of $16.
    (3) James H. M'COBE has taken up a white horse. The horse was appraised at $15 on May 8, 1810.

On the 2nd of July next, there will be a sale of town lots in Shelbyville, Bedford County. Commissioners: Danl. M'KISSICK, Benj. BRADFORD, Berkley MARTIN, John AKINSON, Howel DAWDY, John LANE, William WOODS.

June 1, 1810, Vol. 2, No. 63
    On the 30th, the Sixth Anniversary of the Arlington Shearing was celebrated. Daniel M. CHICHESTER and John C. SCOTT won cups.

The following appointments were made by the President of the United States with the advice of the Senate:
    (1) Buckner THRUSTON, of Kentucky, is a judge of the Circuit Court of the District of Columbia.
    (2) William H. HARRISON is the Governor of the Indiana Territory.
    (3) Cornelius P. VAN NESS, of Vermont, is an attorney of the district of Vermont.
    (4) John WILLARD, of Vermont, is a marshall of that district.
    (5) Joseph CROCKETTE, of Kentucky, is a marshall of the district of Kentucky.
    (6) Return J. MEIGS is the commissoner in charge of the conventions held by Chicksaw Nation and Kentucky,
    (7) John EPPENGER, of Georgia, is a marshall for the district of Georgia.
    (8) Alexander MONTGOMERY, David M'CALEB, Thomas BARNES, Joseph ROBERTS, and Joseph GARSON of Mississippi are members of the Legislative Council of the Mississippi Territory.
    (9) John M'CAMPBELL, of Tennessee, is an attorney for east Tennessee.
    (10) Obadiah JONES, of Georgia, is an additional judge for the Mississippi Territory.
    (11) John E. BECK, of Tennessee, is an attorney for the

district of west Tennessee.
(12) Otho SHRADER, of Pennsylvania, is a judge for the Pennsylvania Territory.
(13) John B. LUCAS, of Pennsylvania, is a judge of the Louisiana Territory.
(14) Stanly GRISWOLD is the Illinois Territory judge.
(15) George WASHINGTON and Park CURTIS are Justices of the Peace for Alexandria County, D. C.
(16) Benjamin HOWARD, of Kentucky, is the Governor of the Louisiana Territory.
(17) Tully ROBINSON, of the Orleans Territory, is an attorney for the district of Orleans.
(18) Oliver FITTS, of North Carolina, is a judge of the Mississippi Territory.
(19) Park WALTEN, of the Mississippi Territory, is a receiver of public monies for lands lying west of the Pearl River.
(20) Lewis SEWALL, of Georgia, is Registrar of the Land Office of the Pearl River.
(21) Jesse SEMER, of New Jersey, is the collector of the district of Great Egg Harbor.
(22) Amos SPAFFORD, of Ohio, is collector of the Miami district.
(23) Thomas H. WILLIAMS, of the Mississippi Territory, is the collector of the Mississippi district.
(24) Archibald BULLOCK, of Georgia, is the collector the district of Savannah.
(25) Parker BARNES, of Virginia, is the collector of Folly Landing.
(26) James SPARKS, of Virginia, is the collector of the district of East River.
(27) Thomas ENGLISH, of Pennsylvania, is Governor in Dublin.
(28) John B. DAVY, of Pennsylvania, is Consul of the Port of Rangoon in the Burmian Empire.

My note is in the hands of William SMITH, Pendleton District, South Carolina for $100. I forewarn all persons against trading for this note as I will not pay unless compelled by law. Hugh DOUGHERTY, Carthage.

The following is a list of estrays in White County, per Jacob A. LANE, d. r. w. c.:
(1) Isaac CRABB, on Calf Killer Fork, has taken a black mare, On April 24, 1810, the horse was given an appraised value of $24.
(2) Arthur NEILLE, on Caney Fork, has taken up a brown mare. On April 3, 1810, the mare's value was $30.
(3) John GREEN, on Lost Creek, has taken up a sorrel mare. On April 28, 1810, the mare's value was $30.
(4) Thomas K. HARRIS, on Green Spring, has taken up a

bay horse. On May 19, 1810, the mare was given an
appraised value of $25.
  (5) William STEWART, on Rutledge Creek, has taken up a
bay mare. On April 28, 1810, the mare was given
an appraised value of $18.
William WARD has commenced the boot and shoemaking
business in Carthage.

June 8, 1810, Vol. 2, No. 64
The following persons have reported estrays in Warren
County, per Richard BURKS, r. w. c.:
  (1) James ENGLISH, at Short Mountain, has taken up a
red bay horse. On May 13, 1810, the mare was given
a value in the amount of $45.
  (2) John GUNTER, on Mountain Creek, has taken up a
brown horse. On May 17, 1810, the horse was valued
at the sum of $17.
  (3) James ROBINSON, on Caney Fork, has taken up a mare.
May 24, 1810, the mare was appraised at $27.50.
  (4) Thomas NEWTY, on Mountain Creek, has taken up a
chestnut sorrel horse. On May 24, 1810, the horse
was given an appraised value of $25.
  (5) John MARTIN, on Sinking Creek, has taken up a bay
mare. On May 14, 1810, the mare was appraised at
a value of $22.
  (6) Isham PERKINS, on Charles Creek, has taken up a bay
horse. On May 16, 1810, the horse's value was $35.
  (7) Julius WEBB, Dry Creek, has taken up a strawberry
roan mare. On May 16, 1810, the mare was appraised
at a value of $20.
  (8) Townsend WEBB, on Dry Creek, took up a chestnut
sorrel horse. The horse was valued at $45.
The following persons have reported estrays in Jackson
County, per James D. HENDLEY, r. j. c.:
  (1) John EAST, on Brook's Bent, has taken up a brown
mare. On May 14, 1810, the mare's value is $40.
  (2) James SHORT has taken up a bay mare. The mare's
value was $9 on May 12, 1810.
  (3) Lewis BUCHANNON, on Little Caney Fork, has taken up
a bay horse. On May 10, 1810, the mare was given
an appraised value of $25.
  (4) Orson MARTIN, on the Cumberland River, has taken up
a black mare. On May 26, 1810, the mare was given
an appraised value of $30.
  (5) William RUDKINS, on Walton's Ferry, has taken up a
bay horse. On March 22, 1810, the horse was given
an appraised value of $45.
  (6) Thomas PESSONS, on Jinnings' Creek, has taken up a
bay horse. On March 22, 1810, the horse was valued

at $35 on March 22, 1810.
(7) Ralph ROGERS, two miles from Fort Blount, has taken up a sorrel mare. The mare's value is $6.
(8) Jacob REAGLE, on the Cumberland River, has taken up a sorrel mare. On May 1, 1810, the mare was given an appraised value of $15.
(9) James JONES, on Doe Creek, has taken up a horse. The horse was valued at $12.50 on March 26, 1810.

The following persons have reported estrays in Warren County, per James M'EWEN, r. r. w. c.:
(1) William MITCHELL, on Hickory Creek, has taken up a mare. On March 31, 1810, the mare's value is $30.
(2) Henry AVENT, on Hickory Creek, has taken up a bay mare. On April 17, 1810, the mare's value is $20.
(3) James EVANS, on the Stones River, has taken up a sorrel horse. On April 7, 1810, the horse was appraised at a value of $23.
(4) Rueben HAMPTON, on Hickory Creek, has taken up a brown mare. On May 3, 1810, the mare was given an appraised value of $25.
(5) John ROGERS, on Collin's River, has taken up a sorrel mare. The mare's value was $20.
(6) William PITTMAN, on Collin's River, has taken up a sorrel mare. The mare's value was $20.
(7) John DONALDSON, on Charles Creek, has taken up a sorrel mare. The mare's value was $2.

The following appointments in the Navy of the United States were made by the President:
(1) Jacob JONES was made Master Commandent.
(2) Geo. W. RODGERS, George C. READ, Henry E. BALLARD, and Thomas GAMBLE were promoted from acting lieutenants to lieutenants in the Navy.
(3) Henry FORD, James H. BOYLES, and Joseph FOSTER were promoted from second lieutenants to first lieutenants in the Marine Corps.
(4) Nicholas MARTIN, of Maryland; Samuel G. HOPKINS, of Kentucky; Nathaniel ALLEN, of Georgia; Francis D. CUMMINGS, of Georgia; Thomas WOODSON, of Tennessee; Francis THORNTON, of Virginia; Robert B. RIDONAL, of Maryland; Joseph MOSELY, of Kentucky; James M. BROWN, of Delaware; Charles S. HANA, of Kentucky; and Alexander G. SEVIER, of Tennessee, received promotions to second lieutenants in the Marines.
(5) John RANDAL is Navy Agent at Annapolis.
(6) Constant TABOR is Navy Agent at Newport, R. I.

John MARSH, on the Barren, Smith County, has taken up a sorrel horse. The horse's value was $12. B. SHAW, r. s. c.

The copartnership of John HARWOOD, jun., and his wife Elizabeth HARWOOD. is dissolved by mutual consent.

On the 26th of May last, a negro man about 30 years old and a woman 25 to 27 years old ranaway from the subscriber. James NORRIS.

June 29, 1810, Vol. 2, No. 67

The following persons have reported estrays in Overton County, per B. TOTTEN, d. r. o. c.:

(1) George FOROTS, on the Roaring River, has taken up a black horse. On May 26, 1810, the horse was given an appraised value of $35.

(2) William EVANS, on the Wolf River, has taken up a bay mare. On June 16, 1810, the mare was appraised at a value of $15.

(3) Joseph CAMPBELL, on the Wolf River, has taken up two horses. On June 9, 1810, their value was given at the sum of $15.

(4) Isaac VANHOOZER, on the Obed's River, has taken up a sorrel mare. On June 11, 1810, the mare was appraised at $15.

Will all those indebted to the estate of Randolph CHEEK, dec., please come forward. Nancy CHEEK, Admx.

On the 5th of July next at the house of Dr. Charles F. MABIAS, dec., his estate will be offered for sale. Susanna MABIAS and William LANE, Admins.

July 6, 1810, Vol. 2, No. 68

The following persons have reported estrays in Smith County, per B. SHAW, r. s. c.:

(1) Jones BALOTE, on Mulherrin, has taken up a bay mare. On June 13, 1810, the mare was appraised at the sum of $15.

(2) Thomas MADDEN, on Goose Creek, has taken up a brown mare. On May 12, 1810, the mare's value was $22

(3) John PITT, on Smith's Fork, has taken up a sorrel horse. On May 14, 1810, the horse's value was $20.

(4) William INGLISH, on Clear Fork, has taken up a brown mare. On May 19, 1810, the mare was given an appraised value of $20.

(5) John SOAN, on the east fork of Peyton's Creek, has taken up a yellow bay mare. On May 19, 1810, the mare was appraised at $19.

(6) Robert STROTHER, on M'Clure's Bent, has taken up a brown mare. On May 17, 1810, the mare was given an appraised value of $12.

(7) Thomas RALPH, at the mouth of Hickman's Creek, has taken up a brown bay horse. On May 15, 1810, the horse was appraised at $37.50.

(8) Pleasant CHITWOOD, on Salt Lick Fork of the Big Barren, has taken up a bay horse. The horse was

appraised at $30 on May 1, 1810.

(9) Frederick EARLY, on Hurricane Creek, has taken up a grey mare. On May 11, 1810, the mare was appraised at a value of $60.

(10) Henry BEASLEY, near Bledsoesborough, has taken up a bay filly. The filly's value was $8.

(11) Charles M'MURRY, on Dixon's Lick Creek, a sorrel horse. On May 12, 1810, the horse's value was $18.

(12) William BAKER, on the south side of the Cumberland River, has taken up a sorrel horse. The value of the horse was given at $5 on June 2, 1810.

(13) Uriah CARSON, on the east fork of Goose Creek, has taken up a sorrel mare. On April 30, 1810, the mare was appraised at $15.

(14) Ruebin GOARD, on Peyton's Creek, has taken up a bay horse. On JUne 5, 1810, the horse was given an appraised value of $20.

(15) William M'GINSON, on Smith's Fork, has taken up a bay mare. On May 17, 1810, the mare was given an appraised value of 417.

(16) William CARMAN, on the east fork of Goose Creek, has taken up a sorrel mare. On June 1, 1810, the value on the mare was $60.

(17) Wilson TAYLOR has taken up a black horse. The horse was valued at $8 on June 11, 1810.

(18) Wilson CAGE, on Dry Lick Creek, has taken up a horse. On June 18, 1810, the horse was given an appraised value of $20.

(19) John CASEY, on Puncheon Camp Creek, has taken up a bay horse. On June 7, 1810, the horse was given an appraised value of $20.

By virtue of an order of sale directed to me by the court of Overton County, there will be exposed to sale at the court house at Monroe on Saturday the 18th of August, 1810, the right, title, interest and claim that William MATLOCK and Samuel STOCTON have to two lots in said town. James M'DANIEL, s. o. c.

By virtue of an alias order of sale directed to me by the court of Pleas and Quarter Sessions held for Overton County, there will be sold at the court house in Monroe on the 18th of August next the right, that James PATTERSON has to an occupation claim on the Wolf River, The property was taken to satisfy an execution obtained by John ROSS. James M'DONALD, s. o. c.

On the 18th of August next, there will be a public sale directed by the White County court of several tracts, that are the property of Jesse TERRY, dec. The property was taken at the influence of James ALCORN. Wm. PHILIPS, s. w. c.

By virtue of an order of sale directed to me by the court

of Overton County, there will be a public sale in the town
of Monroe of a lot is said town, that is the property of
Robert SEVIER, Samuel STOCKTON, and Rutherford WITT. James
M'DONALD, s. o. c.

The following is a list of letters remaining at the post
office at White Plains, per D. ALEXANDER, p. m.: Richard
AUSTIN, John ANDERSON, Robert ARMSTRONG, James BROWN, Thomas
BUFORD, Joseph BOYD, John H. BADGER, Thomas CLARK, Jacon
CHENEY, Andrew DERRYBERRY, Amos GODMAN, William HUSBAND,
Maj. Wlliam HUGHTELL, Isaac JOHNSON, Richard M'KAY, Joseph
PARKER, Job PATIET, Jessee RUSTICK, Alexander SHERRILL, Mrs.
Lise STEWARD, Joseph STEWARD, Zebadiah STOCKSTILL, Nicholas
TEEL, Thomas WILCHOR, jun., Benjamin WOLKMAN, Jesse YOUNG.

The following persons have reported estrays in White
County, per J. A. LANE, d. r. w. c.:
(1) Carter DILLON, near Rock Island, has taken up a
    sorrel mare. The mare's value was $7.50.
(2) William ROBINSON, two miles below Sparta, has taken
    up a bay mare. The mare's value was given at $20.
(3) Andrew SMITH, in the Bar Cove, has taken up a bay
    mare. The mare was appraised at $15.
(4) William SHAW has taken up a bay horse.
(5) John M'COUN, above Sparta, has taken up a sorrel
    horse. On June 1, 1810, the horse was appraised
    at the value of $25.
(6) John TERRY has taken up a grey horse. The horse
    was valued at $18 on May 21, 1810.
(7) James FULKERSON, in Hickory Valley, has taken up a
    bay horse. On June 13, 1810, the horse was given
    an appraised value of $18.
(8) Robert JOHNSTON, living on the Turnpike Road that
    leads from South West Point to Carthage, has taken
    up a brown mare. On June 15, 1810, the mare was
    appraised at $25.
(9) Joel MELTON has taken up a bay mare.

The following persons have reported estrays in Smith
County, per B. SHAW, r. s. c.:
(1) Thomas NASH, on Dixon's Creek, has taken up a bay
    mare. On June 15, 1810, the mare was appraised at
    a value of $17.
(2) James MURPHY, on east Goose Creek, has taken up a
    brown horse. On June 11, 1810, the mare was given
    an appraised value of $5.
(3) Josiah STRANGE, at the mouth of Caney Fork, has
    taken up a bay mare. On June 21, 1810, the mare
    was appraised at $25.

July 20, 1810, Vol. 2, No. 70
On the 10th of June in the town of Philadelphia, Major

75

Dennis DOGAN died. He was a formerly an officer in the British Army.

The following is a list of estrays in Smith County, per Basil SHAW, r. s. c.:

(1) Charles CONNOWAY has taken up a bay mare. The mare was appraised by Killis OLIVER and David LINCH on June 23, 1810 at $3.

(2) John BUCLEY, at Liberty, has taken up a sorrel mare. On June 25, 1810, the mare was appraised at the sum of $20.

On the 6th a duel was fought between Robert TAYLOR and William PATTON at the Wythe County court house. Mr. TAYLOR fell in the second fire. The duel was over a young lady.

At the Clermont merino sheep shearing on the 15th at the home of Robert LIVINGSTON in Clermont, the following persons made toasts: Samuel L. MITCHELL, Elkanah WATSON of Massachuetts, Stephen VAN RENSSELAER, Robert D. LIVINGSTON, Col. D. HUMPHREYS, Dittmas BASSEMULLER late of Germany now of Pennsylvania.

July 27, 1810, Vol. 2, No. 71

The following is a list of letters remaining at the post office in the town of Carthage, per Charles HERVEY, p. m.: James ALEXANDER, Richard BROWN, Susanna BROWNFIELD, Mrs. BALAYADA, Thomas BARNS, Elizabeth COTREL, David COFFEE, Nathaniel CARTER, Elizabeth DORRIS, Nathaniel DICKERSON, James EWINGS, James EATON, Edward FOSTER, William FLOWERS, Lewis FORD, Timothy GARRET, Jonathan GRIFFING, Stephen HANEY, Stephen HOWE, Edward HATY, Joshua JONES, Benjamin JOHNS, William W. LEGON, William LANE, Obadiah MASH, Joseph MARSH, Adam MARLY, John MANN, Robert NIXON, Mr. OVERALLS, William PUGH, Jacob POOL, Jonathan B. ROBERTSON, David ROBERTSON, Thomas SMITH, George SMITH, Lee SULLIVAN, Mary SPARKS, David STETEVILLE, Timothy SHAW, William SHAW, Benjamin SHAW, William SHAW, Ichabod THOMAS, Richard and J. TAYLOR, Green TRUMP, Samuel VARNUM, Thomas WEST, Shadrack WILLIAM, James WALLIS, Mark WOODCOCK, Nathal. W. WILLIAMS.

The following is a list of letters remaining at the post office at Dixon's Springs on July 1, 1810, per Tilmon DIXON, p. m.: Abraham BRITTON, Walter BEAN, Benjamin BURNET, Amos ELLISON, Thomas CRUTCHFIELD, Henry COCKRUM, Jacob DIER, Elizabeth DORRIS, Thomas DIAS, Japthan (sic) DWEHAN, Henry FALEY, Wm. FERGUSON, Thomas FRIZZEL, Eishu HATCHET, Thomas JONES, Thomas MARSHALL, Justus ROLLMAN, Vincent RUST, Josiah RUCKS, James SPAIN, Washington STINSON, Wm. THOMPSON, James VINTRESS, Thomas WILLIAMSON, John WILLIAMS, John WARREN, Henry WILMON.

Wanted salt petre. Edward FOSTER.

Died at Falmount, Jamaica on the 15th, Ann SLVESTER. She

was a free black woman, who was at the advanced age of 133 years. She lived in the neighborhood of DUNCAN's at the time of the great earthquake at Port Royal in the year of 1692. By her account, she was 15 years old. At one time she had children, grandchildren and great grandchildren to the number of 82.

The following is a list of letters remaining at the post office in Williamsburgh on July 1, 1810, per S. WILLIAMS, p. m.: John ALLEN of Joshua BURLET, John AMSTRONG, John ALDRIDGE, James or William BIRDWELL, Stewart DOSS, William HOGAN, William M'DONALD, Samuel M'ADOW, George PRICE or Andrew HAMPTON, James WARD, John WIGHT.

The following persons have reported estrays in Smith County, per Basil SHAW, r. s.:
    (1) Eby BURTON, at Littleberry, has taken up a sorrel mare. On July 7, 1810, the mare's value was $25.
    (2) Matthew DAVID, on Defeated Creek, has taken up a sorrel horse. On July 7, 1810, the horse was given appraised value of $20.

On the second Saturday in September next in the town of Gallatin, there will be a public sale directed by the court of Sumner County of 100 acres on the Cumberland River, that is the property of John LAFFERTY. The property was taken at the influence of Robert RALEIGH and Thomas MORSE. W. M. DOUGLASS, d. s.

On the second Saturday in September next in the town of Gallatin, there will be a public sale directed by the court of Sumner County of 100 acres on Station Camp Creek, that is the property of John BRIGANCE. The property was taken at the influence of Jonathan TROUSDALE and Thomas J. OVERTON. W. H. DOUGLASS, d. s.

On the second Saturday in September next in the town of Gallatin, there will be a public sale directed by the court of Sumner County of two tracts of land, that is the property of Armstead STUBBLEFIELD. The property was taken at the influence of Jacob MERCER. W. H. DOUGLASS, d. s.

The following persons have reported estrays in Jackson County, per Nathan SMITH, d. j. c.:
    (1) John BROW, om Walton's Road, has taken up a sorrel mare. On July 25, 1810, the mare's value was $20.
    (2) William SOINER has taken up a bay horse. The horse was appraised at $5 on July 9, 1810.

August 3, 1810, Vol. 2, No. 72

On the second Monday in September next, there will be a public sale directed by the court of Sumner County of two lots, that are the property of John MITCHELL. The property was taken at the influence of Zacheus WILSON, deceased. William WILSON and John WILSON, adm. John Y. BYRN, d. s.

The following persons have reported estrays in Warren County, per James M'EWEN, d. r.:

(1) T. WEBB, on Day Branch, has taken up a sorrel horse. On June 16, 1810, the horse was given an appraised value of $62.

(2) Absalom BROWN, on the Collin's River, has taken up a sorrel mare. On July 5, 1810, the mare was given an appraised value of $25.

(3) William THOMPSON, on Hickory Creek, has taken up a black mare. On June 26, 1810, the mare was valued at the sum of $15.

(4) Charles CAGLE, on the Collin's River, has taken up black horse. On June 30, 1810, the horse was given an appraised value of $2.

(5) Jesse HODGE, the Stone River, has taken up a sorrel horse. On June 16, 1810, the horse was appraised at the value of $40.

(6) John FALING, on the Stone River, has taken up a bay horse. On June 30, 1810, the horse was appraised at the sum of $40.

(7) Thomas CROMPTON, on Hickory Creek, has taken up a bay mare. On July 7, 1810, the mare was appraised at the sum of $20.

(8) James Y. BLOOD has taken up a bay mare.

(9) James GUNTER, on Mountain Creek, took up a horse.

The following persons have reported estrays in Franklin County, per John YOUNG, r. f. c.:

(1) George TUBB, jun., has taken up a bay horse. On May 12, 1810, the horse was appraised at $15.

(2) Sampson REESE has taken up a bay mare. The mare was appraised at $20 on March 31, 1810.

(3) George ROWLAND, on the Elk River, has taken up a gray mare. On April 17, 1810, the mare was given an appraised value of $27.

(4) James BARLOW has taken up a black mare. The mare was valued at $20 on March 13, 1810.

(5) Francis NABOURS, on Bradley's Creek, has taken up a sorrel mare. On April 19, 1810. the mare was given an appraised value of $22.

(6) William Moore, on the Elk River, has taken up a gray mare. On April 17, 1810, the mare's value was $27.

(7) John WILKERSON, on the Elk River, has taken up a bay mare. The appraised value of the mare was $15 on April 20, 1810.

(8) Alexander BROWN, on Big Praire, has taken up a gray mare. On April 23, 1810, the mare's value was $20.

(9) Robert STERN has taken up a bay mare. The mare was appraised at $20 on May 7, 1810.

(10) Thomas HAMBLETON, on Norwood's Creek, has taken up

78

chesnut sorrel horse. On May 7, 1810, the horse
was appraised at the sum of $40.
(11) John HUNT, on the Elk River, has taken up a bay
mare. On May 15, 1810, the mare's value was $15.
(12) John OWEN, on Bean Creek, has taken up a sorrel
horse. On June 18, 1810, the horse was appraised
at the value of $20.

August 24, 1810, Vol. 2, No. 75
The following is a list of letters remaining at the post
office at White Plains, per D. ALEXANDER, p. m.: Richard
AUSTIN, John AUSTIN, John BUSSELL, Perry BUCKINHANON, John
FERGUSON, Wilson and Seaton BRUCE, Sterling COLLIER, George
DOUGHERTY, Elijah HOWELL, Joshua HARVY, Harry HILL, Abraham
HOLLINGSWORTH, John JONES, Peter JONES, John KEITHLEY, John
MORGAN, Daniel M'DANIEL, Andrew MEANS, John PERKINS, John
PURKEN, Patrick and Samuel POOL, Elisha ROBERTS, Marg.
ROGERS, William RODER, Isaac TAYLOR, James TAYLOR, Samuel
THOMAS, George WALLACE, John WOODLOW.
The following persons have reported estrays in Smith
County, per B. SHAW, r. s.:
(1) John BAKLEY, near Bledsoesborough, has taken a roan
mare. On August 2, 1810, the mare's value was $12.
(2) Moses FURGESON, on Peyton's Creek, has taken up a
sorrel chesnut mare. On June 26, 1810, the mare's
value was appraised t $15.
(3) John TROUSDALE, on the Cany Fork, has taken up a
bay mare. On August 1, 1810, the mare was given an
appraised value of $25.
The following persons have reported estrays in Jackson
County, per James D. NENDLEY for Nathan SMITH, d. r. s. c.:
(1) David DICSON, jun., living on Jinning's Creek, has
taken up a dark bay horse. On May 31, 1810, the
mare was appraised at $20.
(2) John DICKSON, on Jinning's Creek, has taken up a
brown bay mare. On June 7, 1810, the mare's value
was placed at $14.
(3) Mathias SWEENY has taken up a sorrel mare. The
mare's value was $30 on June 2, 1810.
(4) Mark MORGAN, near the head of Cain Creek, has taken
up a roan mare. The mare's value was $20.
(5) Joseph SHAW, on Walton Road, has taken up bay mare.
On June 30, 1810, the mare's value was $15.
(6) William RUDKINS, on Walton Road, has taken up a bay
mare. On June 4, 1810, the mare's value was $9.50.
(7) Howel HERN, on the Roaring River, has taken up bay
mare. On June 30, 1810, the mare's value was $15.
(8) Sampson WILLIAMS has taken up a bay mare. The mare
was appraised at $25 on July 16, 1810.

(9) Henry KERR has taken up a black mare. The mare's value was $12 on July 14, 1810.

Seth ADAMS has arrived at this place on the 9th. He was on his way to Kentucky and Tennessee with 176 merino sheep from the flock of Col. HUMPHRIES of Connecticut.

Miss Tryphose BUTLER on the 20th between 4 am and 40 minutes pass 7 pm, spun 11 skeins of woolen yard.

The following persons were mentioned in an extract from a letter from the West Florida Conventions:

For New Feliciana: William BARROW, John MILLS, John H. JOHNSON, John RHEA.

For Baton Rouge: Thomas LILLY, Phillip HICKORY, Edward HAUSE, William MORGAN.

For Tanahipaho: Mr. COOPER.

September 21, 1810, Vol. 2, No. 77

The following persons were mentioned in an article concerning the West Florida Convention: Charles Dehault DELASSUS, John H. JOHNSON, Phillip HICKEY, Manuel LOPEZ, John W. LEONARD, Thomas LILLY, John MILLS.

On the first of February next in the town of Monroe, there will be a public sale of 100 acres, that is the property of William CAMPBELL. The tract was taken at the influence of William DALE. James M'DONNOLD, shff.

On the first of February next in the town of Monroe, there will be a public sale of 300 acres on the Obed's River, that is the property of Benjamin HUEY. The property was taken at the influence of George GORDON. James M'DONNOLD, shff.

On the first of February next in the town of Monroe, there will be a public sale of lot no. 70, that is the property of Charles CHADICK. The property was taken at the influence of Robert ADKINS. James M'DONNOLD, shff.

On the first of February next in the town of Monroe, there will a public sale of 35000 acres, that is the property of Samuel A. MARTIN. The property was taken at the influence of Moses WOOTON. James M'DONNOLD, shff.

On the first of November, the marriage of Capt. James ISOM of Maury County to Miss Polly GAYLES of Smith County will be performed by Rev. WISEMAN.

March 22, 1811, Vol. 2, No. 97

The following persons have reported estrays in Warren County, per James M'EWEN, r. w. c.:

(1) John PRICE, on Hickory Creek, has taken up a yellow bay mare. On December 22, 1810, the mare was given an appraised value of $10.

(2) William KEELY, on the Long Fork of the Barren, has taken up a bay mare. The mare's value was $15.

(3) Thomas WOOD, on Fall Creek of the Cany Fork, has taken up a bay mare. On December 22, 1810, the mare's value was given at $9.51.

(4) David SPREADLIN, on Hickory Creek, has taken up a red sorrel filly. On January 13, 1811, the filly was appraised at a value of $15.

(5) Ezekiel HATLEN, on Collin's River, has taken up a sorrel horse. On January 21, 1811, the horse was valued at the sum of $40.

(6) Jesse DRAKE, on the Rocky River, has taken up a sorrel horse. On January 24, 1811, the horse was given an appraised value of $9.

(7) Josiah JARVIS, on Hickory Creek, has taken up a sorrel mare. On January 31, 1811, the mare. was given a value of $10.

(8) William LOW, on Hickory Creek, has taken up a brown mare. On February 4, 1811, the appraised value of the mare was $20.

(9) James ENGLISH, on Short Mountain, has taken up a bay mare. On February 13, 1811, the mare was given appraised value of $40.

The following persons have reproted estrays in Smith County, per B. SHAW, r. s. c.:

(1) James CATHEY, on Goose Creek, has taken up a bay horse. On February 9, 1811, the mare was appraised at the sum of $25.

(2) John FITE, on Smith Fork, has taken up a bay horse. On December 20, 1811, the mare's value was $11.

(3) Jud STRUTHER has taken up a sorrel mare. The value of the mare was $30 on January 36, 1811.

(4) John BAKER, near Carthage, has taken up a sorrel horse. On January 7, 1811, the mare was appraised at the sum of $10.

The following persons have reported estrays in Overton County, per B. TOTTEN, d. r. s. c.:

(1) Walter FISK has taken up a brown horse, The mare was valued at $20 on November 25, 1810.

(2) James GOODPASTER, near Standing Stone, has taken up a sorrel horse. On February 15, 1811, the horse was appraised at $15.

On the 20th of April next in the town of Monroe, there will be a public sale of of two town lots, that belong to Charles SEVIER and William CARPENTER. The property was taken at the influence of the commissioners of Monroe. James M'DONNEL, shff.

On the 10th of May next in the town of Carthage, there will be a public sale of 400 acres, that is the property of Samuel M'FERRIN. The tract was taken at the influence of John H. BOWN and Benjamin BURTON. George MATLOCK, shff.

Overton County, Tennessee, February Sessions. James M'DONNOLD, sheriff and collector, reports that the following persons still have unpaid taxes for 1810. B. TOTTEN.

Reputed Owners	Acres	Situation
Samuel HOPKINS	110	Obey's River
Ruebin PERKINS	25	Obey's River
Ruebbin DOBKIN	125	Obey's River
William LITTLE	4300	Obey's River
Hugh MARTIN	200	Obey's River
Samuel A. MARTIN	5500	Obey's River
John SEVIER	16508	Obey's River
William ROAD's heirs	5000	Warr. No. 3285
		Ent. Oct. 9, 1809
Thomas GAORE	150	Spring Creek
Thomas GOOR	100	Spring Creek
Thomas GOORE	100	Spring Creek
David GRAHAM	220	By occupancy
Thomas CAMPBELL	200	Roaring River
David ROSS	3000	Wolf River
John M'IVER	40000	Donnelson's Cave
Samuel M'GEE	150	Wolf River
William ARMSTRONG	400	
Nathan ROBERTSON	143	Donnelson's Cave
Redmond D. BARRY	1700	Spring Creek

The following tracts are liable for a double tax:

Reputed Owners	Acres	Situation	Grant
Josiah COLLINGS	2500	Obed's River	307
		W. 470, Oct. 25, 1788	
Moor STEPHENSON	200	Roaring River	
Charles PETTEGRUE	800		
Josiah COLLINS	1280	G. John GADDY	
James BROOKS and			
James WOODS	640		257
George CAMPBELL and			
Robert ELLIOTT	400	Blair's Creek	261
Andrew ALEXANDER	1000	Roaring River	394
Thomas HOUSTON	640	Wolf River	209
Epraim DUNLAP	640	Cumberland Riv.	262
Epraim DUNLAP	640	C. River	260
Epraim DUNLAP	400	C. River	258
William M'CRARY	800	C. River	254
William M'CRARY	300		253
William M'CRARY	4000		252
William M'CRARY	1000		251
William M'CRARY	640		250
Landen CARTER's heirs	1260	Brimstone Creek	164
James DANDER	640	Spring Creek	181
James DANDER	400	Spring Creek	182

(Continued on following page)

82

(Overton County delinquent tax list continued)

Stokely DONELSON	1000	Obey's River	2729
Richard H. LOVE	1280		302
Isaac M'COMMON	257	Langham's Creek	3352
Joseph MUCKETRATH and			
Murlin YOUNG	600	Wolf River	
Vincent BENHAM	349	Dec. 24, 1798	862
Vincent BENHAM	349	Dec. 24, 1798	860
Allen RAMSAY	646	May 20, 1795	1615
Allen RAMSAY	365	Roaring River	2071

On the 9th of May next in the town of Monroe, there will be a public sale of two lots, that are the property of Charles SEVIER. The property was taken at the instance of John BEATY. James M'DONNOLD, shff.

On the 9th of May next in the town of Monroe, there will be a public sale of 790 acres, that belongs to Edward CORMICK. The property was taken at the influence of Thomas ELLIOTT. James M'DONNOLD, shff.

On the 10th of May next in the town of Carthage, there will be a public sale directed by the court of Smith County of 213 acres, that is owned and occupied by Michael MURPHEY. The property was taken at the influence of the commissioners of Williamsburgh. George MATLOCK, shff.

On the 10th of May next in the town of Carthage, there will be a public sale directed by the court of Smith County of two town lots, that are the property of Lemuel PURNELL. The property was taken at the influence of John HARMAN. George MATLOCK, sheriff.

The following persons have reported estrays in Sumner County, per Will. TRIGG, jr., r. s. c.:

(1) Moore COTTON, on Station Camp Creek, has taken up a bay mare. On December 13, 1810, the mare was given an appraised value of $10.

(2) William NAIL, on Rocky Creek, has taken up a sorrel horse. On December 4, 1810, the horse was given an appraised value of $55.

(3) William MARTIN, on the east fork of Drake's Creek, has taken up a bay mare. On December 7, 1810, the mare was valued at $25.

(4) Henry YOUNG, on Second Creek, has taken up a sorrel horse. On December 4, 1810, the horse was given an appraised value of $25.

(5) Will. TRIGG, jr., has taken up a dun mare. The mare was appraised at $18 on January 3, 1811.

(6) James DOUGLASS, in Cage's Bent, has taken up a bay horse. On December 25, 1811, the horse was valued at the sum of $20.

(7) James CROCK, on Spring Creek, has taken up a roan mare. The mare's value placed at $20.

(8) Daniel LEGIT, about one mile above Montgomeries Mill (sic), has taken up a sorrel mare. The mare was valued at $9 on January 1, 1811.

(9) John PITT, on Station Camp Creek, has taken up a bay mare. On January 7, 1811, the mare was given an appraised value of $20.

(10) James SAUNDERS has taken up a sorrel horse. The horse was valued at $20.

The following persons were mentioned in a list of Acts passed at the third session of the Eleventh Congress: George ARINROYD; the name change of Lewis GRANT to Lewis Grant DAVIDSON; John Eugene LEISENDORFER; Nathaniel F. FOSDICK; William MILLS; Peter AUDRAIN; John MACNAMARA; Richard TERVIN, Mississippi Territory; Edwin LEWIS, Mississippi Territory; Samuel SIMS, Mississippi Territory; and Joseph WILSON, Mississippi Territory.

In the year of 1808, I gave a note to Henry TURNEY for $50. I will not pay said note. Matthew DUKE.

On the 13th of April next in the town of Carthage, there will be a public sale directed by the court of Davidson County of 2500 acres, that is the property of the heirs of Matin ARMSTRONG, dec. His heirs are Thomas ARMSTRONG, John H. ARMSTRONG, Joseph W. ARMSTRONG, William HEWLETT and his wife, the daughter of said ARMSRTONG, and Alexander M'CALL and his wife, the daughter of said ARMSTRONG. George MATTLOCK, sheriff of Smith County.

Isaac WALTON on Walton's Ferry, Smith County, has taken up a bay horse. On February 22, 1811, the horse was appraised at $42.50. B. SHAW, r. s. c.

April 12, 1811, Vol. 2, No. 97

The following is a list of letters remaining at the post office at Carthage on March 31, 1811, per Basil SHAW, p. m.: Jas. BIRCHET, William BALDRIDGE, Henry CORNWELL, William EWEL, Henry DRYDON, Stephen FARMER, Archibald or Elijah FULKS, John GORDON, Abil HUTSON, William HANKINS, Leander HUGHES, Nathan and Claiborne HALL, Joseph JOHNSON, Halloway KEE, Phil LYON, James LYON, Charles LEWIS, Samuel MILLER, James MILLS, Malcolm M'MILLIAN, Joseph MORGAN, Alexander M'CALL, William PARKER, James PAIN, Joseph D. SMITH, William TAYLOR, James VANCE, Robert WILBURN, Samuel WALKER, Horation WALKER, Col. Wm. WALTON.

On the first Saturday next in Carthage, there will be a public sale of 400 directed by the court of Smith County, that is the property of Jonathan ELSTON. The tract was taken at the influence of Charles KAVANAUGH, John GORDON.

On the third Saturday next in the town of Williamsbourgh, there will be a public sale directed by the court of Jackson County of 146 acres, that is the property of Willeroy PATE.

The tract was attached by James RAY. J. COOK, sheriff.

The following persons have reported estrays in Jackson County, per Samuel D. HENDLEY by Nathan SMITH, d. s. j. c.:

(1) Sylvanus FOWLER, on the Cumberland River, has taken up a bay horse. On January 11, 1811, the horse was appraised at the value of $11.

(2) John ROBINSON, on Brimstone Creek of the Cumberland River, has taken up a sorrel mare.

(3) Robert STEWART, in Williamsburgh, taken up a mare.

(4) William WHITEFIELD has taken up a brown bay mare.

(5) Joseph LOCKE, on Jinnings Creek, has taken up a bay brown horse. On January 11, 1811, the horse was appraised at $16.

The following persons have reported estrays in Sumner County, per William TRIGG, jun., r. s. c.:

(1) Bingham KEY, on Roger's Fork of Bledsoe's Creek, has taken up a grey horse. On January 5, 1811, the horse was appraised at $70.

(2) Smith HAUDSBOROUGH, near Henderson's Mill, took up a sorrel horse. On January 19, 1811, the horse was appraised at $27.50.

(3) Richard JOHNSON, on Bledsoe's Creek, has taken up a sorrel horse. On February 16, 1811, the horse was valued at the sum of $70.

(4) Ezekiel THOMAS has taken up a sorrel horse. The horse was appraised at $35 on February 25, 1811.

On the third Saturday next in the town of Williamsburgh, there will be a public sale directed by the court of Jackson County of 201 acres, that is the property of John JAMES. The land was taken at the influence of Benjamin CLERCK. J. COOK, sheriff.

On the third Saturday in May next in the town of Williamsburgh, there will be a public sale directed by the Jackson County court of 60 acres, that belong to Nicholas TEEL. The land was taken at the influence of James HOND. J. COOK, sheriff.

On the 10th of May next in the town of Carthage, there will be a public sale of 213 acres, that is owned and occupied by Michael MURPHEY. Also for sale, there were 100 acres that is occuppied by John BRANSFORD. The property was taken at the instance of the commissioners of Williamsburgh. George MATLOCK, sheriff.

On the 10th of May next in the town of Carthage, there will be a public sale of 70 acres, that is owned and occupied by William JINKINS. The property was taken by the state. George MATLOCK, sheriff.

On the 10th of May next in the town of Carthage, there will be a public sale directed by the Smith County court, of town lot no. 84, that is the property of Lemuel FARWELL. The land was taken at the influence of John HARMAN. George MATLOCK, sheriff.

On the 10th of May next in the town of Carthage, there will be a public sale directed by the Smith County court of 400 acres, that is the property of Samuel M'FERRIN. The land was taken at the influence of John H. BOWEN and Benjamin BURTON. George MATLOCK, sheriff.

On the third Saturday in May next, there will be a public sale directed by the Jackson County court of 150 acres, William TACKET. The property was taken at the influence of Jacob BAKER and John FITZGERALD. J. COOK, sheriff.

On the third Saturday in May next, there will be a public sale directed by the Jackson County court of 640 acres, that is the property of Joseph CHAFFENHAN. The land was taken at the influence of Thomas BELLENSLEY. J. COOK, shff.

The following appointments were confirmed by the Senate during the late session of Congress:

(1) Augus C. LUDLOW, Fitzhenry BABBIT, Walcot CHAUNCEY, William CARTER, jun., John H. ELTON, Joshua WATSON, Edmund P. KENNEDY, Jesse WILKINSON, Horace WALPOLE, and Alexander J. DALLAS, to be Navy Lieutenants.

(2) Robert GREENLEAF and John WILLIAMS are promoted to Capt. of Marines from First Lieutenants.

(3) William S. BUSH and John M. GAMBLE are promoted to Marine First Lieutenants from Second Lieutenants.

(4) William STRONG, and John URQUHART are now Second Lieutenants of the Marine Corp.

(5) J. A. BRERETON from Surgeon's Mate to Surgeon in the Navy.

(6) Joseph G. ROBERTS and Walter NEW to be Surgeon's Mates.

On the fourth Saturday in May next in the town of Williamsburgh, there will be a public sale directed by the Jackson County court of three lots, that are the property of Samuel WILSON. The land was taken at the influence of the commissioners of Williamsburgh. J. COOK, shff.

On the fourth Saturday in May next, there will be a public sale in the town of Williamsburgh, directed by the Winchester Superior Court in Carthage, of 120 acres, that is the property of Benjamin BLACKBURN. The property was taken at the influence of John DILLINHAM. J. COOK, sheriff.

For sale, 400 acres in Overton County. John SCROGGAN.

Reward $20. On the 31st of January, a negro man named HARRY ranaway from the subscriber in Overton County. He is the property of Col. William ROBERTSON, of Claiborne County. John TATE.

Wanted a paper maker. William MOORE.

The stud horse Alborak will stand this season at my stable on Goose Creek. Richard BRITTELL, Smith County.

June 6, 1811, Vol. 2, No. 105

The following is a list of letters remaining at the post office in White Plains on April 1, 1811, per William QUARLES, p. m.: Major John ARMSTRONG, Benjamin BLACKBURN, Thomas CRUTCHER, Major James CHISOM, William EATON, Moses FISK, Col. Isaac GOARE, James LYON, Washington LEDBETTER, WIlliam MARCHBANKS, Jobe MARTIN, Jobe MORGAN, George RAINS, Capt. Joseph SMITH, William WLLIAMS, James G. WISTLE, Benjamin WEAVER.

The following persons have reported estrays in Sumner County, per Will. TRIGG, r. s. c.:

(1) Thomas KEEFE, on the middle fork of Station Camp, has taken up a yellow sorrel mare. The mare was valued at $10 on March 12, 1811.

(2) James BRACHAN, on the Sulpher Fork of Drake Creek, has taken up a black horse. On February 28, 1811, the horse was appraised at the sum of $35.

(3) James GREER, on the north fork of the Red River, has taken up a sorrel mare colt. The colt was appraised at $16 on February 25, 1811.

(4) James ODAM, living near Gallatin, has taken up a bay mare. On March 26, 1811, the mare was given an appraised value of $30.

(4) Harvey WILLIS, living on the west fork of Station Camp, has taken up a grey mare. On April 23, 1811, the mare was appraised at $5.

(5) Samuel FLINNEN, living on Manscoes Creek, has taken a sorrel mare. On April 10, 1811, the mare was valued at the sum of $50.

(6) Thomas NEAL, on Bledsoes Creek, has taken up a bay mare. On April 10, 1811, the mare's value was $15.

(7) John BRIGANN, jr., on Station Camp, was taken up a bay horse. On April 10, 1811, the horse was given an appraised value of $10.

(8) Polly YOUNG, on Second Creek, has taken up a bay horse. On April 26, 1811, the horse was given an appraised value of $25.

The following persons have reported estrays in Warren County, per James M'EWEN, r. w. c.:

(1) Stephen LOONY has taken up a sorrel horse on the Barren Fork of the Collin's River. The horse was valued at $40 on April 4, 1811.

(2) Thomas GARNER, jun., on Hickory Creek, has taken up a sorrel mare. On April 1, 1811, the mare valued at the sum of $20.

(3) Claiborne GUNTER, on Mountain Creek, has taken up a sorrel mare. On April 5, 1811, the horse was given an appraised value of $25.

(4) Bazil RIDDLE, on Collin's River, has taken up a bay

mare. On April 12, 1811, the mare's value is $16.
(5) Benjamin HAWKINS, on the Collins River, has taken
    up a sorrel horse. On April 6, 1811, the horse was
    appraised at the sum of $25.
The following persons have reported estrays in Jackson,
per Nathan SMITH, d. r. j. c.:
(1) Edward ROBERTSON, on the Roaring River, has taken
    up a bay horse. On March 27, 1811, the horse was
    appraised at a value of $25.
(2) William GOODING, on the north fork of Indian Creek,
    has taken up a bay mare. On March 25, 1811, the
    horse was appraised at $17.
(3) Benjamin HOLLADY, four miles below Williamsburgh,
    has taken up a brown mare. The mare was appraised
    at $12 by Philip BRYANT and James BREEDING before
    James ROBERTS, j. p.
    John B. GILLIAM, cabinetmaker, has commenced business at
Dixon Springs.
    Sumner County, Tennessee, March Term, 1811. William
HALL, sheriff and collector, reports that the following
tracts of land still have unpaid taxes for the year 1810.
David SHELBY, clerk.

Reputed Owners	Acres	Situation
Oliver SMITH heir's	lot	Cairo
William DICKSON	lot	Cairo
William MORGAN	lot	Cairo
Thomas CAMPBELL	lot	Cairo
Edwin SMITH	lot	Cairo
John LAWRENCE	lot	Cairo
George REES	lot	Cairo
James SIMPSON	lot	Cairo
William DENNIS	500	Caney Fork
Jacob JONES	228	Adj. Thomas GROVER
William DENNIS	100	Drakes Creek
James M'KNIGHT	lot	Cairo
Edward HUDSON	lot	Cairo
John PEARSON	lot	Cairo

Wanted beef steers and barren cows. John MURPHEY.
    The following persons have reported estrays in Overton
County, per B. TOTTEN, d. r. s. c.:
(1) John MILLER, on Dry Fork of the Obed's River, has
    taken up a brown mare. On March 30, 1811, the mare
    was appraised at $18.
(2) William MARCHBANKS, on the Ft. Blount Road, has
    taken up a bay horse. On April 11, 1811, the horse
    was valued at $26.
(4) John LEATHERWOOD, near Monroe, has taken up a brown
    filly. On April 15, 1811, the filly's value is $18.
(5) Charles SEVERE, in Monroe, has taken up a horse.

The following persons have reported estrays in Smith County, per B. SHAW, r. s. c.:
(1) Josiah STRANGE, has taken up a brown mare. The mare was appraised at $14 on April 24, 1811.
(2) Wyat GRANT, near Carthage, has taken up a brown mare. On May 1, 1811, the mare was valued at $15.

I want to forewarn the public from trading or dealing with my wife Elizabeth JINNINGS. She has left my bed and board without cause or provocation. Edmond JINNINGS.

The following persons have reported estrays in Jackson County, per Nathan SMITH, d. r. j. c.:
(1) John B. PARTNER, living on the Cumberland River, has taken up a black mare. On May 20, 1811, the mare was appraised at $35.
(2) John SHOEMAKER, on Martin's Creek, has taken up a sorrel horse. On May 22, 1811, the horse was given an appraised value of $35.
(3) Emanuel HOLMES, on Brimstone Creek, has taken up a sorrel mare. The mare's value was $40.
(4) Yelvalon NEVILL has taken up a bay mare. The mare was valued at $12 on May 15, 1811.

June 17, 1811, Vol. 3, No. 107
There was a letter to the editor from Joel DYER.

The following persons have reported estrays in Smith County, per B. SHAW, r. s. c.:
(1) Robert COOPER has taken up a brown mare. The mare was valued at $8 on May 11, 1811.
(2) Edward WILLIAMS, on Holmes Creek, has taken up a sorrel horse. On April 17, 1811, the horse was given an appraised valued of $15.
(3) Thomas DRIVER, on White Oak Creek on the Barren River, has taken up a black mare. The mare's value on April 27, 1811 was $20.
(4) Dale EVANS, at Liberty, has taken up a bay mare. On May 8, 1811, the mare was valued at $15.
(5) William CHAPMAN, on Hickman's Creek, has taken up a grey horse.
(6) Seth BURTON has taken up a sorrel mare. The mare was valued at $5 on May 25, 1811.
(7) Charles FORRESTER, on Dry Fork, has taken up a grey mare. On April 9, 1811, the mare was appraised at the sum of $10.
(8) Jesse BEASLEY, Indian Creek, has taken up a grey mare. On May 1, 1811, the mare's value was $18.
(9) Claiborne WRIGHT, on Sullivan's Fery, has taken up black mare. On May 26, 1811, the mare was given an appraised value of $40.
(10) Joseph NASH, on the Long Fork on the Barren, has

taken up a bay mare. On May 27, 1811, the mare was valued in the amount of $35.

(11) Elizabeth WILSON, near Liberty, has taken up a white horse. On May 11, 1811, the horse was given an appraised value of $4.

(12) John HAIL, on Clear Fork, has taken up a bay mare. On April 31, 1811, the mare was valued at $10.

(13) Joseph SNOW, on Dry Fork, has taken up a horse.

(14) Charles CONAWAY has taken up a bay mare. The mare was appraised at $11 on June 4, 1811.

(15) Edward DALE, at Liberty, has taken up a bay horse. On May 30, 1811, the mare was valued at $40.

(16) Jesse POWEL, on Cany Fork, has taken up a horse. On May 22, 1811, the horse was appraised at $35.

(17) Daniel BURFORD, near Carthage, has taken up a bay horse. On June 6, 1811, the horse's value is $15.

(18) Isaac MONGLE, on Goose Creek, has taken up a sorrel mare. On May 26, 1811, the mare's value was $20.

(19) Horatio WALKER has taken up a black filly. The filly was valued at $14 on May 20, 1811.

(20) John PRITCHER, on Defeated Creek, has taken up a mare. On June 5, 1811, the mare's value is $20.

(21) David MNEELY has taken up a sorrel filly The filly was appraised at $20 on June 5, 1811.

(22) Charles CONNOWAY has taken up a grey horse.

July 11, 1811, Vol. 3, No. 111
The following is a list of letters remaining at the post office on July 1, 1811, per B. SHAW, a. p. m.:   Harmonious ALKIRE, Nathaniel BREWER, Heze. BLANKINSHIP, John BRANSFORD, Jesse BURTON, Henry CORNWALL, Alex. CAMPBELL, John CANADY or Shadrick PHILLIPS, Joseph CALLOWAY, Rueben EWEL or William JAMES, Malachi EWEL, Hanson G. FOWLER, William FARQUAHAR, Phillip FOX, John GORDON, Benj. GOODSON, William GILL, Allen HOLLIDAY, Jordon HICKS, John HICKS, John HARRIS, James HARVEY, John S. HARMAN, Mark HOLLOMAN, Charles JENNINGS, John LITTLE, W. P. LAWRANCE, James LYON, Roger LARKINS, John MARTIN or George PAINE, William MARCUM, Joel MANN, Matthew PATTON, Moses RHOADES, Hazel M. C. RICE, Col. ROBERTSON, William SMART, Millington STALLIONS, Joshua SHORT, Martha TURNEY, N. W. WILLIAMS, Evan WILLIAMS, John WARREN, Jonas WHITLEY, Charles WHITSON, James WHITSIT.

July 24, 1811, Vol. 3, No. 112
For sale, assorted merchandise. Robert and William ALLEN.
On the 21st, Nathaniel WILLIAMS married Miss Sally WALTON, daughter of Col. William WALTON.
The partnership of John ALLEN and Robert ALLEN of Dixon Springs and Gallatin is dissolved by mutual consent.

The following persons have reported estrays in White
County, per J. A. LANE, d. r. w. c.:
  (1) William ROLTON has taken up a bay horse. The horse
      was appraised at $20 on May 14, 1811.
  (2) Clement CIMENTS, on Cany Fork, has taken up a
      sorrel horse. On May 21, 1811, the horse was given
      an appraised value of $15.
  (3) James M'CATIN, on Calf Killer Fork, has taken up a
      sorrel mare. On May 25, 1811, the mare was valued
      at the sum of $22.
  (4) William CRIEN has taken up a black mare. The mare
      was appraised at $20 on May 27, 1811.

August 7, 1811, Vol. 3, No. 114
    Jackson County, Tennessee. The following tracts of land
still have unpaid taxes for the year 1810 and they will be
sold on the first Monday in next . J. COOK, shff.

Reputed Owners	Acres	Situation
Bejamin BLACKBURN	300	
Edward FITZPATRICK	100	Walton's Road
Joshua GORE	150	Mill Creek
Orson MARTIN	640	Cumberland River
David MITCHEL	50	Nob Creek
John MARTIN	640	Line Creek
David MEADOW	250	
Hardy MURFREE's heirs	1536	
Robert BROOKS	120	Brook's Bent
John JAMES	201	Jinnings Creek
Isaac MOORE's heirs	2106	
Daniel CHERRY	274	Walton's Road
Stokely DONALSON	640	Grant No. 2814
Solomon PREWITT's heirs	640	
George HERNDON	320	Occ. by Abner LEE
John PAYTON	640	Occ. by David DIXON
		and the GRIFFITHS
James BRAKEN	70	Adj. Stephen MARAIGN
John HOWARD	2450	Roaring River
Benjamin BASHAW	640	Occ. James RAY, sen.
David WILSON and		
John DIXON	640	War Trace
John BLACK's heirs	640	Cumberland River
Richard MITCHELL	320	Occ. Joel ALEXANDER
David ROSE	270	
William P. ANDERSON	640	Occ. John CUNNINGHAM
Richard MITCHELL	300	Imp. Woolsey PEARCE

    On the first Monday in September next, there will be a
public sale directed by the Smith County Court of 200 acres
in Overton County, that is the property of Benjamin SAVAGE.
The property is occuppied by Ruebin DOBKIN. The tract was

taken at the influence of Thomas DILLIN. J. M'DONNOLD.
The following is a list of letters remaining at the post office in Williamsburgh on July 21, 1811, per Sampson WILLIAMS, p. m.: Richard ANDERSON, John J. ANDERSON, Philip BRYANT, Charles CROOKER, Richard COUDREA, Isaac CARLOCK, John GATITS, James D. HENLEY, John LYTTLEPUTE, Clemment MOSS, Richard MANSELL, James M'CLAIN, Robert PALMER, Stephen MARAIGH, James RAGLM, John ROGERS, Romulus SAUNDERS, John THOMPSON, John WHEELER, Joseph WINIELY.
The following is a list of estrays remaining in Smith County, per B. SHAW, r. s. c.:
(1) Arthur S. HOGUN has taken up a sorrel mare. The horse was valued at $7.50 on June 11, 1811.
(2) William JUSTICE, on the Barren River, has taken up a bay horse. On April 30, 1811, the horse was appraised at $40.
(3) Thomas CRUTCHFIELD, on Hogun's Creek, has taken up a bay horse. On June 29, 1811, the horse was given an appraised value of $15.
(4) Thomas JOHNSON, on Indian Creek, has taken up a sorrel filly. On June 22, 1811, the filly was valued at the sum of $25.
(5) Thomas G. WALTON, on Snow Creek, has taken up a bay horse. On July 6, 1811, the horse was appraised in the amount of $10.
(6) William PAYNE has taken up a bay mare. The mare was valued at $18 on July 12, 1811.
(7) Claiborne DENNY has taken up a sorrel mare. The mare was valued at $18 on July 12, 1811.
(8) Thomas BOREING has taken up a bay mare. The mare was valued at $13.50 on June 27, 1811.
(9) Charles BOULTON has taken up a sorrel horse colt. The colt was valued at $10 on July 13, 1811.
Smith County, Tennessee, March Term, 1811. John BAKER, collector, reports that the following tracts of land still have unpaid taxes for the year 1810. Joseph W. ALLEN.

Reputed Owners	Acres	Situation
Robert BANKS	182	
Rueben YARBURY	357	
Samuel HOWARD	lot	Carthage
Robert BROWN	426	
John HUSTON	100	
William WOOD	640	
John M'QUISTEN	640	
John M'NAIRY	1020	
Anthony HART's heirs	640	
Gidean and Wm. PILLOW	594	Cany Fork
Henry CHANDLER	196	Cany Fork

(Continued on following page)

(Smith County delinquent tax list continued)
```
John W. NICKLES            122      1 white poll
Stephen MONTGOMERY         237      Goose Creek
Washington L. HANUM       1000      1808, 1809, 1810
James ABERCREMY           1560      1808, 1809, 1810
Robert FENNER             1800      1808
JOHN G. BRAHEN            1280
Thomas PARLENA's heirs    4800      Cany Fork
```
Reward $15. A man named William M'DANIEL who is on Indian Creek, near his brother-in-law John SADLER stole a grey stud horse. John HAZLET.

August 21, 1811, Vol. 3, No. 116

Murdered in his house on Saturday last, Jesse JACKSON of this county. It is believed that he was murdered by his wife. She has been committed to jail.

The following persons have reported estrays in Smith County, per B. SHAW, r. s. c.:
(1) Thadeus ARMSTEAD, on Snow Creek, has taken up a sorrel mare. On August 3, 1811, the mare was given an appraised value of $20.
(2) Elias JOHNS has taken up a bay mare. The mare's value on August 1, 1811 was $5.
(3) Daniel BUFORD has taken up a black mare. The mare was valued at $15 on August 1, 1811.
(4) James BALLEW, Salt Lick Creek, has taken up a bay horse. On July 19, 1811, the horse was valued at the sum of $17.
(5) John HANCOCK has taken up a black horse. The horse was valued at $30 on July 17, 1811.
(6) On July 25, 1811, Isaac GREEN, on Peyton's Creek, has taken up a black mare valued at $16.
(7) Charles CONAWAY has taken up a grey gelding. The horse was valued at $4.50 on August 17, 1811.
(8) David M'NEELY, on the Cany Fork, has taken up a bay horse. On August 17, 1811, the horse was appraised at the sum of $20.

The following persons have reported estrays in Warren County, per James M'EWEN, r. w. c.:
(1) Walter WOOD, on Hurricane Creek, has taken up a bay mare. On June 12, 1811, the mare was appraised at a value of $10.
(2) William PANE, on Piney Creek, has taken up a bay mare. On June 25, 1811, the mare was given a value in the amount of $7.
(3) Sarah ELAM, on the east fork of the Stones River, has taken up a bay mare. On June 28, 1811, the mare was appraised in the amount of $25.
(4) James SWANN, three miles west of M'Minnville, has

has taken up a yellow bay mare. On June 11, 1811, the mare was appraised at the sum of $23.
(5) A chestnut sorrel horse was taken up a William KEY on Hickory Creek. The horse was valued at the sum of $15 on June 20, 1811.
(6) Jacob BOLINGER, on Hickory Creek, has taken up a sorrel horse. On July 31, 1811, the appraised value of the horse was $30.
(7) Micajah NEWSAN, on the Collins River, has taken up horse. On August 1, 1811, the horse was appraised at the sum of $25.
(8) Peter FITLE, on Mountain Creek, has taken up a bay mare. The mare was appraised on August 25, 1811.
(9) David HAY, on Cany Fork, has taken up a horse.
(10) Benjamin WOOTON, on Hickory Creek, has taken up a yellow sorrel horse. On August 6, 1811, the horse was appraised at $25.

September 4, 1811, Vol. 3, No. 118
New York, August 7th. Patrick and William PHELAN, two passengers from the ship Belisariou from Dublin, were removed by the British sloop Atlanta. Upon the arrival of the Atlanta at Halifax, the following persons were removed to a sloop which sailed for the Isle of St. Johns with orders, that they were to be put on the estate of Lord James TOWNSEND: Richard KING, Jane KING, James KING, Mary KING, Jane KING (sic), John GILBERT, John BIRK, Eliza BIRK, Thomas WALSH, Thomas NEWNAM, Lawrence CURRENT, Thomas BIRD, Mary BIRD, Valient NEEDHAM, Cath. NEEDHAM, Eliza NEEDHAM, Joseph GILBERT, Ann GILBERT, Ally BURTON, Michael MURPHY.
The following men were impressed: Richard LANGAR, Peter DOLEY, James GRAHAM, John DUNN, James COSTEGAN, William TURNER, Edward DORE, William MORGAN, Peter COURTNEY, Michael M'HOLLAND, Mathew MURPHY, William SUTTON, Bartle TURNER, Edward LATELEY, Thomas WALSH, Martin BAMBRICK, Michael BAMBRICK.
Dr. LAWRENCE has returned to Smith County and is opened for business.

October 2, 1811, Vol. 3, No. 121
For sale, dry goods and groceries. Joel B. HARPER.
On the 2nd of November next in the town of Carthage, there will be a public sale directed by the Smith County court of the property, that belongs to Dr. Charles F. MABUIS, dec. Susannah MABIUS and Wm. LANE, admin.
On the 23rd of November in the town of Williamsburgh, there will be a public sale directed by the Jackson County court of 221 acres, that is the property of John JAMES. The property was attached by Benjamin CLARK. J. COOK, shff.

The following persons have reported estrays in Overton County, per B. TOTTEN, d. r. o. c.:
(1) Solomon ALRCE, on the west fork of the Obeds River, has taken up a sorrel horse. On July 15, 1811, the horse was appraised at the sum of $32.
(2) George CHRISTIAN, on the Roaring River, has taken up a grey horse. On August 1, 1811, the horse was valued at the sum of $15.
(3) William CHASEY, on the Obeds River, has taken up a bay mare. On August 7, 1811, the mare was valued in the amount of $40.
(4) John M'COUCE, on Roaring River, has taken up a roan mare. On August 8, 1811, the mare's value was $25.
(5) James WATTS, on the Wolf River, has taken up a bay mare. On August 13, 1811, the mare was appraised in the amount of $20.

October 16, 1811, Vol. 3, No. 122

I want to forewarn the public against trading with my negroes. Francis GILDART.

The following is a list of letters remaining at the post office at Carthage on October 1, 1811, per B. SHAW, a. p. m.: Jacob ADAMS, John BROWN, Hezekiah BLANKENSHIP, John BASSINGER, David HOPKINS, Hubbard BREWER, Samuel BAIRD, William CAGE, John COOOPER, Jonathan COTTINGHAM, Joel DYER, James DAUGHERTY, John DIEL, Robert DABNEY, William FLOWERS, John GALES, Thomas GRAHAM, Samuel GIBBONS, Winston HIGH, Arthur S. HOGAN, Josiah B. HARREL, Stephen JOHNSTON, Thomas JONES, John KIRK, John LYON, Barnet LEE, William M'CORLEY, Andrew M'CLAIN, Anthony MATCALF, sen., Joseph MORGAN, Jacob MILLER, William PISTOLE, Edward POWEL, Mrs. Nancy ROBERTS, John RUSSEL, Samuel ROBERTSON, William SHAW, Mary LEXTON, Malcolm SMITH, Moses SCRIVNER, George L. TRAVERS, Henry TOLLEY, Henry WATTERSON, Jonathan WISEMAN, Ephraim WINKLE, Capt. WHITE, James or Daniel WITCHER.

For sale, the 100 acres, that I now occuppy. Lewis SMITH.

For sale, 640 acres on Hickman's Creek. R. B. ROBERTSON.

The following persons have reported estrays in Franklin County, per James THOMPSON, d. r. f. c.:
(1) Jeremiah SMITH, jun., near Caldwell's Bridge, has taken up a sorrel mare. The mare's value is $55.
(2) John DOBS, on the Elk River, has taken up a sorrel mare. The mare's value is $20.
(3) John DELOAH, on Elk River, has taken up a sorrel mare. The mare's value is $30.
(4) Perry YOUNG, on Soaps Ford, has taken up a grey horse. The horse was appraised at the sum of $55.
(5) Burrel THOMPSON has taken up a sorrel horse.

(6) Nathaniel RUSSELL, on the Elk River, has taken up a bay mare. The mare was given an appraised value in the amount of $20.

(7) John JOLLY, on the Rolling Fork of the Elk River, has taken up a bay mare. The mare's value is $25.

(8) Solomon GEORGE, below Winchester, has taken up a brown mare. The mare's value is $15.

(9) William TUBBS has taken up a sorrel mare. The mare was valued at $20.

(10) John GLASCOW, on the Elk River near M'Queen's Ford, has taken up a sorrel mare.

(11) John WINN has taken up a brown mare. The mare was appraised at the sum of $20.

(12) Isaac HUNT has taken up a brown colt worth $15.

(13) Jessee ARMSTRONG has taken up a bay mare, that is as appraised at $20.

(14) John BROW has taken up a sorrel horse.

(15) Daniel HILL, on the Elk River, has taken up a mare.

(16) Francis CRABB, on the Elk River, has taken up a brown bay mare. The mare's value is $12.

(17) John BROWN has taken up a bay mare.

The following persons have reported estrays in Jackson County, per Nathan SMITH, d. r. j. c.:

(1) Joseph HUNTER, on Falling Water, has taken up bay horse.

(2) Benjamin FORD has taken up a brown bay mare.

(3) Thomas CASSILY, on Salt Lick Creek, has taken up a brown horse.

All persons are forewarned against trading for a note given to William STEVENSON about the 20th of October, 1800. I was defrauded on said note. Land SHAWMAKER.

On the 30th of November next in the town of Carthage, there will be a public sale of 470 acres, that is owned and occuppied by the heirs of Charles F. MABIUS, dec. The property was taken at the influence of Richard CHAPMAN. John GORDON, d. s.

On the 15th of November next in the town of Carthage, there will be a public sale directed by the Smith County court of two lots, that are the property of Lemuel PURNELL. The property was levied on the hand of Thomas WILKERSON by John BAKER. The orginal attachment was by William MOOR. George MATLOCK, shff.

The following persons have reported estrays in Sumner County, per Wm. TRIGG:

(1) John LASLEY, on Drake's Creek on the Cumberland River, has taken up a sorrel mare. The mare was appraised at $15 on May 6, 1811.

(2) Fanney ARTHBURTHNOT (sic) has taken up a sorrel filly. On July 28, 1811, the filly's value is $10.

(3) James HARRISON, on Bledsoes Lick, has taken up a
     bay mare. On May 6, 1811, the mare was apprasied
     in the amount of $4.
(4) Humphrey BATE, on the Cumberland River, has taken
     up a bay horse. On May 6, 1811, the appraised value
     of the horse was $20.
(5) Samuel BRINKLEY, on the Red River, has taken up a
     sorrel horse. On May 20, 1811, the horse was given
     an appraised value of $32.50.
(6) Lewis CRANE has taken up a sorrel mare. The mare
     was appraised on June 5, 1811 at $10.
(7) Richard ALLEN, on Bledsoes Creek, has taken up a
     sorrel mare. On May 25, 1811, the mare was valued
     in the amount of $45.
(8) Mary RICHMON, on the west fork of Goose Creek, has
     taken up a brown mare. On June 1, 1811, the mare
     was appraised at $30.
(9) James SMOTHERS, on Drakes Creek, has taken up a
     sorrel horse. On June 22, 1811, the horse was
     appraised at $13.
(10) William CARR, on Goose Creek, has taken up a brown
     mare. The mare's value on June 1, 1811 was $5.
(11) John JOHNSON, four miles above Gallatin, has taken
     up a bay horse. On June 29, 1811, the horse was
     appraised at $25.
(12) William BOYLE, on Sulpher Fork, has taken up a
     mare. On July 12, 1811, the mare's value was $25.
(13) Henry BELOTE has taken up a sorrel mare. The mare
     was valued at $9 on July 23, 1811.
(14) James GOHERN, on Bledsoes Lick, has taken up a
     sorrel horse. The horse's value is $18.
(15) David BRYANCE, on Station Camp, has taken up an
     iron grey horse. The horse was given an appraised
     value of $60 on August 28, 1811.
(16) Thomas BLACKMORE, on Rocky Creek, has taken up a
     grey mare. On August 31, 1811, the mare was valued
     at $6 on August 31, 1811.

November 9, 1811, Vol. 3, No. 125
     George ALLEN, age 61, died on the 4th. On the following
day, Elizabeth ALLEN, his wife, died.
     Smith County, Circuit Court, September term, 1811. Arley
YOUNG by Stephen MARAIGN, her next friend vs. J. YOUNG,
Petiton of Divorce. On the fourth Monday in March next in
the town of Carthage, J. YOUNG is ordered to appear in
court. Robert ALLEN, clerk of Smith County.

November 16, 1811, Vol. 3, No. 126
     Uriah DRAKE, the son of William DRAKE of Norton, Delaware

County, Ohio, was murdered by a free negro by the name of Bill JACKSON. Mr. DRAKE has been working in Lower Sandusky and had left about noon.

I expect to leave the state in six months. Will all those indebted please come forward and settle their accounts. Barnet E. LEE.

Charleston, October 9th. A swindler by the name of Homer G. BOSTICK alias George BROWN was jailed five years after his crime by Ezekial NASH. Nathan JEFFRIES after a long pursuit took him a few days ago at Brier Creek, Burk County, Georgia.

On the first Saturday in December next in the town of Gallatin, there will be a public sale directed by the Sumner County court of 150 acres on Station Camp Creek, that is the property of Archibald MARLIN. The property was taken at the influence of Lemuel PREWT against Nancy BOYCE and Archibald MARTIN, admin. of Nicholas BOYCE, dec. Wm. H. DOUGLASS.

On the first Saturday in December next in the town of Gallatin, there will be a public sale directed by the court of Sumner County of four tracts of land, that is the poroperty of Armstead STUBBLEFIELD. The land ajoins Thomas STUBBLEFIELD. The property was taken at the influence of Jacob MERCER. Wm. HALL, shff.

December 7, 1811, Vol. 3, No. 129

Knoxville, November 18, 1811. There was a pillage of the mail Friday week on the road between John CAINS and Maj. LEA's. The following pieces were recovered: A letter dated New Orleans, October 25, 1811, from Augustus INGLEHAM to Messers. FERGUSON and DAY of New York; One from Charles M. FLETCHER to Thadeus MAYHAM of New York, dated New Orleans, October 18, 1811; One from Jacob TRIMBLE & Co. to Joel WEST & Co. of New York, dated New Orleans, October 12, 1811; One from TALCOTT & POWER to Robert BUSH & Co. of New York, dated New Orleans, October 10th and that mentions a Mr. WILLIAMS and a delivery by the ship Broker, STEPHENS, master; One from R. M. WILLIAMS to R. F. DUNLAP of New York, dated New Orleans, October, 1811; One from WINER & HARMAN to Messers. SHELL, SING & Co. announcing the arrival of Capt. HULL, dated New Orleans, October 10, 1811; One to George JOHNSTON a merchant of New York, to his brother at New Orleans, dated October 11, 1811; One dated New Orleans, November 9th from George WILLIAMSON to Francis ABRAMS, of Orange County, Virgina, giving an account of ABRAMS' brother's death; There is a bill of execution drawn by TALCOTT & BOWERS on Messers. W. and D. TALCOTT, New York, in favor of Abraham RUSSEL, jr.; there are two bills of exchange in French dated April 20, 1803, and July 7, 1803 with a second endorsement by RICHARDS, dated October, 1810, that is payable to T. P. L.

WIRBITTING on October the 18th at New Orleans; A note made payable to J. P. SHIBETTER.

The Cotton Factory of George EDDY & Co. has a variety of goods for sale.

On the 13th of January next in the town of Monroe, there will be a public sale of 200 acres, that is occuppied and owned by Joseph CRAWFORD. The property was taken at the influence of George ARMSTRONG. J. M'DONNOLD, shff.

On the 13th of January next in the town of Monroe, there will be a public sale directed by the court of Overton County of 428 acres, that is the property of Joseph CRAWFORD. The property was taken at the influence of Joseph BATES and David WHITMAN. J. M'DONNOLD, shff.

On the 13th of January next in the town of Monroe, there will be a public sale directed by the Overton County court of 50 acres, that is the property of Robert JOHNSON. The property was taken at the influence of Stephen MAYFIELD. J. M'DONNOLD, shff.

A negro woman named SARAH, age 40, was committed to the jail of Smith County. She says that she is the property of Hugh CRAWFORD, Station Camp, Sumner County. B. SHAW, jailor. The following persons have reported estrays in Smith County, per B. SHAW, r. s. c.:

(1) Robert CLARK, on Payton's Creek, has taken up a bay mare. On August 27, 1811, the mare's value is $12.

(2) James AULTON, on Snow Creek, has taken up a bay mare. On August 24, 1811, the mare's value is $11.

(3) Robert BASWELL, on Caney Fork, has taken up a bay horse. On September 2, 1811, the mare was given an appraised value of $6.50.

(4) Samuel B. CRUTCHFIELD, on Hogin's Creek, has taken up a bay filly. On September 10, 1811, the filly was valued at the sum of $20.

(5) George DOOLEY, on Round Lick Creek, has taken up a sorrel mare. On October 2, 1811, the mare's value was given at $16.

(6) Mathew KIRK, on Beech Bent, has taken up a bay mare. On September 18, 1811, the mare was valued in the amount of $17.

(7) Henry M'WHORTER, on the Long Fork of the Barren, has taken up a bay horse. On October 28, 1811, the horse was appraised at $20.

(8) Charles BOULTON has taken up a bay horse. The horse was valued at $20 on November 2, 1811.

(9) William HARVEY, on Hickman's Creek, has taken up a sorrel filly. On November 9, 1811, the filly was appraised at $10.

(10) Nathaniel BURDINE, on Round Lick, took up a horse. On November 1, 1811, the horse's value was $8.

The following persons have reported estrays in White County, per Jacob A. LANE, d. r. w. c.:

(1) John ROBERTSON, on Cane Creek, has taken up a bay mare. On August 30, 1811, the mare was appraised at the sum of $14.

(2) Michael HIROR, on Falling Water, has taken up a bay mare. On September 10, 1811, the mare was given an appraised value of $20.

(3) Randolph RAMSEY, on Falling Water, has taken up a horse. On September 19, 1811, the horse was given an appraised value of $40.

(4) Eliheu SAUNDERS, near Cook's Ferry, has taken up a bay horse. On October 5, 1811, the horse was given an appraised value of $10.

On the 14th, Jacob R. TAYLOR, the son of John B. TAYLOR, of Philadelphia, was murdered and at the same time another man named COLLINS was killed. He was the Second Mate to the Brig Hetty, Capt. Wm. FOUNTAIN, master.

The following persons have reported estrays in Overton County, per B. SHAW, r. s. c.:

(1) Junious HOOPER, on the Obeds River, has taken up a bay horse, which was worth $26 on October 11, 1811.

(2) Jacob SMELSOR, on Donelson's Cove, has taken up a horse, that was worth $25 on October 21, 1811.

(3) Arthur BEEL has taken up a sorrel horse. The value of $20 was given on November 9, 1811.

(4) William HAYS has taken up a brown horse. The horse was valued at $25 on November 9, 1811.

(5) Stephen MAYFIELD has taken up a bay horse.

On the fourth Saturday in February next in the town of Williamsburg, there will be a public sale of 640 acres, that is the property of Benjamin BLACKBURN. The land was taken at the influence of George RAMSEY. James COOK, shff.

On the 13th of January next in the town of Monroe, there will be a public sale directed by the court of White County of 90 acres in Overton County, that is the property of William PHILLIPS. The property was taken at the influence of Alexander LOWERY, William GIST, Jacob A. LANE, and Ephraim ALEXANDER. J. M. M'DONNOLD.

December 21, 1811, Vol. 3, No. 131

Rev. Freeman KILLINSWORTH, magistrate of Johnson County, North Carolina, was apphrended on a charge of counterfeiting silve dollars.

On the 8th of February next in the town of Sparta, there will be a public sale directed by the White County court of 115 acres, that is owned and occuppied by William RIDGE. The property was taken at the influence of William MARCHBANKS. Isaac TAYLOR, jr., shff.

The Democratic Clarion and Tennessee Gazette
Published by Thomas G. Bradford

January 17, 1810, Vol. III, No. CIII

The following is a list of letters at the post office at Franklin On January 1, 1810, per D. SQUIER, a. p. m.: John ANDREWS, William ANTHONY, John A. ANDERSON, George BURNETT, John BURGRESS, Elias BRIDGEWATER, Joseph BLYTH, Elizabeth BAILY, William BLACK, William BANKS, Etheldred BEYET, Newton CANNON, Thomas CALIEN, Robert W. CARTER, Samuel CARTER, Daniel CAMPBELL, Thomas DUTTON, William DEAN, Thomas GOFF, Shadrick GARDNER, Brice M. GARNER, Isaac FERGUSON, Edward HORD, Thomas HARDEN, John HAMER, Mr. HESS, Thomas HARDEMAN, N. P. HARDEMAN, Kemp HOLAND, Archibald HOLMES, John HILL, David HOLLADAY, James JACKSON, Joseph JACKSON, Matthew JOHNSON, Henry JACKSON, Felix KICKPATRICK, Briant LYNCH, James F. LONG, Francis LONG, Lucy M'REYNOLDS, Lynch M'GEE, Colin M'DANIEL, Thomas M'CRORY, David MONTGOMERY, William M'GAUGH, Charles M'CLELLAN, Mary M'CALL, Jacob M'COLLAN, Jared M'COOICO, Charles MURPHRY, George OLIVER, Allen PURVES, Joel PARRISH, Leroy POPE, Ruebin PHILIPS, N. G. PINSON, Nelson PATTERSON, James PUGH, Alexander PICKARD, junr., Giles PAGE, Thomas H. PERKINS, Archibald RUTHERFORD, Mahew RUSSEL, Alexander RICKEY, Ruebin RIGGS, Jo STACY, Jordan SOLOMON, Richard SMITH, William ROBERTS, John STEWAT, Benjamin SMITH, Thomas E. SUMNER, John SMITH, James SHANNON, Joseph TAYLOR, Charles TULLEY, John TUCKER, John THOMPSON, Harden TILMON, Levi UNDERWOOD, Andrew WHITE, John WHITE, James WILSON, Susan WHEDBEE, Ann WILSON, John WILKINS, Abraham WALKER, John WITHERSPOON, William WILSON, Patterson WALKER, Thomas YOUNG.

For sale, salt petre. Geo. POYZER.

The subscriber will not take cotton in payment of debts as of the 15th of January next. J. B. CRAIGHEAD.

The following persons have reported estrays in Bedford County, per Howel DAWDY, ranger:

(1) James BEAVERS, Cany Spring Creek, has taken up a sorrel mare. On December 16, 1810, the mare was appraised at $50.

(2) Samuel FLEMING, on Rock Spring, has taken up a bay horse. The horse's value was 12-1/2 cents.

(3) Thomas MUSGROVE, on Weakley's Creek, has taken up a bay mare. On December 13, 1810, the mare was appraised at $18.

(4) William B. BURNOM has taken up a brown horse. The horse was appraised at $47 on December 22, 1810.

The horse Wonder will stand this season at my stable on the west Harpeth on Lieper's Fork. David DUNN.

Strayed April 23rd last, two hogs. J. W. THOMAS.

On the 28th of December in Nashville a bank note for $50 was found. J. P. M'CONNELL.

The undersigned obtained from the Court of Pleas of Bedford County, September Sessions, 1809, the letters of administration on the rights and chattels of John COUNTS, jun., dec. Will all persons who have debts due for the following estates come forward. Rosa. COUNTS, adx., and John SLOR, adm., Bedford County, December 15, 1809.

(No Date), Vol. III, No. CV

The house lately occuppied by R. STAINBECK is for rent. Interested persons apply to E. TALBOT.

There will be delay in the drawing of the lottery. Sampson SAWYERS.

A female seminary will be opening in the situation adjoining Nashville, that was the property of Mr. WHITE and lately occuppied by John ANDERSON. Mrs. TARPLEY.

I am ready to make title to Enoch HEATON for the tract of land, that I gave my bond for about the 15th of January. O. WILLIAMS.

On the 5th of next month at the court house in Franklin, a negro man, the property of John TAPLEY, dec., is for sale. Thomas H. PERKINS and Th. EDMISTON, adm.

For sale, land. Young A. GAY.

On the 16th, two negroes, FRANK, age 25 or 26, and his wife DORCAS, age 19 or 20, ranaway. There is liberal reward for their capture. R. P. CURRIN.

On the 14th of March next, there will be a public sale directed by the court of Wilson County of 300 acres, warrant no. 51, entry no. 311 and 200 acres, warrant no. 5408, entry no. 245; that is the property of Willie CHERRY. On August 31, 1807, the property was taken at the influence of John and William ALLEN. Th. BRADLEY.

On the 17th of March next in the town of Lebanon, there will be a public sale of 100 acres, that is the property of Jared BETTS. The property was taken at the influence of John INON vs. James BETTS, Samuel HAR--, and John B. WALKER. Wm. WOODARD, dep. shff.

On the 29th of December, Barber TRIM married Miss SOPHY of Nashville.

On the 25th of December, a bank note given by me to Mr. WILLIAMS to Edley EWING for $11 was lost. Nathan OWEN.

On the 1st of February next, the flat bottom boat Farmer, Rueben PAYNE, master, will sail for New Orleans. Interested persons apply to the master or Stephen CANTREL, Nashville.

On the 15th of March next in the town of Lebanon, there will be a public sale directed by the court of Wilson County of 250 acres, that is the property of Micajah VERITT. The property was attached by Samuel THOMAS. Th. BARDLEY.

Bedford County, Tennessee, December term, 1809. Benjamin
BRADFORD, sheriff, reports that the following tracts of land
still have taxes remaining due for 1809.

Reputed Owners	Acres	Situation
Alex. WILSON's heirs	440	Bradshaw's Creek
Joseph ANDERSON	300	Duck River
John BRIMAGER	2684	
William BLACK	750	
William BRANCH	200	
Uriah BASS	640	Elk River
Clemment CANNON	250	
Nicholas CONRAD	274	
Stephen CLOYD	150	
Zadock DANIEL	600	
Ephraim DAVIDSON	150	
Amos FREEMAN	100	
William HENRY	1550	
Tignate JONES	100	Rock Creek
Amos JOHNSTON	640	
Thomas LOGAN	100	
David BUCHANNON	1307	
EDMISTON & BERRY	1660	
William GILBREATH	716	Sug Creek
Joshua WILLIAMS	640	
Howell LOYD	40	
Jesse MAXWELL	320	
George MAXELL	58	
A. PEADY and Jo. COOL	5000	
Elijah PATTON	240	Mulberry
Nathan PATTERSON	200	Duck River
William STAMPER	300	Duck River
James FROTZE	2500	
Howell TATUM	529	.
David VAUGH's heirs	640	
Oliver WILLIAMS	320	
Robert W. SMITH	5000	Duck River
David SHANNON	100	Mulberry Creek
Daniel WILLIAMS	620	
Joseph COCK	200	
Roger SNELL	234	
Samuel WILSON	320	Swan Creek
William MORRISON	100	Weakley's Creek
NOBLE & MERIDETH	400	Mulberry
William EDMISTON	1200	
William LYTLE	640	
William CASWELL	1280	
Thomas HICKMAN	640	Cane Creek
William P. ANDERSON	100	Kelly's Creek

(Continued on following page)

(Bedford County delinquent tax list continued)

Martin ARMSTRONG	5000	Coldwater
John ALCORN	40	M'Cullock's Crek
John BAKER	640	Duck River
John BOYD	500	Duck River
Joseph COLEMAN	275	War Trace
Geo. DOHERTY	5000	Swan Creek
Tilmon DIXON	640	Cove Spring
James GREENLEE	500	Cove Spring
John HILL	2560	Duck River
John HAYWOOD	260	Duck River
Thomas KEEFE	274	Duck River
John KENNEDY	1000	Cane Creek
John M'NAIRY	640	Kelley's Creek
Hardy MURPHREE	700	Duck River
Henry MONTFORD	50	Cove Spring
Thomas M'CURREY	1000	Elk River
James NORWORTHY	428	Sugar Creek
Francis NASH	640	Duck River
Thomas POLK	5000	Elk River
William POLK	640	
William PATTERSON	375	
Henry M. RUTLEDGE	1675	Swan Creek
John SMITH, sen.	1000	Elk River
John STROTHER	248	Duck River
John FILSEY's heirs	120	Kelly's Creek
John EDMONSTON	1200	Elk River
John INSKEEP	1000	Duck River

The following lands were not listed for taxes in 1809 and are liable for a double tax.

Reputed Owners	Acres	Situation
Jesse FRANKLIN	1000	Elk River
LOOMAS & DILLAHUNTY	640	
John MOTHERALL	228	Elk River
John TALLIFERIO	1000	No. 1267
John YOUNG	357	Norisse's Creek
Michael CAMPBELL	640	Norisse's Creek
CAMPBELL & PHILLIPS	1000	Norisse's Creek
SWAIN & STUBBLEFIELD	2550	Sec. 4, Range 4
Joel HOBB's heirs	640	

The following lands were not listed for taxes in 1808 and are liable for a double tax.

Reputed Owners	Acres	Situation
Richard COOK	640	Sc. 1, Rn. 2, Et. 15
Arthur BROOKS, ass.	640	Sc. 1, Rn. 5, Et. 176
Daniel GILLISPIE	1000	Rn. 4, Et. 170
Daniel M'GAVOCK	1000	Sc. 1, Rn. 5, Et. 118
William BRYAN	1000	Rn. 4, Et. 237

(Continued on following page)

(Bedford County delinquent tax list continued)

Miles WATSON	150	Sc. 1, Rn.5, Et. 483
Robert NEALY	63	Sc. 1, Rn. 1, Et. 38
Robert NELSON, assig.	182	Ent. 637
John GORDON	160	Elk River
Ephraim DAVIDSON	100	Sc. 2, Rn. 5, Et. 183
Joseph GRAHAM	618	Sc. 2, Rn. 5, Et. 337
John M'CORKLE	649	Bradshaw's Creek
John STEEL	1280	Elk River

On the 17th of March next in the town of Lebanon, there will be a public sale directed by the court of Wilson County of 90 acres, occupied by Drury PERRY,and 28 acres on Little Creek, that is the property of Daniel THYLMAN, Drury PERRY and Lanclott VIVRETT. The tracts were taken at the influence of Christopher COOPER. Thomas BRADLEY, shff.

For sale, 274 acres, fourteen miles below Nashville, on which I now live. Ivy WALK.

The following persons were mentioned in an article regarding the sale of lottery tickets: James HICKS, Charles BOILES, C. B. NIEISON, George HULL, all of Williamson Co., Tennessee; and Harrison BOYD, Jacob SCOTT, Spencer GRIFFIN, John MILLER, all of Maury County, Tennessee; James ALLISON, Brice M. GARNER.

The following persons were mentioned in an article regarding cut money: E. S. HULL & Co., James WITKERALD, George POYZER, BUSTARD & EASTIN, DEADERICK & SETTLER, W. and G. MORGAN, John H. SMITH, J. H. PLUMUR, John ANDERSON, Tho. KIRKMAN, Alexander PORTER, J. B. CRAIGHEAD, Tho. MASTERSON, Tho. CHILDRESS, Dun. ROBERTSON, Thomas MASTERSON, W. TRIGG & Co., and W. LYTLE & Co.

Lost on the road from Nashville to Columbia or in Franklin, a plane (sic) chain and key. There is a reward for whoever delivers them to me in Williamson County or to Jo. LITTLES on Spencer's Creek. Jason HOPKINS.

(No. Date), Vol. III, No. CVI

The following persons have reported estrays in Wilson County, per E. CRUTCHER, d. r.:

(1) Joshua WHITE, on Spencer's Creek, has taken up a bright bay horse.

(2) George SMITH has taken up a bay mare.

(3) ROBERT SHIELDS took up a bay mare.

(4) Thomas M'CALPIN, near Lebanon, took up a bay mare.

(5) John M'FARLEN, on Sumner's Creek, took up a mare.

Will all those indebted to the estate of Aaron WILSON, dec., please come forward and settle theirs debts, John GRAVES, admin., Davidson County, December 6, 1810.

The copartnership of E. BENOIT, Henry WYAND, and William SCHOBE is hereby dissolved by mutual consent.

105

The RICKARD family is leaving Tennessee on the first passage down river.

For sale, the tract formerly occuppied by Rees PORTER, sen., about one and a half miles from HAYSBOROUGH. Those interested apply to Ress PORTER or Elias PORTER in the town of HAYSBOROUGH.

The following persons have reported estrays in Sumner County, per Wm. TRIGG, jun., ranger:

(1) Carson DOBBINS, living about six miles from the town of Gallatin, has taken up a brown sorrel mare. On October 30, 1809, the mare was valued at $50.

(2) Josiah PERRY, living on Mansker's Creek, has taken up a bay horse. On November 28, 1809, the mare was given an appraised value of $20.

(3) Isaac PARCE, on Drake's Creek about two miles below Henderson's Mill, has taken up a sorrel horse. The Horse was valued at $1 on December 1, 1809.

(4) John WHITE, living on Duha's Creek, has taken up a black mare. On December 5, 1809, the mare's value was given at $20.

(5) Robert STEEL, sen., living on Bledsoe's Creek, has taken up a yellow bay horse. On December 12, 1809, the horse was appraised at $8.

(6) George M'GUIRE, on Bledsoe's Creek, has taken up a colt. On December 12, 1809, the colt was valued at the sum of $20.

(7) John MILLS, on Goose Creek, has taken up a horse. On December 18, 1809, the horse was valued at $15.

(No Date), Vol. III, No. CVIII

Wanted, furs to purchase. J. LOWERY & Co.

For sale, drugs, medicine, and paint. J. R. BEDFORD.

Wanted to purchase, two negro men. S. SHANNON.

The following is a list of letters remaining at the post office in Jefferson on January 1, 1810, per John SPENCE, p. m.: Thomas ASHLY, Francis ADAMS, Ransom ATKINS, Frederick BURNS, Richard BULLARD, James ANDREWS, David AMSFIELD, John BULLARD, John BYLER, Dr. A. BARKER, George BLAIR, William BAILY, Owen BULLARD, David BANE, John BREMEN, John BURNES, Ambrose BARKER, James BARRONTON, Solomon BEASELEY, Abraham BYLER, Nancy BLAKE, Charles BROOKS, John BRADLEY, Benjamin BRADFORD, Stephen BOOTHE, O. M. BURGE, Moses CHASEN, Robt. BANKHEAD, James CHANDLER, Anthony CLOPTON, Henry CONWAY, Donelson COFFERY, William COLDWELL, Jesse DUNN, John DRAKE, Benjamin DOLE, Jonathan DENNESON, David DICKEY, William DAVIDSON, John DAVIDSON, George DAVIDSON, John EARWOOD, Gen. Joseph DICKSON, James ESTILL, Jacob ELLER, William FINCH, William FINNEY, Charles FARIS, Ruth FULLER, Absalom FEY, Hizekiah FARIS, Thomas FULTON, James FARIS, George GROSON,

Malcolin GILCHRIST, Christopher CASE, sen., George GANTER, John GARNER, James GIVENS, Andrew GAMBLE, Claibrone GOODMAN, John GRIFFIN, Magaret GARNER, George GRISHAM, Vance GREER, John GREER, Col. Alexander GREER, Thomas GREER, George HILL, William HALL, Joseph HASTING, Henry HARRISON, ---- HARRIS, Samuel HASTINGS, Kitchen HOLLIMAN, Hance HAMILTON, Michael HARISON, Major HARELSON, Nimrod JINKINS, James JONES, John JACKSON, Lewis JONAKIN, Joseph ISAAC, John JAY, sen., Robt. KENNEDY, Charles A. LEWIS, Jacob LEWIS, Peter LEATH, John LEWIS, Phillip LOWE, Peter LEGRAND, Elizabeth MAIN, John M'CRORY, William MITCHELL, Jacob M'RIERY, Humphrey MOUNT, John M'CLURE, John M'QUEEN, John M'PEKE, James M'REYNOLDS, Mary MAXNT (sic), Alexander M'MILLON, Thomas MARTIN, Thomas MARLEY, Isaac M'MECLAY, Amos M'COY, John MANN, Archibald MUCKLEROY, Edward MITCHELL, John MACK, sen., Robert MACK, James M'KISSICK, Mark MITCHELL, Polly MARTIAL, Mary OWENS, Alexander OUTLAW, William PITMAN, James PATTON, Johnathan PHARR, Thomas PARKER, Ezekiel PITTS, John I. PHARR, William RAWLINGS, John REYNOLDS, Hugh ROBINSON, General ROBERTSON, Rev. James RUCKER, David ROGERS, Jincy ROBERTSON, WIlliam SULTON, French H. STROTHER, Calib STVELL, James SCOTT, John STROTHER, Elizabeth SMITH, William SMITH, John SMITH, Patrick SITWEN, Stephen TALOR, William TRIVEAT, John WINN, Jeremiah THORTON, Randolph TALOR, John THORNTON, Thomas C. VAUGHAN, Alexander VINCENT, Robert WOLSON, Abner WEAKLEY, Jesse WILSON, John WARNER, John L. WOOD, Win WILLIED (sic), Baisel WEST, Elizabeth WHITWORTH, Oliver WILLIAMS, John WALLITE, James WILSON, Joseph WALKER, Sara WHITE, Andrew YOUNGBLOOD.

In November, 1809, a red morocco pocketbook was lost from the Tombigby settlements. Included in the contents was a note on John WIRK for $47.50, dated November the 18th. In order to collect the reward, please deliver to me in Columbia. Burwell KANNON.

On the 17th of March in the town of Columbia, there will be a public sale under the direction of the Maury County court of 5000 acres located at the mouth of Robinson's Creek, that is the property of Henry HARMAN. The tract was taken under attachment by Joseph LAND. Saml. H. WILLIAMS.

For sale, an assortment of goods. John BAIRD.

On the 17th of March next in the town of Columbia, there will be a public sale directed by the Maury County court of 5000 acres, that is the property of Spencer GRIFFIN. The tract was entered in the name of Michael BACON and granted to Robert HILL, Warrant No. 574. The property was taken at the influence of John SAMPLE. Saml. H. WILLIAMS.

Mr. and Mrs. GREEN will be opening a seminary for young ladies in the town of Nashville.

The public is cautioned against trading for a title bond

given to James MEANS for 50 acres. Wm. M'CLURE.
Roane County, Tennessee, January Sessions, 1810. John
BROW, sheriff, reports that the following tracts of land
still have unpaid taxes for 1809. Henry BREAZEALE, clerk by
his deputy John PURRIS.

Reputed Owners	Acres	Grant No.	Date
Wm. TERRILL	300	208	January, 1795
Stockley DONELSON	500	581	July 11, 1788
Thomas and Robert KING	1000	577	July 11, 1788
Isaac TAYLOR and			
Robert YOUNG, sen.	640	110	November 16, 1795
Stockly DONELSON and			
William TERRILL	1000	258	March 7, 1796

The following persons have reported estrays in Bedford
County, per Howell DAWDY, r. b. c.:
(1) James PATTERSON, on the Barren Fork, has taken up a
     sorrel horse. On January 15, 1810, the horse was
     appraised at $20.
(2) A sorrel horse was taken up by David YAIS living on
     Huricane Creek. The horse was valued at $20.
(3) Stephen BRANDAGE, on Haricane Creek, has taken up a
     chestnut sorrel horse. On January 6, 1810, the
     horse was valued at $12.
(4) Jacob HARRINGTON, on Thompson's Creek, has taken up
     a bay mare. On January 17, 1810, the horse was
     appraised at $20.
The following persons have reported estrays in Wilson
County, per E. CRUCTHER, d. r.:
(1) John ALCORN, in Lebanon, has taken up a filly.
(2) Robert SHARONS has taken up a sorrel mare.
(3) Allanson TRIGG has taken up a sorrel mare. The mare
     was valued at $15 on January 6, 1810.
(4) Joshua KELLY has taken up a black horse. The horse
     was valued at $6 in February, 1810.
(5) George CUMMINGS, on Hurricane Creek, has taken up a
     yellow bay mare. On February 10, 1810, the mare
     was appraised at $20.
On the 24th of February, there will be a public sale
directed by the Superior Court of the Washington District,
in place of holding court in Bedford County, of 300 acres,
that was the property of Archibald SIMPSON. The property
was taken at the influence of George MAXWELL and his wife.
Benj. BRADFORD, sheriff.

(No Date), Vol. III, No. CIX
For sale, a negro boy. Charles ANDERSON.
On the 24th of March next in the town of Franklin, there
will be a public sale directed by the court of Williamson
County of 50 acres on Arrington's Creek, that belongs to

108

Enoch HEATON. The property was taken at the influence of DEADERICK & SOMERVILLE. Wm. HULME, sheriff.

The following persons have reported estrays in Sumner County, per WM. TRIGG, jr., ranger:

(1) Edward SAUNDERS has taken up a yellow bay mare. The mare was valued at $15 on December 19, 1809.

(2) Isaac WALTON, on Mansker's Creek, has taken up a bay horse. On December 22, 1809, the horse was appraised at $40.

(3) George SMITH, near the mouth of Drake's Creek, has taken up a bay horse. On December 20, 1809, the horse was appraised at $25.

(4) Solomon BANDY, on Drake's Creek, by permission of Thomas MASTEN, has taken up a bay mare. The mare was valued at $30 on December 19, 1809.

(5) Lewis CRANE, on Cage's Bend, has taken up a black filly. On December 7, 1809, the filly was valued in the amount of $7.50.

(6) James SANDERS, at the mouth of Drake's Creek, has taken up a bay horse. On January 5, 1810, the value of the horse was placed at $70.

(7) Cato MOSS, by permission of David KING, has taken up a bay mare. On January 19, 1810, the mare was appraised at $30.

(8) Isaac PIERCE has taken up a brown gelding. The value of the gelding was $20 on January 1, 1810.

On the 19th, Willis TYLER, apprentice to the saddler's business, eloped from the subscriber. He is 22 years old, 5 ft., 9 in. tall, and has a swarthy complexion. There is a reward of one cent offered for his return. J.S. WILLIAMSON.

I wish to employ a miller. Anyone interested, please apply at Station Camp Creek. R. D. BARRY.

Norfolk, January 31st. Captain LANGDON arrived from Cadiz this morning on the schooner Ann Ballard.

Davidson County, Janaury Sessions, 1810. Michael C. DUNN, sheriff and collector, reports that the following tracts still have taxes due for 1809. The property will be sold on the first Monday in April next in the town of Nashville. Andrew EWING, clerk.

Reputed Owners	Acres	Situation
Peter PINKLEY	100	1 white poll
John CAGLE	100	
Jeremiah ELLIS	50	1 white poll
Sampson FLAKE	215	1 white poll
Russel GOWER	80	1 white poll
Hererally DAVIE	lot	Nashville
William GILMON	640	
Thomas HARNEY	lot	1 white & 1 black poll

(Continued on following page)

109

(Davidsn County delinquent tax list continued)

John HAMILTON	1000	1808, and 1809
John IRWIN	540	Lot in Nashville
Nicholas LONG	274	
Henry LEACY	300	
Abraham NOLIN	41	1 white poll
John PANS	640	
Robert READING	63	
Henry RICHARDSON	136	1 free poll
William RICHARDSON	120	1 free poll
Benjamin SEAWELL	320	1 black poll
James D. SHARP	150	1 white poll
Wm. TRIGG	300	
John MYERS	274	1 white poll
Charles SURES' heirs	100	
Philip WOLF	100	1 white poll

March 2, 1810, Vol. III, No. CX

For sale, a lot in Gallatin that adjoins David SHELBY's lot. Nath. PERRY.

The copartnership of Alex. and A. PORTER is hereby dissolved by mutual consent. Alex. PORTER, sen.

My wife Sara has forsaken me since the first of December last. She has barred the door and excluded me with out just cause from her chamber. I will not pay any of her contracts. John WATKINS.

Open, a military school in Columbia. Wm. H. SHILTON.

On the 14th of April next in the town of Nashville, there will be a public sale directed by the Davidson County court of lot no. 27, that is the property of James DEATHERAGE. The land was taken by Geo. HAMBLET against James BYRNS, John DEATHERAGE and Foster SAYRE. M. C. DUNN, shff.

On the 14th of April next in the town of Nashville, there will be a public sale directed by the Davidson County court of 100 acres, that is the property of Robert PORTER. The tract adjoins the lands of the heirs of Drury SMITH and Samuel BELL. The property was taken at the influence of Jonathan PHILLIPS and John M'KINNEY. M. C. DUNN, shff.

On the 14th of April next in the town of Nashville, there will be a public sale of 50 acres on Mill Creek. The tract adjoins Henry HYDE, where Joseph GARNER lately lived. Also for sale is 50 acres, which adjoins Wm. EWING, where Samuel MADON lives. The tracts were taken at the influence of John H. SMITH and Elizabeth EDWARDS. M. C. DUNN, shff.

On the 10th of December last at the post office in Charlotte, Virginia, several notes were stolen, that were enclosed in a letter addressed to Col. William CHRISTMAS. Joseph WATKINS.

Will those indebted, please come forward and settle their

accounts as I am leaving the country. John B. CRAIGHEAD.

On the 10th of April next, I shall make an application for a certificate on North Carolina Grant No. 448, dated June, 1793, for 640 acres at the office of the Commissioner of West Tennessee. John COCKRIL, sen.

On the 14th of April next in the town of Nashville, there will be a public sale directed by the Davidson County court of 414 acres, that is owned and occuppied by George WADE. The property was taken at the influence of William GRIMES. John C. HALL, d. s.

John BRADBERRY, jun., on Cedar Lick, Wilson County, has taken up a bay mare. The mare was valued at $20.

Richard GARRETT, waggon-maker, has opened for business one mile south of Nashville where John MACKLIN formerly lived.

March 9, 1810, Vol. III, No. CXI

For sale, good whiskey. Eleazer and Thomas J. HARDEMAN.

The following persosn have reported estrays in Sumner County, per Wm. TRIGG, jr., r. s. c.:

(1) Wm. C. ANDERSON, on Desha's Creek, has taken up a black mare. On January 12, 1810, the mare was given an appraised value of $12.

(2) Phillip RAMER, near Henderson Mill, has taken up a sorrel mare. On Janaury 10, 1810, the mare was valued in the amount of $20.

(3) Nancy BOYCE, on Station Camp, on sorrel horse. The horse was valued at $43 on February 6, 1810.

The following persons have reported estrays in Wilson County, per Edmund CRUTCHER, d. r.:

(1) David HANKS, on Round Lick, has taken up a grey mare. The mare was appraised at $15.

(2) Thomas DOOBY, on Cedar Creek, has taken up a bay horse. The horse was valued at $13.

(3) Henry MCFALL, for Thomas WATSON, near Drake's Lick, has taken up a black horse. On February 12, 1810, the horse was appraised at $70.

(4) Edmund CROFORD, on Pond Creek, has taken up an iron grey horse. On March 1, 1810, the horse was valued in the amount of $40.

Reward $5. A bay mare strayed or was stolen from John SMITH on Overall's Creek, Rutherford County, in November. Anyone finding said mare deliver to me or George SIMPSON in Jefferson to collect the reward. Daniel H. HENDERSON.

On the 10th of March next, I shall apply to the office of the Commissioner of West Tennessee for a certificate on Grant No. --, dated July 12, 1789, for 640 acres, that was issued by North Carolina to Nancy SHEPPARD, and Oliver SMITH. The wife of Oliver SMITH was formerly known as Nancy SHEPPARD.

The property was conveyed by Nancy SHEPPARD to Hardy MURFEE. David DICKSON, admn.

On the 14th of April next in the town of Nashville, there will be a public sale directed by the Davidson County court of 410 acres, that is owned and occuppied by Ezekiel DOUGLASS. The property was taken at the influence of James BERMINGHAM against DOUGLASS and Wm. MILLER, his sercurity. John C. HALL, d. s.

The noted horse Afton will stand this season at the house of Wm. SAUNDERSON. Wm. DAVIS will testify to his pedigree. Joseph SCALES.

March 16, 1810, Vol. III, No. CXII

On the 14th of April next in the town of Nashville, there will be a public sale directed by the Davidson County court of 265 acres, that is owned and occuppied by William NEWSAM. The property was taken at the influence of James and Washington JACKSON, HAZARD & CABOT, and Alexander & A. PORTER. John C. HALL, d. s.

In the town of Nashville on the 14th of April next, there will be a public sale directed by the court of Davidson County of 160 acres, that is owned and occuppied by John B. JACKSON. The property was taken at the influence of Ira BRADFORD. John C. HALL, d. s.

Mexico, a large jack, will stand this season at my stable on White's Creek. Thos. RIVERS.

On the 13th of April next, bids will be taken for the building of a jail. Commissioners: David M'EWEN, James HICKS, Richd. STEELE, and Ewen CAMERON.

On the 23rd of April next in the town of Jefferson, there will be a public sale directed by the Davidson County court of two rights of occupancy, that is the property of James BELL. The rights were taken at the influence of Dav. ORTON. N. JINKINS, d. s.

March 23, 1810, Vol. III, No. CXIII

Maury County, December term, 1809. John SPENCER, sheriff and collector, reports that the following tracts of land will be sold for taxes on the first Monday in April next. Joseph B. PORTER, clerk.

Reputed Owners	Acres	Situation
Martin ARMSTRONG	5000	Sec. 4, Ran. 1
William P. ANDERSON	400	Elk River
Edley ALEXANDER	600	
John G. BLOUNT	65	Sec. 2, Ran. 13
James BRIGHT	255	Richland Creek
John BLAIR	300	Fountain Creek
Richard COOK	726	Richland Creek

(Continued on following page)

(Maury County delinquent tax list continued)

Martin ARMSTRONG	250	Grant No. 68
John CHILDERESS	1000	Fountain Creek
James CONNER	600	
Benjamin CARTER	2100	Carter's Creek
Samuel CHAPPEL	274	30 mile tree
Francis CHUDS	3000	Elk River
George DOHERTY	5000	Sec. 3, Ran. 1
Divess. Geo. DOHERTY	1000	
DEADRICK & TATUM	1250	Duck River
Edward HARRIS	274	Sec. 1, Ran. 14
Nicholas HARDEMAN	2000	Globe Creek
Washington SHANNON	1000	Fountain Creek
Haywood TURNER	6000	
John L. HICKMAN	2040	Globe Creek
John JOHNSTON, sen.	250	Cedar Creek
James LEWIS	1500	Globe Creek
Joel LEWIS	1280	Richland Creek
Micajah G. LEWIS	5000	Richland Creek
John M'NAIRY	500	Richland Creek
Henry MONTFORD	5000	
Hardy MURFEE	600	Elk River
James MCUESTION	325	
John NELSON	5000	Richland Creek
Jessy MAXWELL	400	
William PHILLIPS	853	
Thomas POLK	5000	
CAMPBELL & PHILLIPS	640	Rutherford Creek
Nicholas PERKINS, jun.	1500	Globe Creek
PATTON & IRWIN	2500	Richland Creek
Sterling ROBERTSON	1000	Fountain Creek
Elridge ROBERTSON	1000	Fountain Creek
James ROBERTSON	1000	Fountain Creek
Henry RUTHERFORD	231	
Robert THOMPSON	1000	Duck River
Howel TATUM	640	Duck River
Heydon WELLS	940	Flat Creek
Abraham WALKER	150	Robertson Creek
Wm. WALLACE	1800	Fountain Creek
J. GILSPIE's heirs	220	Big Tombigby
James TRIMBLE	5000	Carter's Creek

The following lands were not listed in 1809 and are liable for a double tax.

Reputed Owners	Acres	Situation
James DANIEL	300	Duck River
John IRWIN	440	
John BIGHAM	3200	
Edward KEARBY	600	Haywood and Richland

(Continued on following page)

113

(Maury County delinquent tax list continued)

Legatees of H. DICKSON	1500	Duck River
John DICKSON	1000	Tombigby
Henry MONTFORD	300	
Simon ELIOTT	1000	
John GILLISPIE	750	Smith's Creek
Alexander M'CORKLE	2411	Fountain Creek
John M'CAUDLESS	1000	Duck River
Thomas POLK	2000	Stinking Creek
Thomas OWENS	5000	Rice's Creek
John PORTERFIELD	5000	Globe Creek
John RUTHERFORD	5000	Duck River
Griffith RUTHERFORD	1000	Duck River
Thomas HARRIS	5000	Duck River
Matthew M'CAULLY	3200	Rice's Creek
Thomas PARSONS	320	Snow Creek
Henry RUTHERFORD	113	Duck River
Elizabeth BARROW	640	Porterfield's Creek
James DANIEL	300	Duck River
STONE & HART	2000	Fountain Creek
David ROSS	600	Duck River
Benj. M'CULLOCH	640	Elk River
Samuel THOMPSON	400	Duck River

Maury County, December term, 1809. John SPNCER, sheriff and collector, reports that the following persons had lots in the town of Columbia were not listed for taxes in 1809. The properties are liable for a double tax, per Joseph B. PORTER, clerk: Kinchin ANDERSON, Norton GIN, Allen YATES, Peter CHEATHAM, Henry ANDERS, James DOBBINS, John WILLIAMS, David HUGHES, John WILLIAMS, John RUSSELL, Dennis WRIGHT, Thomas HARNEY, Jabius NOWLIN, Joseph LAYMASTER, Edmund HARRISON, John WILLIAMS, John LYON, John PALMER, OLDHAM & ONEAL, Joseph RHOADS, Alex. M. GILBERT, John WILLIAMS, John BELL, Rich. HANKS, Robt. HANKS, William BADGER, Foulker COX, Samuel CANNON, Thomas DEADERICK, Wm. LEINTZ, Jas. GULLET, Peter BASS, J. W. BRUCE, NELSON & CANNON.

On the 28th of April next in place of holding court in Bedford County, there will be a public sale directed by the Superior Court of the Mero Distrct of 300 acres, that is owned and occuppied by John THOMPSON. The property was taken at the influence of Thos. BLACKMORE. J. WARNER, d. s.

Will all those indebted, please come forward and settle. R. M. HARWELL.

Elijah MILTON, in Giles County, has taken up a sorrel mare. Lewis Clark, r. g. c.

Edmund COLLIN, on Bledsoes Creek in Sumner County, has taken up a sorrel mare. On February 12, 1810, the mare was appraised at $20. Wm. TRIGG, jr. r. s. c.

Abner GILMORE, on Bledsoes Creek, has taken up a sorrel

114

horse, that was valued on February 15, 1810. Wm. TRIGG.

March 30, 1810, Vol. III, No. CXIV

Dr. Thomas A. CLAIBORNE, of Nashville, married Mrs. Isabella Charlotte H. WOOLDRIDGE at Natchez on Thursday, March the 14th.

One day last week, William COBELL of this county being intoxicated fell from his horse and broke his neck.

London. January 12th. The American frigate John Adams landed Mr. FENWICK with dispatches for Mr. ARMSTRONG.

Open, a house of entertainment in the town of Franklin in the place lately occuppied by Clayton TALBOT. Thomas SAPPINGTON.

John REID, attorney at law in Franklin, is open for business in the house lately occuppied by Peter R. BOONE.

For rent, the house and lot that adjoins Mr. HALL. Joseph ENGLEMAN.

The following persons have reported estrays in Maury County, per Joseph BROWN, r. m. c.:
  (1) Thomas CATES, on Swan Creek, has taken up a sorrel horse. The horse was valued at $47.
  (2) Jacob SCOTT, on Flat Creek, has taken up a sorrel mare. The mare was valued at $11.
  (3) Edward WILLIAMS, on the Duck River below Columbia, has taken up a sorrel mare, that was valued at $50.
  (4) Henry DAMEWOOD, on Bear Creek, has taken up a bay mare. The mare was valued at $11.
  (5) Isham JOHNSON, on Knob Creek, has taken up a sorrel horse. The horse was valued at $19.
  (6) Joseph B. PORTER, on Lytle's Creek, has taken up a grey mare. The mare was valued at $12.
  (7) Duncan GILCREASE has taken up a yellow sorrel mare. The mare was valued at $35 on March 20, 1810.

The following persons have reported estrays in Sumner County, per Wm. TRIGG, jr., r. s. c.:
  (1) Solomon RUYLE, on Mansker's Creek, has taken up a brown horse. On February 24, 1810, the horse was given an appraised value of $17.50.
  (2) Thos. BRINKLEY, on the Red River, has taken up a black mare. On February 23, 1810, the mare was valued in the amount of $9.

April 6, 1810, Vol. III, No. CXV

The following is a list of letters remaining at the post office at Franklin on April 1, 1810, per D. SQUIER, a. p. m.: Peter ALEXANDER, Eleaza. ANDREWS,, Ephm. ANDREWS, James ANDREWS, James ALLISON, George ADAMS, Fred. BROWDER, Rueben BOOTH, Daniel BECLER, Gab. BUMPASS, Kinch. BALDWIN, John BYERS, William BURKETT, Elizabeth BOND, Stephen BROOKS, Nel.

VIELDS, Rev. L. BLACKMORE, Eliza. BAILY, Benjamin BUGG, Nel.
CHAPMAN, Samuel CHAPMAN, Eliza. CORDEL, John CALVERT, Jos.
CARSON, J. A. CAMPBELL, Clem. CANNON, Wm. DOWINING, William
M. DAVIDSON, James DOTY, Chris. FITXPATRICK, Robt. GRAHAM,
Abner HOLT, Sion HUNT, Thos. HARDEMAN, Wm. HOLLIMAN, Robert
HAMILTON, Arch. or Moses HOLMES, Dav. HOGAN, Henry INGRAM,
James JULIN, Geo. JULIN, John IRON, Eliza LOCKE, Wm. LOGAN,
Richd. S. LOCKE, Jas. F. LONG, Jacob LINDSAY, Samuel LEE,
Benj. LANCASTER, Nath. LAIRD, Jas. LAULIN, jr., Dav. M'CORD,
Hen. LANDRUM, Josiah LEACH, Thos. M'CRORY, Samuel MOORE,
Daniel or Samuel M'COLLOM, Ch. HURPHEY (sic), Henry MAY,
Isaac M'COLLOM, Jared M'CONICE, Sarah M'BRIDE, Nath. MOSS,
John M'CLARAN, Jas. M'DONALD, Alex. M'CLARAN, John M'BRIDE,
Jeffery MURRELL, Wm. MEARS, John NEELY, sen., Francis NUNN,
Peter PERKINS, jr., N. T. PERKINS, James PERRY, John PORTER,
Thos. S. PARSONS, Abner PILLOW, Giles PAGE, Hen. RUTHERFORD,
Wm. RODGERS, Saml. SHELBOURNE, James STONE, Stephen SMITH,
jas. SHORTER, Drury SCRUGGS, Polly SHANNON, Jonathan WOOD,
W. WARRINGTON, Susan WHEDBEE, John WILLEY, Maryann TAYLER,
Thos. S. TROTHER, Pett. WOODARD, Nich. WILBURN, Job WIGLEY,
John WHITE, S. D. WADDEL.
To the public, there has been an advantage taken of me on
a subject considered criminal for the purpose of destroying
the public's confidence in me as well as strip me of my
property. I hope the public will suspend their opinions
until court. The character of William Terril LEWIS is well
known. B. P. PERSON.
Moses SPRENKLE, in Maury County, has taken up a black
mare. Joseph BROWN, r. m. c.

April 13, 1810, Vol. III, No. CXVI

We gave notes to James SMITH, of Bedford County, for
lottery tickets. The lottery was not drawn and we will not
pay. Asey STREET, James NICHOLAS, Jane DANIEL.
On the 28th of November last, Alex. and A. PORTER put a
package of notes (halves), which have been stolen from the
mail. The first halves were sent to Samuel CASWELL,
merchant of Philadelphia.
The following is a list of letters remaining at the post
office in Columbia, per L. B. ESTE, a. p. m.: James BOWMAN,
Charles ANDERSON, Robert BEATY, Molly BRIDGES, Benjamin
BARTON, Dillen BLEVINS, Robert BRYD, Peter BODERHAMER, Aaron
CUNNINGHAM, Daniel SMITTEN, Stephen CLARK, George CRAWFORD,
Richard COOK, Littleberry CHEATHAM, Littleton CAPLE, William
DEAN, John DRAKE, John DANIEL, George DAVIDSON, Joel GLASS,
Moses DRIVER, William R. DAVIS, John GORDAN, James GRAHAM,
William GRAHAM, Julia GIBSON, Owin GRIFFIN, Hardy HOLLMAN,
Calib HENLEY, Henry GOODKNIGHT, Isaac HUTCHISON, Rev. Thomas
HELLUMS, James HARDEUSOLE, Durgens HARDIN, John HENDRIX, Wm.

M'MAHON, William MIXFIELD, James M'KESICK, Humphrey LEACH, Rev. Thos. HELLUMS, Lewis JONIHAN, Miss Mary Myrna JONES, John KEER, Jones KINDRICK, Samuel LUCK, Andrew LOPP, David LAURANCE, Humphrey LEACH, Edmund MANTOX, Archibald M'CORKLE, James M'CORLEY, Capt. John MEDEARIS, John MITCHELL, Samuel M'CULLUM, Joshua NEUMAN, Robert ORR, Widow Lucy PERRY, John PARKER, Charles PINCKNEY, Thomas PORTER, James PARRY, Lewis PROBERT, John PURR, Capt. John PATTESON (sic), Nancy PAXTON, James PHURRISS, Jonathan PIRKINS, Thomas PUTTON, Thomas RUBY, Col. William PILLOW, Wm. PENCOCK, James READ, Benjamin H. ROLLINS, John RICHESON (sic), Swepsin SIMS, Wm. SHERROD, Joel SHERROD, Joseph SEWELL, Winkfield SHOPSHIRE, John TONEY, John M. TAYLOR, Jeremiah TUCKER, Washington WALKER, George WHALEY, George WOLF.

I shall apply to the Commissioner of West Tennessee on the 5th of May next for a certificate on Grant No. 2815, issued by North Carolina, to myself as the assignee of Enoch KING on May 20, 1793. John WILSON.

The following persons have reported estrays in Wilson County, per E. CRUTCHER, d. r. w. c.:

   (1) James DOOLY, on Big Spring, has taken up a bay mare. On March 1, 1810, the mare was appraised at the sum of $15.

   (2) Joseph BARTON, on Big Spring, has taken up a bay filly. On March 1, 1810, the filly was given an appraised value of $12.

   (3) Britten DRAKE has taken up a bay mare. The mare was valued at $2 on March 1, 1810.

   (4) Joseph CRABTREE, on Drake's Lick, has taken up a bay horse. On March 4, 1810, the horse's value was placed at the sum of $5.

   (5) William GREY, on Spencer's Creek, has taken up a bay horse. On February 21, 1810, the horse was appraised at $30.

   (6) Dempsey MASSEY, on Cedar Creek, has taken up a sorrel mare. On March 7, 1810, the mare was given an appraised value of $8.

   (7) John JINNING, on Smith's Fork, has taken up a bay mare. On March 15, 1810, the mare's value was $30.

   (8) William ALSUP has taken up a sorrel mare. The mare was valued at $20 on March 15, 1810.

   (9) John ROACH, on Sugg's Creek, has taken up a bay horse. On March 15, 1810, the horse was given an appraised value of $15.

 (10) Swan WARN has taken up a bay mare. The mare was valued at $70 on March 21, 1810.

 (11) George PUGH, on Purtle Creek, has taken up a grey mare. On March 19, 1810, the mare's value was $25.

 (12) Britten DRAKE has taken up a bay horse. The horse

was appraised at a value of $11 on March 23, 1810.
(13) Isham DAVIS, on the Cumberland River, has taken up
a white horse. On March 16, 1810, the horse was
appraised at a value of $20.

April 20, 1810, Vol. III, No. CXVIV
The following is a list of letters remaining at the post
office at Jefferson, per John SPENCE, p. m.: Thos. BEDFORD,
Jesse BEAN, Col. J. BLACKWELL, Ransom ATKINS, Jas. BARKLEY,
Hen. W. or Thos. BUTLER, Jas. BARRONTON, John BEREMON, Dr.
John R. BEDFORD, Robt. BANKHEAD, John COOK, Wm. CARNEY, John
CRAWFORD, J. DAVIDSON, John FRAZIER, Asa FONVILLE, Thomas
GREEN, Jas. GRIER, Jona. GREAN, Joel GOODE, John HUGHITT,
Eli HARRAL, William C. HOGAN, Lewallen JONES, Col. William
LOFTEN, Benjamin H. LEWIS, John LAURENCE, Thomas MOORE,
Samuel M'NEES, Saml. MUSGROVE, Hum. MOUNT, John M'CRORY,
Saml. MITCHELL, Isaac M'NEALY, Jas. MCKLERPY, Hum. NELSON,
William NORMAN, Saml. PATTON, Abell PURSELL, Bazewel PAYNE,
Samuel RAMSEY, A. RAWLINGS, Benjamin RANSOM, John RIVES,
William ROUNDTREE, Thomas SAPPINGTON, William STAMPS, Jos.
THOMPSON, Thos. C. VAUGHN, Jas. WILSON, Lewis WATSON, Capt.
John WARREN, Abner WEATHERLEY.
On the 16th Gen. William WASHINGTON died at Sandy Hill,
South Carolina. He is a hero of the Revolution and a nephew
of the late President WASHINGTON.
The following persons have reported estrays in Giles
County, per Lewis CLARK, r. g. c.:
(1) James WILFORD, on Robertson's Fork, has taken up a
grey mare. On March 12, 1810, the mare was given
an appraised value of $11.
(2) James REED, on Richland Creek, has taken up a black
mare. On March 19, 1810, the mare's value was $17.

April 27, 1810, Vol. III, No. CXVIII
For sale, New England cheese. D. C. SNOW.
To hire, a negro carpenter. Wm. PURNELL, Haysborough.
On the 9th of June next in the town of Nashville, there
will be a public sale directed by the Ciruit Court of the
United States District of West Tennessee of 203-1/2 acres,
that is the property of Howel TATUM in Bedford County. The
tract is occupied by John M'CUESTION, Shedrick BROWN, and
Mathew PHILLIPS. Also for sale is lot no. 86 in Nashville,
that was lately occuppied by Dr. CATLET and is now occupied
by Peter MYERS. The property was taken at the influence of
Peter and John HUFFMAN. John CHILDRESS, jr.
I am offering a reward for the capture and conviction of
the villian who broke in my shop. Francis MAY, Nashville.
Boston, April 7th. Capt. SUTTON arrived yesterday by the
brig Sally from London bringing the London newspapers.

On the 2nd of June next in the town of Columbia, there will be a public sale directed by the court of Maury County of one house and three lots in said town, that is the property of Perry COHE. The property was taken at the influence of Simon JOHNSTON. W. BRADSHAW, d. s.

On the 2nd of June in the town of Columbia, there will be a public sale directed by the Maury County court of lot no. 20 in said town, that is the property of Allen YATES. The property was taken at the influence of James DOWNS against Howard D. HARDEN and Allen YATES. S. H. WILLIAMS, shff.

A negro woman called NELLY, age 30, ranaway from the subscriber living on Swan Creek, Lincoln County. In order to collect the reward, please deliver said negro to me or Nimrod WILLIAMS. Nimrod WILLIAMS for Joseph GARNER.

May 4, 1810, Vol. III, No. CIX

The folllowing persons have reported estrays in Wilson County, per E. CRUTCHER, d. r. w. c.:
   (1) Duncan JOHNSON, on Round Lick, has taken up a bay horse. On March 3, 1810, the horse was given an appraised value of $35.
   (2) Alexander KIRKPATRICK, on the Cumberland River, has taken up a bay horse. On April 11, 1810, the horse was appraised at a value of $30.
   (3) Samuel CALHOON has taken up a grey mare. The mare was valued at $20 on April 21, 1810.
   (4) James MACLIN, on Bradley's Creek, has taken up a blue roan mare. On April 21, 1810, the mare was appraised at a value of $40.

John HARDING pleads the gambling act on the 27th of April before Benj. J. BRADFORD, Mayor of Nashville, at the lost of Thomas GIBBS.

Will all those indebted please come forward and settle their debts. Henry REED.

I caution the public against taking assignments on a note, that I gave to John A. S. AANDERSON (sic) and Wm. P. ADERSON (sic). Joshua TOWNSEND.

May 11, 1810, Vol. III, No. CXX

For sale, a nail factory. Wm. CARROL & Co.

On the masthead of this issue was handwritten Capt. J. C. HALL.

Wanted, hides at the tanyard or at KRISERSWILL's or at Capt. STONE's Mill. Peter BASS.

On the 23rd of June next in the town of Lebanon, there will be a public sale directed by the court of Wilson County of 133 acres, that is the property of Solomon BASS, dec. The property was taken at the influence of N. W. WILLIAMS

against BASS and David THYLMAN. Thomas BRADLEY, shff.
The following persons have reported estrays in Lincoln County, per Philip KOONCE, ranger, by his deputy Brice M. GARNER:

(1) Charles HAYS, on Mulberry Creek, has taken up a horse. The horse was valued at $4.
(2) Alex. MOORE, on Cane Creek, has taken up a bay horse. The horse was value at $3.
(3) Wm. DICKSON, on Mulberry Creek, has taken up a bay horse. The horse was valued at $8.
(4) Jeremiah ETHERAGE has taken up a white mare.
Wanted, furs. Moses EAKIN.

The following persons have reported estrays in Maury County, per Joseph BROWN, r. m. c.:

(1) Samuel WATKINS, on Duck River, has taken up a bay horse. On April 7, 1810, the horse was appraised in the amount of $8.
(2) Doc. James C. O'RIGHLY, on Bear Creek, has taken up a black horse. On April 13, 1810, the horse was appraised at a value of $2.
(3) Nathaniel THOMPSON, on the Tombigby, has taken up a bay mare. On April 14, 1810, the mare was given an appraised value of $2.
(4) Abner PILLOW, on Rutherford's Creek, has taken up a horse. On April 19, 1810, the horse's value was $4.
(5) John CHAMBERS, on the Duck River, has taken up a horse. On April 17, 1810, the horse was given an appraised value of $25.
(6) Joseph JOHNSON, on Knob Creek, has taken up a black horse. On April 21, 1810, the horse was given an appraised value of $30.
(7) John BUTLER, on Flat Creek, has taken up a chesnut yellow sorrel mare. On April 28, 1810, the mare was valued at $16.
(8) William WEBB, in the neighborhood of James LEWIS, has taken up a sorrel horse. The horse was valued at $30 on April 28, 1810.

The following persons have reported estrays in Wilson County, per E. CRUTCHER, d. r. w. c.:

(1) Isaac B. ESTICK, on Bradley's Creek, has taken up a bay horse. On April 21, 1810, the horse was given an appraised value of $34.
(2) Joseph YOUNG, on South Fork, has taken up a bay mare. On April 24, 1810, the mare was appraised in the amount of $8.50.
(3) Aaron LAMBERT, on Spring Creek, took up a sorrel filly. On May 5, 1810, the filly's value is $15.

William SNEED married on Tuesday last Miss Nancy KEELING. They are both of this county.

120

The following persons have reported estrays in Giles County, per Lewis CLARK, r. g. c.:
(1) William BUCKMAN, on Richland Creek, has taken up a bay horse. The horse was valued at $20.
(2) Thomas PACKSTON, on Bradshaw's Creek, has taken up sorrel filly. The filly was valued at $47.50.

The following persons have reported estrays in Sumner County, per Wm. TRIGG, jr., r. s. c.:
(1) Wm. C. ANDERSON, on Deshay's Creek, has taken up a bay filly. On March 26, 1810, the filly was given an appraised valued of $1.
(2) Wm. ALLEN, in the town of Gallatin, has taken up a sorrel horse. The horse was given an appraised value of $60 on March 27, 1810.
(3) Thomas BRITTON, on Mansker's Creek, has taken up a bay mare. On March 26, 1810, the mare was given an appraised value of $28.
(4) Wm. VINEYARD, on Drake's Creek of the Big Barren, has taken up a horse. On March 27, 1810, the horse was valued at $2.
(5) Mrs. Martha ALVIS, on Goose Creek, has taken up a yellow bay horse. On March 3, 1810, the horse was appraised at $14.

May 18, 1810, Vol. III, No. CXXI

Smith County, Tennessee, March term, 1809. John GORDON, collector, reports that the following tracts will be sold on the first Monday in November next to satisfy the unpaid taxes for the years 1807 and 1808. George MATLOCK, sheriff.

Reputed Owners	Acres	Situation
Thomas HAMILTON	1280	1807
F. CHILD's heirs	2560	Cany Fork, 1808
John DAVIS	440	1808
Moses DULEY	----	A stud horse, 1808
Thomas HAMILTON	1280	1808
John NELLY's heirs	320	1808
Daniel WILBOURN	300	1808
Robert MADEN	75	1 white & 1 black pol
Archibald CANAN	50	1 white
Abram ELLIS	100	1 white
Joseph RUMBLER	30	1 white
John HARVEY	200	A stud horse

On the 18th of June next in place of holding court in Lincoln County, there will be a public sale directed by the court of Bedford County of 200 acres, that is the property of Henry LOFTON. The property was taken at the influence of Richard WIATT. Cornelius STATER, shff.

On Wednesday evening last by Rev. James WHITESIDE, David Calvin SNOW married Mrs. Hannah GLEASON, both of this county.

The following persons have reported estrays in Lincoln County, per Brice M. GARNER for Philip KOONCE, ranger:
(1) Abner WELLS, on Will's Creek, has taken up a bay horse. The horse is valued at $15.
(2) William ALLEN, on Will's Creek, has taken up a sorrel horse. On April 27, 1810, the horse was given an appraised value of $5.
(3) John WINTAKER, jun., on Mulberry Creek, has taken up a black horse.

June 1, 1810, Vol. III, No. CXXIII
On the 10th of May last, Stephen WARREN, coming from Natchez on his way home to Lexington, Kentucky, left a jenny. The jenny is the property of Maj. John PRUETT. The owner should come claim his property. Martin STANLEY, Williamson County.

On the second Thursday in July next, there will be a public sale of lots in Shelbyville, Bedford County. Commissioners: Danl. M'KISSICK, Benj. BRADFORD, John LANE, Berkley MARTIN, John AKINSON, Howel DAWDY, William WOODS.

For sale, land warrants. Roger B. SAPPINGTON.

For rent, a house in lot in Columbia. Alexander MEBANE and Joseph HODGE.

MCLAURINE and THOMAS, cabinet-makers, have commenced business in the house next to Mrs. WINN.

Benedict THOMAS has served his apprenticeship under me and also worked as a journeyman with me. I certify, that when he left my employment that he was a master of his trade. Porter CLAY, Lexington, May 7, 1810.

On the 28th, a grey horse strayed from the plantation of Charles LATTEMORE. To collect the reward, please deliver the horse to Charles LATTEMORE in Sumner County. Oliver JOHNSON.

In the town of Jefferson, there will be a public sale directed by the Davidson County court of two rights of occupancy to 156 acres, that is the property of James BELL. The tracts were taken at the influence of David ORTON. Nimrod JENKINS, d. s.

The following persons have reported estrays in Rutherford County, per Neil B. ROSE for Wm. HOWELL, r. r. c.:
(1) James FURGUSON, near Jefferson, has taken up a black mare. The mare was valued at $13.
(2) Wm. LOCK, near Jefferson, has taken up a sorrel mare. The mare was appraised at $15.
(3) John M. GENAERY, on the east fork of the Stones River, has taken up a bay horse valued at $10.
(4) Lewalling JONES, on the west fork of the Stones River, has taken up a black mare valued at $12.
(5) Thos. BEDFORD, near Jefferson, has taken up an iron

grey horse. The horse was appraised at $35.
(6) Richard W. CUMMINS, at Cummin's Mill, has taken up
    a sorrel mare. The mare is valued at $35.
(7) Abner DEMENT, near Cummin's Mill, has taken up a
    sorrel horse. The horse is valued at $23.
(8) Joseh JONES has taken up a bay mare.
(9) Francis YOURE, living on the main road from the
    town of Jefferson to Garrison, has taken up a mare.
(10) John EDWARDS, near Cummin's Mills, has taken up a
    grey mare. The mare was valued at $25.
(11) Wm. LOCK, near Jefferson, has taken up a mare.
(12) Wm. ROBERTSON, near Cummin's Mill, has taken up a
    colt. The colt is valued at $15.
    Miss Eliza RIDLEY, about 15 years old, died last Friday
last at Maj. BUCHANON's. She has just completed her
education at Mrs. CLOPTON's school.
    Smith County, Tennessee, March term, On the first Monday
in November next, the lands are to be sold to satisfy the
unpaid taxes for 1809 at the direction of George MATLOCK.
Joseph W. ALLEN, clerk.

Reputed Owners	Acres
William HUGHLET	100
Francis SAUNDERS	200
Griffith RUTHERFORD	620
Alexander BRADEN	640
Charles CROUGHTON	900
Edward GWIN	180
Thomas HARDEMAN	640
John RUMBLER	50
George WILSON	120
William WHITE	355
John LEE	120
James GLEN	100
Peter KING	---
Augustus CARTER	lot
Thomas KING	640
William LARNS	175
Richard CANTREL	100
James BLACKMORE	98
John M'NAIRY	900
Daniel PROPS	283
James WINCHESTER	502
Gifford DUDLEY	339
Thomas HICKMAN	3734
T. HICKMAN's heirs	2148
James HEMPHILL	640
William SMITH	878
Henry DICKENS	135

(Continued on following page)

Jesse NICKLES	244
Robert HAMILTON	2000
Thomas JOHNSTON	640
Marenda MATHEWS	1000
Plotomy POWELL	1000
Jesse PARSONS	640
Roger PARSONS	640
William TRIGG, jr.	640
William TRIGG, sen.	1000

June 15, 1810, Vol. III, No. CXXV

For sale, blue grass seed. Andrew EWING.

On the 9th of May, Mary Jane CONDON, the infant daughter of James CONDON, died.

New York, May 19th. The brig Camilla commanded by Capt. SHALER arrived from St. Sebastian. John GRISWOLD brought dispatches.

I want to forewarn all persons from taking assignments on a note drawn by Mrs. Martha WEIS and her son in favor of Porter ALLEN with a bearing date of March 28, 1808. Lemuel T. TURNER.

Thomas HITER, clock and watch-maker, silversmith and jeweler is open for business.

The following persons have reported estrays in Wilson County, per E. CRUTCHER, d. r. w. c.:

(1) Alanson TRIGG, on Fall Creek, has taken up a yellow bay mare. The mare is valued at $25.

(2) Ruebin BULLARD, on Barton's Creek, has taken up a sorrel mare. On May 17, 1810, the mare was given an appraised value of $8.

(3) Solomon RUSSELL has taken up a bay mare. The mare was valued at $12 on May 5, 1810.

(4) John TILFORD, on Jenning's Fork on Round Lick, has taken up a bay horse. On May 23, 1810, the horse was appraised at a value of $27.

(5) John KELLEY, on Smith's Fork, has taken up a sorrel roan horse. On May 24, 1810, the horse was given an appraised value of $15.

(6) Joseph WEATHERSPOON, on Sander's Fork, has taken up a bay mare. On May 12, 1810, the mare was valued at the sum of $43.

(7) John GOODLOE, on Cedar Creek, has taken up a horse. On May 10, 1810, the horse was valued at $50.

(8) Archibald SHANKS, at the tanyard, has taken up a bay mare. On May 16, 1810, the mare's value is $40.

(9) John TAYLOR, on Round Lick Creek, has taken up a black mare. On May 12, 1810, the mare was given an appraised value in the amount of $12.

(10) Elias PAUL, on Stewart's Ferry, has taken up a bay
     horse. On May 15, 1810, the horse's value is $25.
     On the 28th of July next at the court house in Warren,
there will be a public sale directed by the court of Warren
County of three tracts of land, that are the property of
Alexander CARMICHAEL. Absolom and Elisha PEPPER occuppy the
tract on Hickory Creek. The second tract, of 35 acres,
adjoins John TILLEY and the third adjoins Joseph COVILLE.
The property was taken at the influence of Joseph COLVILLE.
Wm. BARNETT, sheriff of Warren County.
     The following persons have reported estrays in Bedford
County, per Howel DAWDY, r. b. c.:
     (1) John COARTS, on Big Flat Creek, has taken up a
         horse. The horse was valued at $70.
     (2) John JACKSON, on the Garrison Fork, has taken up a
         horse. On May 18, 1810, the horse was appraised at
         a value of $25.
     (3) Wm. ELUM, jr., on Garrison Fork, has taken up a bay
         mare. On May 8, 1810, the mare's value was $45.
     (4) Daniel BANCROFT, on Powell's Creek, has taken up a
         bay horse. On May 13, 1810, the horse was given an
         appraised value of $15.
     (5) Thomas BURNOM, on War Trace, has taken up a horse.
     (6) George BIERT, on War Trace, has taken up a horse.
     (7) Wm. LONGMIRE, on Garrison Fork, took up a horse.
     (8) Christopher LANDERS, on Thompson's Creek, has taken
         up a bay horse. The horse was valued at $22.
     (9) Howel DAWDY, jr., the son of Howel DAWDY, sen., has
         taken up a sorrel horse. The horse's value is $22.
     (10) John SADDER, on Butler's Creek, took up a horse.

June 22, 1810, Vol. III, No. CXXVI
     Reward $40. On Sunday laast, a mulatto named DICK, also
known as Richard INGRAM, ranaway from a boat on the Harpeth.
John B. CRAIGHEAD.
     The following persons have reported estrays in Sumner
County, per Wm. TRIGG, jun., r. s. c.:
     (1) James SANDERS has taken up a black horse. The value
         of the horse was $10 on May 5, 1810.
     (2) James GUIN has taken up a mare. On May 19, 1810,
         mare was valued at $35.
     (3) Isaac STREET, on the Cumberland River, has taken up
         a sorrel horse. On May 14, 1810, the horse was
         appraised at a value of $21.
     I shall apply to the Commissioner of West Tennessee on
the 21st of July for a certificate on North Carolina Grant
No. 1616, dated April 27, 1793, for 640 acres, that was
issued to the heirs of Daniel SELLARS. Thomas JOHNSON.
     The Hiram Lodge No. 55 will have a meeting on the 24th in

the town of Franklin. Wm. HULME, Sec'ry pro-tem.
The copartnership of NEILSON, KING & MITCHELL is hereby dissolved by mutual consent. Charles B. NEILSON and John MITCHELL, surviving partners.

June 29, 1810, Vol. III, No. CXXVII
Benj. WHITE was convicted before the federal court of robbing the mail.
Died on Thursday the 28th, Capt. George WEST, late of Montgomery County, 52 years old. He was a native of North Carolina and an officer in the Navy.
Will all those indebted to the estate of Gray WASHINGTON, dec., please come forward. Elizabeth WASHINGTON, admin.
On the 15th of July next, I shall apply to the Commissioner of West Tennessee for a certificate on North Carolina Grant No. 1057, dated November 26, 1789 for 640 acres, that was issued to James Cole MONTFLORENCE conveyed by deed to Nicholas H. S. FOURNIER. This application was made for the benefit of the heirs. Joseph GREER, extr.

July 6, 1810, Vol. III, No. CXXVIII
The following persons have reported estrays in Wilson County, per Edmund CRUTCHER, d. r. w. c.:
  (1) Dennis KELLY, on Smith's Fork, has taken up a brown horse. On May 18, 1810, the horse was appraised at a value of $16.
  (2) James DOD, on the west fork of Round Lick, has taken up a bay mare. On May 17, 1810, the mare was appraised at a value of $20.
  (3) William SPICER, on Little Cedar Lick, has taken up a sorrel horse. On June 4, 1810, the horse was given an appraised value of $16.
  (4) Drury PERRY has taken up a bay horse. The horse's value was given at $27.50 on June 8, 1810.
  (5) John G. GRAVES, on Stoner's Creek, has taken up a bay horse. On June 8, 1810, the horse was given an appraised value of $60.
  (6) Joshua ANDERSON, on Barton's Creek, has taken up a white horse. On June 20, 1810, the horse was given an appraised value of $15.
  (7) Joseph CASON has taken up a black mare. The mare was valued at $8 on June 12, 1810.
  (8) Peter MOORE, on M'Knight's Creek, has taken up a sorrel mare. On June 23, 1810, the mare was given an appraised value of $28.
  (9) Moses OWEN has taken up a sorrel horse. The horse was valued at $28 on June 23, 1810.
  (10) Blake RUTLAND, on Stoner's Creek, took up a colt. The colt was valued at $10 on June 24, 1810.

(11) Jehu FERRINGTON, on Spring Creek, has taken up a
mare. On June 26, 1810, the mare's value is $11.
The subscriber in Sumner County, near Gallatin, will dig
wells. Joseph MOTHERAL.

July 13, 1810, Vol. III, No. CXXIX
The name of A. M'DOWELL was written on the masthead of
this issue.
The following is a list of letters remaining at the post
office in Franklin, per Gurdon SQUIER, a. p. m.: Valentine
ALLEN, John AUSTIN, Jno. ATKINSON, John ANDREWS, Bartlet
BASHAM, John BAYET, Frede. BRAWDER, James BRAWDER, Samuel
BROWN and John SMITH, Noel BROWN, Hugh BARR, John BARNAN,
James BURGESS, Joseph BRITTAIN, Jeremiah BURNES, Mr. DAVIS,
John CURRITHERS, Josiah CATE, Moses CHAMBERS, John BURNES,
Joseph CRAVENS, Benj. CARTER, David CAMPBELL, James CLINTON,
Saml. CRAWFORD, Samuel DODSON, Elisha DODSON, Wm. DUBERRY,
William DANIEL, James DAVIS or H. BRADFORD, John ELLISON,
Newton EDNEY, Robert ETTES, Absalom FRY, William GRIFFIN,
Wm. HARNER, Benj. HASSEL, Robert HALL, Isaac HALLIS, Thomas
HARVEY, Malachi HALIMAN, Charles GUNTER, William HENDERSON,
John JACKSON, Jesse JACKSON, Mary H. JONES, Chas. KAVENAUGH,
Benj. KING, David LOVE, Henry LANFORD, John H. LANG, Josiah
LEECH, Daniel LEE, Jas. or Dan MUSE, Neely M'MULLEN, William
M'LAIN, John M'CRORY, John MOODY, James M'CRACKIN, Saml.
M'CRACKEN, Mr. NEELY, Joshua OWENS, Sampson POWEL, Israel
PHILLIPS, John M. PHILLIPS, Alex. PERRYMAN, Horatio PETTIS,
Eliz. PORTER, James PUGH, Frederic PEEBLES, Pleasant RUSSEL,
Hen. RUTHERFORD, Mr. RANDOLPH, Aaron RUNALDS, John RECCARD,
Alex. RICHEY, Wm. SMITH, C. A. SMITH, Jonathan SPYKER, John
THOMPSON, Joseph TAYLOR, James TROUSDALE, Haden TILMON, Joel
WALLER, Robert WHITE, Jas. WILLIAMSON, Susan WHEDBEE, David
WOODS, Martha WEAVER, Jo. WITHERSPOON, German WINSETT, Dav.
and P. WALKER, Col. FRANC WILLIS, Richard YORK.
The following is a list of letters remaining at the post
office in Lebanon, per Jonathan PICKETT, p. m.: Wm. ADDISON,
William ALGOOD, James BRINSON, Samuel BURNEY, Henry BROOKS,
Elliott BROWN, Saml. BRAWNING, William K. BENNET, Richard
BANKS, Jonathan DAWDY, John EDWARDS, Polly FAITNER, Step.
GALLIGLY, William GRIFFITH, Sarah GALLIGLY, John GREGRY,
Benjamin HICKS, Micajah HALLIS, George HARPAN, John HILL,
Samuel MASER, Isham JOHNSON, sen., Philip JOHNSON, John
LEWELLING, Robert LEONARD, Benj. MARSHALL, Adam MASER, Peter
MOORE, Ang. M'DUGARD, John M'PEAK, David M'GAHEY, Jer.
M'KINSEY, Alexander OUTSLER, Edmund PARSONS, Drury PERRY,
John SPRING, Thomas RHODES, Pettis RAGLAND, Doct. TRIGG, Wm.
THOMPSON, W. G. WILLIAMS, Solomon THOMAS, John WILLIAMSON,
Will H. WADE, Judia WILLIE, Hardy C. WILLIS, John K. WYNN.
Will all those indebted to John T. PICKERING, please come

forward and settle their accounts. Spencer PICKERING. Green (sic) County, Tennessee. At the Court of Pleas and Quarter Sessions on the fourth Monday in January, 1810, Andrew PATTERSON, collector, reports the following tracts of land have unpaid taxes for the years of 1806 and 1807. The properties will be sold in the town of Greenville on the 1st of November, 1810. Andrew PATTERSON.

For the year 1806:

Reputed Owners	Acres	Situation
Mary BRUMLEY	171	Chuckey
Wm. DONELSON	250	Chuckey
Philip MOSER	100	1 white poll
Alex. CURREY	274	Lick Creek
James GLASS	200	Lick Creek
Christi. FRAKER	150	Lick Creek
Andrew STEEL, agent for		
James RAMSEY, dec.	400	Horse Fork
James ALLEN	100	Horse Fork
Enoch GRENIER	33	Horse Fork
Crawford JONES	101	Horse Fork
Sol. BOWHARD	100	Horse Fork
Abn. CHAPMAN	324	Horse Fork
David HUTTON	133	1 white poll
J. KILLINGSWORTH	100	Horse Fork
Levi MOORE	100	Horse Fork
Jas. KIRPATRICK	150	Bent Creek
Tho. BLACKBURN	181	1 white & 1 black
John DARMON	300	Camp Creek
John STINSON	240	Little Chucky
Solomon FAN	50	Little Chucky
John BOILS	40	1 white poll
Isaac FRISBEY	40	Little Chucky
Ha. HUTCHINSON	540	Brush Creek
Isaac SHERRILL	50	Cove Creek
Dan. ARMSTRONG	40	1 white poll
Hen. CONWAY	177	Lick Creek
John LOYD	25	1 white poll
Grif. RUTHERFORD	1	1 white p. & store
Wm. NEEL	50	1 white poll
Web. DENNISS	1	1 white & 1 black
Wm. DREW	---	1 white & 1 black
Geo. HARRISON	lots	1 white & 1 black
John MORRIS	100	1 white poll
Thos. MORGAN	50	
Step. WOOLSEY	100	1 white poll

For the year 1807:

Reputed Owners	Acres	Situation
Sa. ROBERTSON	550	Duck Creek

(Continued on following page)

128

(Greene County delinquent tax list continued)

Name	Acres	Situation
H. HUTCHINSON	150	Duck Creek
Dav. WILLIAMS	300	Chucky
Hen. CONWAY	---	Three town lots
J. LINGESELTER	200	1 white poll
H. M'BROOM	---	
George CASSELT	100	1 white poll
Nero CAMPBELL	---	Improvement

For the year 1810:

Reputed Oweners	Acres	Situation
Harrison HUTCHINSON	150	1 white poll
Philip TAYLOR	10	1 white & 4 black
Joseph WILLIAMS	200	Cedar Creek
Philip WYGRAM	325	1 white poll
Drury MORRIS	200	

The following persons have reported estrays in Maury County, per Joseph BROWN, ranger:

(1) John M'CAULEY, on Green's Lick Creek, has taken up a sorrel mare. On June 25, 1810, the appraised value was given at $30.

(2) Steph. SMITH, on Green's Lick Creek, has taken up a brown mare. On June 12, 1810, the mare was given an appraised value of $40.

(3) Eleazer ALEXANDER, on Carter's Creek, has taken up bay horse. The horse was valued at $40.

(4) Robert HILL, on Silver Creek, has taken up a bay horse. On June 19, 1810, the horse was given a value of $37.50.

(5) George DICKEY, on Green's Lick Creek, has taken up a bay horse. On June 6, 1810, the horse was valued at $12.50.

(6) David ORTON, on Rutherford's Creek, has taken up a sorrel horse. On June 2, 1810, the horse was given an appraised value of $30.

(7) John GRIFFIN, on Lytle's Creek, has taken up a bay horse. On June 25, 1810, the horse's value is $75.

The following is a list of persons in Rutherford County, reporting estrays, per Neil B. ROSE for Wm. HOWELL, ranger:

(1) James CLEMMONS, on Hurricane Creek, has taken up a sorrel horse, that is valued at $10.

(2) James GARRET has taken up a sorrel horse.

(3) Wm. BASKINS, on the Stones River, has taken up an iron grey horse, that is valued at $40.

(4) Nimrod INGRAM, on Bradley's Mill, has taken up a bay horse, which is valued at $23.

(5) Richard STEPHENS, near the Old Garrison, has taken a sorrel mare, that is valued at $13.

(6) Robert OVERALL, on Wright's Mill, has taken up a black mare, that was appraised at a value of $35.

(7) Wm. D. HILL, in Jefferson, has taken up a sorrel mare, that was appraised at $23.

(8) Wm. DELOCH, on Ready's Mill, has taken up a sorrel mare, that was given an appraised value of $23.

(9) Joseph BURDETT, on Hurricane Creek, has taken up a grey horse, which was valued at one cent.

(10) Wm. WHORRY, on Ready's Mill, has taken up a sorrel horse, that is valued at $15.

(11) John T. WILLIAMS, on Overall's Creek, has taken up a horse, that is valued at $25.

(12) James RUCKER, jun., at Rucker's Mill, has taken up a grey horse.

(13) Wm. LOCK, near Jefferson, has taken up a mare.

(14) Wm. MAHAN has taken up a grey horse.

The following is a list of letters remaining at Columbia, per B. ESTES, a. p. m.: Thos. ARNOLD, Gilbert BERRY, Jane C. BLAKE, Alex. BOWLING, Duncan BROWN, Rev. Dun. BROWN, Jno. BROWNING, Woodles BERILE, Wm. M. BERRYHILL, Drury BRIDGES, Wm. BURROW, Jno. BROADWAY, Robt. BEATY, Dr. Jas. BOYER, Geo. COCKBURN, George CAULTER, Bethsheba BYLER, Wm. CARUTHERS, Aaron CUNNINGHAM, Peter CHEATHAM, James CRISPASS, Wm. DUKE, Eli COCKRUN, John DUNN, James DOBY, Miller DOGGETT, Michael EZETE, Dav. ERWIN, John ESTES, Moses DIBER, Wm. DICKSON, Jas. DOUGAN, John DABNEY, Geo. DAWSON, John EMERSON, David FOSTER, Wm. FARIS, John FOURY, Isham FUQUA, Thos. C. FOSTER, Geo. GILE, George GRAY, James GORDON, David HUNT, James HOLLAND, Moses HALNEY, James HANNA, John HURMAN, Wm. LANE, John HELSHOURER, Isaac HARDIN, Jos. HERNDON, Calib HENBY, Isaac HUTCHERSON, Martin JONES, James JOHNSON, Charles IRBY, Harry JOHNSON, Hyther JAGGERS, Mary H. JONES, John LAIRD, Robt. LOONEY, Washington LEDBETTER, James KIDD, Saml. KING, Jos. KIRKPATRICK, Thomas LANE, James LEDBETTER, Elizabeth LAURENCE, John LOVE, Maj. Jas. LEWIS, Benj. H. LEWIS, Jas. LOVE, Jas. MORRASON, Abraham MAYFIELD, Daniel M'CLEAN, John M'JIMSEY, Samuel M'CAWLEY, Daniel M'COLLUM, Samuel M'CONNEL, Daniel M'BEAN, William F. M'DUFF, John W. GIMPSEY, William MARTIN, Wm. M'MICKEN, Thos. M'LAUGHLIN, Thomas NEX, Henry NORMAN, Richd. M. NOWLEN, John NELSON, sen., Jos. PORTER, Hariet PAXTON, Ambrose POWELL, James PEERY, John PICKARD, Samuel RAMSEY, Will RUSH, Col. Albert RUSSEL, Sarah ROLLINS, Aaron REYNOLDS, Jos. ROSBOROUGH, John SCOTT, James SPEAD, Henry SCALES, Judah SIMS, William SIMS, Paris SIMMONS, Richd. SCOTT, Thos. SUTHERLAND, Thomas SMITH, Ruebin SMITH, Henly STONE, Jonathan SPYKER, Moses TOMLINSON, Martin TANGATE, Saml. H. WILLIAMS, John VANPETT, John WOOD, Eliza WRIGHT, Joannah WARRINGTON, Mrs. S. WHIDSEY, William WILLS, Mrs. YEWELL, Britton YARBOROUGH.

The copartnership of the firm of John S. WILLIAMSON and Thomas WILLIAMSON is dissolved by mutual consent.

July 27, 1810, Vol. III, No. CXXXI

Married on Tuesday evening last, Capt. John BRAHAN, cashier at the Nashville Bank, to Miss Polly WEAKLEY. She is the daughter of Col. Rob. WEAKLEY, member of Congress.

Married on Wednesday evening last, John BAIRD, merchant of this town, to Miss Fanny PLUMMER of Robertson County.

Married on Sunday evening last, William WILLIAMS to Mrs. Mary MCALL, both of Williamson County.

Died at Capt. PRYOR's on Monday last, Garret VOORHIES at age 53. He was on a visit to this country to see his children.

Joel BARLOW and Wm. GRAY are opening a woolen factory in Hartford, Connecticut.

Reward $100. On the 27th of May, a negro man named JAMES, age 35, ranaway from the subscriber on Round Lick in Smith County, He is African by birth. His wife is named RACHAEL. James NORRIS.

The following persons have reported estrays in Bedford County, Howel DAWDY, r. b. c.:

(1) William ADAMS, on the Duck River, has taken up a bay filly. On May 18, 1810, the filly was given an appraised value of $8.
(2) Henry SAYLING, on Garrison Fork, has taken up a sorrel horse. On June 7, 1810, the horse was given a value of $20.
(3) Peter RUSHING, on War Trace Fork, has taken up a brown bay horse. The appraised value of the horse was placed at $14 on June 16, 1810.
(4) James A. WILSON, on the Duck River, has taken up a bay horse, that was valued at $35.
(5) Rueben NANCE, on Hurricane Creek, has taken up a sorrel mare. On June 23, 1810, the mare was given an appraised value of $5.
(6) A sorrel mare was taken up on the Duck River by John WARNER. On June 7, 1810, the mare was given a value of $30.
(7) Joel CASEY, on Caney Spring, has taken up a grey filly, that is valued at $8.

On the 1st of September in the town of Columbia, there will be a public sale directed by the court of Maury County of lot no. 93 that is the property of Giles STEWART and John READ. The property was taken at the influence of John ROSS and Isaac ADAIR. W. BRADSHAW, shff.

August 3, 1810, Vol. III, No. CXXXII

Married on 20th of July on Thursday evening last, Zeno CAMPBELL, of Caburrus County, North Carolina, to Miss Ann K. BALCH. She is the daughter of William BALCH of Bedford Co.

In Shelbyville on the 22nd of September, there will be a

public sale directed by the Bedford County court of 140 acres, that is the property of Anderson POWEL. The tract was taken to satisfy a writ of venditioni exponas. Benjamin BRADFORD, sheriff of Bedford County.

In Shelbyville on the 22nd of September, there will be a public sale directed by the Bedford County court of 5000 acres, that is the property of Wm. BRANCH, dec. The tract was taken at the influence of James OVERSTREET. Benjamin BRADFORD, sheriff.

On the 1st of September next, I shall apply to the court for a division of 2550 acres among the heirs of Rev. William HILL. The property was issued on North Carolina Grant No. 1225, dated November 27, 1793, and the second tract on Grant No. 182, dated December 17, 1794. John M. GOODLOE.

On the 22nd of September next in the town of Lebanon, there will be a public sale directed by the court of Wilson County of 50 acres, that is the property of William CLIFTON and Thomas WILLIAMS. William CLIFTON occuppies the land. The property was taken at the influence of James WILIE. T. BRADLEY, sheriff.

The following persons have reported the estrays in Wilson County, per Edmund CRUTCHER, d. r. w. c.:

(1) John M'KNIGHT, on Sand's Fork, has taken up a mare. On July 16, 1810, the mare was valued at $15.

(2) Samuel HARRIS, on Jennings Fork, has taken up a bay horse. On July 21, 1810, the horse's value is $35.

(3) John AFFLAX has taken up a bay mare. The mare was appraised at $31.25 on July 25, 1810.

(4) Middleton BELT, on Fall Creek, has taken up a brown mare. On July 20, 1810, the mare's value is $15.50.

(5) James M'LIN, on Bradley's Creek, has taken up a bay mare. On July 12, 1810, the mare's value is $35.

(6) Samuel CARTWRIGHT, on Jennings Fork, has taken up a mare. On July 25, 1810, the mare's value is $20.

On the 22nd of September next in the town of Lebanon, there will be a public sale of 205 acres, that belongs to Daniel THYLMAN, Micajah VIEVERETT, and Sion BASS. The land is occuppied by Micajah VIEVERETT. The property was taken at the influence of James M'REYNOLDS. T. BRADLEY, shff.

On the 1st of September in the town of Columbia, there will be a public sale of 200 acres, that is the property of Spencer GRIFFIN and Jacob SCOTT. The property was part of Grant No. 574, that was issued to Robt. HILL and was entered in the name of Michael BACON. The tract was taken at the influence of Richard ORTON, Henry BAKER, Robert P. CURREN and Joel R. OLDHAM. Samuel H. WILLIAMS.

The following persons in Rutherford County have reported estrays, per W. HOWELL, r. r. c.:

(1) Luckett DAVIS, at Howell's Mill has taken up a mare.

(2) Caleb ZACHERY, on Hurricane Creek, has taken up a sorrel mare.

(3) James BLACKMAN, on Overall's Creek, has taken up a sorrel mare.

(4) Benjamin CARR, on Overall's Creek, has taken up a sorrel mare.

The following persons have reported estrays in Bedford County, per H. DAWDY, r. b. c.:

(1) Robt. BAKER, on Garrison Fork, has taken up a bay horse. On June 16, 1810, the horse's value is $35.

(2) Wm. POSTON, on Thompson's Creek, took up a black mare. On July 5, 1810, the mare's value was $15.

(3) Anderson DONELSON, on Beach Creek, has taken up a mare. On July 7, 1810, the mare's value was $15.

(4) Benj. DAVIS, on Sinking Creek, has taken up a bay horse. On July 10, 1810, the horse's value is $12.

(5) John STONE, on Sugar Creek, has taken up a mare. On July 13, 1810, the mare was appraised at $18.

(6) Stephen MALIN, on the north fork of the Duck River, has taken up a sorrel roan mare. On June 27, 1810, the mare was appraised at a value of $5.

The following persons have reported estrays in Sumner County, per W. TRIGG, jr., r. s. c.:

(1) Jesse WEAVER has taken up a sorrel horse. The value of the horse was $55 on June 6, 1810.

(2) Thomas WHITE, on Bledsoes Creek, has taken up a horse. On June 15, 1810, the horse's value is $15.

(3) Abraham KING, on Beloat's Ferry, has taken up a bay mare. On June 12, 1810, the mare was valued at $7.

(4) Thomas BLACKMORE, Rockney Creek, took up a mare. The mare's value was $2 on June 6, 1810.

(5) Alexander M'MELLON, on Bledsoe's Creek, has taken up a bay mare. The appraised value of the mare was $15 on June 18, 1810.

August 10, 1810, Vol. ?, No. ?

The subscriber is living at the Daniel VAUIX's, that is six miles from Nashville. I am carrying on the business of architecture. James GUZZARD.

Died on Saturday last, James M'CUTCHEN of Williamson County. He hung himself while drunk. He left a wife and children.

Eli GARRETT, on Swan Creek, Lincoln County, has taken up a sorrel horse. The horse was appraised at $15 on July 12, 1810. Brice M. GARNER for Philip KOONCE.

The following is a list of letters remaining at the post office at Jefferson, per John SPENCER, p. m.: John BEASLEY, Carter ABBOTT, Charles BURNES, Alex. BARNHILL, John BULLARD, Uriah BROCK, Thos. BRENTS, Thos. BROTHERS, Mrs. C. HARDEMAN,

Jesse BEAN, J. BURTON, Benajah (sic) CARLTON, John CHISUM, Robert CLARK, John CRAWFORD, Joel CHILDRESS, Joseph CARNEY, John DAVIS, Henry DAVIS, Samuel DUNAWAY, John DICK, Samuel ERWIN, Dav. ELDER, Moses ECHOLS, William FELEN, Matcomb GILCHRIST, jr., Lewis GILLISPIE, Jos. HERNDON, John HARRIS, Robt. HUDSPETH, William HIGGINBOTHAM, Rezia JARVIS, Samuel JACKSON, William KING, Dr. Charles KAVANAUGH, Peter KING, Richard KEEL, Major William LOGAN, William MATHEWS, James M'QUESTION, Mark MITCHELL, John M'KNIGHT, Tenniri MOORE, John M'PEAK, Samuel M'BRIDE, George MORRIS, John MARSHALL, Adam MILLER, Robt. MILLER, James NEELY, Burrel PERRY, Jos. E. PHILLIPS, John PARKS, William PEACCOCK, John PURKLE, Jeffery PECK, Thomas RUCKER, Jincey ROBINSON, Abraham BAKER John REYNOLDS, Fred. REPLOGLE, Geo. RUMMINGER, John STEWART, John SUTTON, Elizabeth SMITH, Caleb STROVALE, Moses SHORT, James THOMPSON, William TAYLOR, George SIMPSON, John SMITH, Jonathan SPEAKER, Abraham TENNESON, Wm. THOMAS, Wm. WHITE, Barnabas WELLS, William WALKOUT, Maj. Thos. WASHINGTON, John WILSON, Wm. WOODALE, Abner WETHERLY.

August 17, 1810, Vol. III, No. CXXXIV

Williamson County, Tennessee, July Sessions, 1810. Wm. HULME, sheriff and collector, reports the following tracts of land have unpaid taxes for the year 1810. The properties will be sold in the town of Franklin on the first Monday in November next. N. P. HARDEMAN, clerk.

Reputed Owners	Acres	Situation
Nathaniel ARMSTRONG	160	
William ALLEN	---	Two town lots
ALLEN & BURTON	---	Two town lots
Daniel ANDERSON	640	Murfee's Fork
Samuel BLAIR	160	Little Harpeth
Thomas BLOUNT	3642	Arrington's Creek
Joseph BLYTHE	3520	Duck River
Benjamin H. COVINGTON	640	Big Harpeth
John DAVIS	362	
William DONELSON	1421	
Lewis DONELSON	640	Big Harpeth
John DONELSON	2470	
John GILLESPIE	323	Flat Creek
Thomas HOGG's heirs	3976	Big Harpeth
John HASSEL	100	Big Harpeth
Nimrod JENKINS	100	Big Harpeth
Wm. MEDLOCK	80	Little Harpeth
John M'IVER, John PARK, Jas. PARK, and Wm. PARK	3200	Five tracts
Hugh M'CLUNG	120	West Harpeth
George MAXWELL	53	West Harpeth

(Continued on following page)

Wm. RICKARD	1280	West Harpeth
Ann M'ROE	1302	
Samuel RYAN	120	
James SHANNON	216	Haye's Creek
Samuel TENNESSON	40	
James WILSON's heirs	700	Harpeth Lick
Thomas G. WATKINS	1360	M'Crory's Creek
Wm. WALKER	222	Hayes
Abraham WALKER	19	Murfrees Fork
Wm. L. YARBOROUGH	240	Mill Creek
Robt. GOODLOE's heirs	684	Harpeth LICK
John CRAWFORD	137	Big Harpeth
Wm. SLOAN	240	

The following persons were at a convention in West Florida: John RHEA, Dr. Andrew STEEL, George MATHER, John MILLS, Samuel CROCKER, William BARROW, Thomas LILLY, Philip HICKEY, John H. JOHNSON, Edmund HAUSS, William MORGAN.

The following persons have reported estrays in Bedford County, per Howel DAWDY, r. b. c.:

(1) William DITTO, on War Trace, has taken up a brown mare. On July 26, 1810, the mare's value was $20.

(2) John PATTON, on Balch's Fork, has taken up a brown mare. On July 20, 1810, the mare's value was $16.

August 24, 1810, Vol. III, No. CXXXV

Will the Thomas BOATWRIGHT that moved five years ago from Georgia to Tennessee, please contact the editor.

Married on Thursday last, Hugh M'CRARY to Amy MAZE. They are both of this county.

On the 27th of September next in the town of Columbia, there will be a public sale directed by the Williamson County court of 5000 acres lying on both sides of Fountain Creek, Warrant No. 542, that is the property of William GILBERT, dec. The rights to said land belong Jenny GILBERT, the wife of Robert PRINCE; Sarah GILBERT, the wife of James HOLLAD; Alexander M. GILBERT; Milly GILBERT; Sally GILBERT; Fanny GILBERT; Philip GILBERT; William GILBERT; and to Jenny GILBERT and Elizabeth GILBERT to children of John GILBERT, dec. and heirs to Wm. GILBERT, dec. Wm. BRADSHAW, d. s.

Roane County, Tennessee, July Sessions. John BROWN reports the following tracts have unpaid taxes for 1810 and are liable for a double tax. Henry BREAZLE.

Reputed Owners	Acres	Situation
John TIPTON	1000	Emery
Philip EMMETT	80	Ent. 133
Joseph STOUT	50	King Cr., Ent. 147
Mathew ENGLISH	40	King Cr., Ent. 394

(Continued on following page)

(Roane County delinquent tax list continued)

Ambrose BRYANT	83	Ent. 420	
Josiah MONTGOMERY	114	Occ. No. 74	
John JONES	162	Occ. No. 75	
John FLANNAGIN	200	Aj. Saml. ELKRIDGE	
Heirs of James HENRY	1000		
Thomas BUTLER	168		

August 31, 1810, Vol. III, No. CXXXVI
Died at Parkertown, Vermont, Capt. John VINCENT, age 95.
He was an Indian.
Bedford County, Tennessee, March term, 1810. Benjamin
BRADFORD, sheriff and collector, states that the following
tracts of land have unpaid taxes for 1809. The properties
will be sold on the first Monday in November next. Thomas
MOORE, clerk.

Reputed Owners	Acres	Situation
Alexr. NELSON's heirs	4400	Bradshaw's Creek
Stephen BRIMAGER	55	Hurricane Creek
John BRIMIMAGER	262	
Ephraim DAVIDSON	1500	
William HENRY	1500	
Amos JOHNSTON	640	Sinking Creek
William BOWEN	460	Cane Creek
A. PEDDY and Jos. COBB	5000	Elk River
Elijah PATTEN	240	Mulberry
David SHANNON	406	Mulberry
James FRIZLE	2500	
Howell TATUM	529	Elk River
David VAUGHN's heirs	640	
William MORISSON	1000	Weakley's Creek
NOBLE & MEREDITH	400	Mulberry
William CASWELL	1230	
Joseph COLEMAN	275	
John HILL	2560	Duck River
Thomas KEIF	274	Duck River
John KENNESY	1000	Cane Creek
Henry M. RUTLEDGE	1656	Swan Creek
John TILSEY's heirs	120	Kelley's Creek
John INSKEEP	10000	Duck River

Bedford County, Tennessee, March term, 1810. Benjamin
BRADFORD, sheriff and collector, states that the following
tracts were not given in for taxes for 1808 and are liable
for a double tax. They will be sold on the first Monday in
November in Knoxville. Thomas MOORE by Stephen BRADFORD.

Reputed Owners	Acres	Situation
David M'GAVOCK	1000	Sec. 1, Ran. 3
Daniel GALISPIE	1000	Range 4

(Continued on following page)

136

(Bedford County delinquent tax list continued)

William BRYAN	1000	Range 4
Miles WATSON	150	Sec. 1, Ran. 5
John GORDON	160	West Elk River
Ephraim DAVIDSON	190	Sec. 2, Ran. 5
Joseph GRAHAM	648	
John M'CORKLE	649	Bradshaw's Creek
ROLLING & LOFTEN	274	Swan Creek
John STEEL	1280	N. Side Elk River
John SLATE	1280	N. Side Elk River
Henry YOUNG	4218	Sec. 3, Ran. 1
ROBINSON & RAYNES	1280	Sec. 4, Ran. 1
James ROBINSON	640	Sec. 3, Ran. 3
David ROSS	5000	Sec. 5, Ran. 5
Heirs of T. SORREL	640	Sec. 5, Ran. 2
Heirs of Jas. SHIVER	274	Mulberry Creek
Robt. H. DYER	440	Sec. 4, Ran. 5
Anthony FOSTER	640	Sec. 4, Ran. 3
Mathew BROOX	640	Sec. 4, Ran. 2
John COCKRELL	50	Sec. 7, Ran. 4
Michael CAMPBELL	227	Sec. 3, Ran. 7
Wm. CASWELL	278	Sec. 6, Ran. 3
Jacob CASTLEMON	200	Sec. 2, Ran. 3
John YOUNG	375	Sec. 2, Ran. 3
John MOTHERALL	41	Swan Creek
Edward MITCHELL	70	Cove Spring Creek

Married on Tuesday evening last, Capt. RODGERS, of White's Creek, to Miss Juliet MERRYMAN, the daughter of W. MERRYMAN of this county.

Married on Saturday evening last, Daniel YOUNG to Mrs. Peggy BELFORD. They are both of this county.

Charles WILKINS has received a consignment of goods from Col. HUMPHREYS of Connecticut.

September 7, 1810, Vol. III, No. CXXXVII
Bedford County, March term, 1810. Benjamin BRADFORD, sheriff and collector, reports that the following tracts of land were not given in for taxes for 1809 and are liable for a double tax.

Reputed Owners	Acres	Situation
John GORDON	160	Elk and Flint Riv.
Edward GILES	472	Duck River
Daniel GILLISPIE	1000	Flint River
Joseph GRAHAM	612	Sec. 3, Ran. 5
Alexander GORDON	209	
Wm. GILMORE	12	Short Creek
Thomas GEORGE	109	Hurricane
David GILBERT	50	Flat Creek

(Continued on following page)

137

(Bedford County delinquent tax list continued)

Name	Acres	Location
Wm. GIBSON	200	Sugar Creek
Joseph GRAY	30	Bradshaw's Creek
Wm. GRAHAM	390	Rock Creek
Heirs of T. HUNTER	640	Sec. 3, Ran. 2
Thomas HICKMAN	460	Sec. 2, Ran. 4
Samuel B. HARRIS	400	Norrise's Creek
Thomas HOPKINS	100	South Side Elk
Green HILL	640	Cove Spring Creek
Joshua HADLEY	640	Sec. 6, Ran. 4
Richard HIGHTOWER	150	Bradshaw's Creek
Benj. HARNEY	540	Garrison Fork
HIGHTOUR (sic) & PILLOW	213	Bradshaw's Creek
Alex HUGHES	400	Rock Creek
John C. HAMILTON	50	Weakley's Creek
Thos. HOUSTON	640	War Trace
Thos. JOHNSTON	274	Sec. 7, Ran. 5
Wm. ERWIN	50	Big Flat Creek
Isaac WEST	149	Wilson's Creek
John WRIGHT	50	Kelley's Creek
Elijah WEST	500	Duck River
Joseph P. WATKINS	70	Duck River
John YOUNG	375	Sec. 4, Ran. 4
John KELLY	50	
J. LEWIS & others	1000	Sec. 3, Ran. 7
Tipton LEWIS	1500	Sec. 3, Ran. 5
Heirs of J. LAURENCE	640	Sec. 4, Ran. 3
Wm. LYTLE, sen.	150	Sec. 5, Ran. 4
Benj. LITTLE	50	Wilson's Creek
Hezekiah LACETER	50	Rock Creek
John MOTHERALL	41	Swan Creek
Edward MITCHELL	70	Cove Spring Creek
John MEDERAS	170	Sec. 4, Ran. 3
Jos. MOTHERALL	640	Sec. 2, Ran. 3
MOTHERALL & NOBLETT	400	Sec. 2, Ran. 5
Dav. M'GAVOCK	100	Sec. 1, Ran. 2
Rand. M'GAVOCK	225	Sec. 4, Ran. 3
Wm. MARTIN	160	Sec. 1, Ran. 2
Arthur MOORE	250	Big Flat Creek
Wm. MOORE	50	
Robt. MACLEMORE	640	Duck River
James MACKEY	640	Sec. 2, Ran. 3
Samuel MAXWELL	355	Duck River
Mark MITCHELL	50	Hurricane Creek
Amos MACLEMORE	85	Weakley's Creek
James M'ADAMS	100	Hurricane Creek
Daniel MUSE	300	Rock Creek
James MITCHELL	85	Noah's Fork

(Continued on following page)

138

(Bedford County delinquent tax list continued)

Name	Acres	Location
Hugh M'KELVY	45	Upper Spring Creek
O. P. NICHOLSON	640	Sec. 7, Ran. 1
Robt. NELSON	122	Sec. 1, Ran. 1
Wm. NARK	400	No. Side Duck
Wm. NUN	30	No. Side Duck
B. W. BOLAN	40	Sec. 4, Ran. 4
Alex. OUTLAW	312	Duck River
Abel OLIVE	150	Sec. 2, Ran. 1
Jos. OWEN	110	Carr's Creek
Thos. THOMPSON	67	No. Side Duck
Thomp. THOMPSON	60	Sec. 6, Ran. 3
Geo. TILMAN	70	Caney Spring
James TEMPLE	39	So. Side Elk
MOORE & WILLIAMS	100	Swan Creek
Heirs of M. WARD	640	Cane Creek
Robert WHITE	1000	Sec. 4, Ran. 4
Haden WELLS	640	Sec. 1, Ran. 3
James WHITE	1600	Sec. 5, Ran. 6
Dav. WINCHESTER	300	Sec. 5, Ran. 1
Thomp. WRIGHT	425	Sec. 7, Ran. 5
John WHITE	427	
Wm. WHITE	1000	Duck River
Heirs of M. WATSON	240	Sec. 1, Ran. 3
BLAIR & WILBERN	150	Sec. 5, Ran. 6
Joseph WILLIAMS	640	Sec. 2, Ran. 3
John WALKER	167	Flat Creek
James WALL	2560	Rock Creek
John WOODS	200	Sec. 5, Ran. 2
Heirs of A. WILDER	200	Flat Creek
Wm. WOODS	76	Rock Creek
Wm. WYATT	16	Flat Creek
Stephen WHITE	5	Spring Creek
James WRIGHT	25	Kelley's Creek
Edward WADE	50	So. Side Duck
Alexander WHITE	50	Kelley's Creek
Geo. ALEXANDER	1650	Weakley's Creek
Hugh ALEXANDER	300	Cane Creek
COX & ELLISTON	60	Bradshaw's Creek
Wm. ADAMS	74	Carr's Creek
Mathew ARMSTRONG	6	S. S. Cumberland
Moses AYRES	130	Rock Creek
Samuel AUSTIN	30	Kelley's Creek
Heirs of Geo. BELL	640	Sec. 4, Ran. 4
Matthew BROOKS	640	Sec. 4, Ran. 3
Wm. BRYAN	1000	Sec. 5, Ran. 4
Sumner BOOTH	640	Elk River
Wm. BLACK	300	No. Side Duck

(Continued on following page)

139

(Bedford County delinquent tax list continued)

Name	Amount	Location
Thos. R. BUTLER	206	Cove Creek
Edward BYRAN	100	Flat Creek
Hezekiah BROWN	50	Flat Creek
Joel BUTLER	50	Carr's Creek
Dav. BERRY	150	
John COCKRILL	50	Sec. 7, Ran. 4
Thos N. CLARK	60	Kelley's Creek
Isaac CROW	257	Rock Creek
Wm. CASWELL	278	Sec. 6, Ran. 3
A. CUNNINGHAM	640	Mulberry
John CONNER	274	Duck River
M. CUNNINGHAM	428	Sec. 4, Ran. 5
James CHAMBERS	186	Duck River
Wm. CLARK	110	Sec. 7, Ran. 3
Alex. CRAIG	100	Duck River
W. DONALSONKETH (sic)	125	
Isaac CONGER	258	
Wm. DILLARD	225	Sec. 5, Ran. 3
Samuel DOBBINS	640	Sec. 2, Ran. 2
Ephraim DRAKE	640	Sec. 3, Ran. 2
Robt. DYER	440	Sec. 7, Ran. 5
John DAVIDSON	100	Bradshaw's Creek
Amos DAVIS	120	Swan Creek
Walter DANIEL	18	Ryley's Creek
Thos. DOUGLASS	20	Barren Fork
Benj. FIZRANDOLPH	640	Mulberry Creek
Jesse FRANKLIN	1000	Sec. 1, Ran. 3
Anthony FOSTER	640	Sec. 4, Ran. 3
Wm. FOSTER	30	Alexander's Creek
John FISHER	100	Sinking Branch
Elijah PATTON	250	Spring Creek
Francis PATTERSON	640	Sec. 3, Ran. 4
Thos. PERSON	940	
Ephraim PAYTON	640	Sec. 4, Ran. 4
PARKER & BROWN	2500	Duck River
Elisha PREWETT	143	Sec. 4, Ran. 3
Ambrose PORTER	90	Flat Creek
Solomon PLUMLY	100	Sec. 7, Ran. 3
James ROBINSON	640	Sec. 3, Ran. 3
David ROSS	5000	Sec. 5, Ran. 5
Thos. SHUTE	274	N. S. Duck River
Robt. W. SMITH	250	Weakley's Creek
Thos. TAYLOR	93	Sec. 7, Ran. 3
Nath. TAYLOR	640	N. S. Duck River
Heirs of M. THRIFT	640	Mulberry Creek
Geo. TILMAN	75	Flat Creek
Felix ROBINSON	1000	Sec. 4, Ran. 3

(Continued on following page)

140

(Bedford County delinquent tax list continued)

Lavina ROBINSON	640	Sec. 5, Ran. 2
Jordan ROACH	100	Sec. 6, Ran. 6
Michael ROBINSON	50	
Henry RUTHERFORD	60	Sec. 4, Ran. 1
Alexander RUTLEDGE	40	Weakley's Creek
Rowly RIM	50	Swan Creek
Elijah RUTLEDGE	80	Weakley's Creek
Samuel SHANNON	33	Sec. 1, Ran. 2
Daniel SHIP	728	Sec. 1, Ran. 3
STUBBLEFIELD & Others	640	Sec. 2, Ran. 4
Geo. SMITH	640	Cove Spring Creek
William SLODE	132	Sec. 7, Ran. 5
John SKINNER	640	Cove Spring Creek
Amst. STUBBLEFIELD	640	Sec. 2, Ran. 6
Heirs of Thomas SORREL	640	Sec. 5, Ran. 2
Sampson SAWYERS	45	Flat Creek
Swaink (sic) STUBBLEFIELD	2560	
John SLOP	300	Sec. 5, Ran. 5
Heirs of I. SHIVERS	274	Mulberry Creek
Morris SHEAN	200	
Sam SAWYERS	100	Flat Creek

For sale, hemp and bee's wax. W. and G. MORGAN & Co.

Reward $20. On the 12th, a negro man called Richard GRINDALL ranaway from the subscriber. He is about 40 years old and is 5 ft., 10 or 11 in. tall. He has a pass signed by Maj. C. KILE. To collect the reward, please deliver said negro to me in Jackson County, Georgia. Samuel GARDNER.

Reward $30. On the 7th, three negroes belonging to the estate of H. MURFEE, dec. ranaway. They are DREAD, age 35, 5 ft., 4 or 5 in. tall; SAM, age 22, 5 ft. 10 in. tall; and WILLIS about 17 years old. D. DICKSON, admn.

For rent, a two story log house opposite Mr. CHEATHAM's tavern. For terms, see Mr. MARTIN, merchant. M'GILVEY and M'PHAIL.

Reward $10. In the middle of last April a sorrel mare strayed or was stolen from the subscriber on Bigby Creek, Maury County. Duncan M'INTRYRE.

The following persons have reported estrays in Wilson County, per Edmund CRUTCHER, d. r.:
(1) Rueben BULLARD, on Barton's Creek, has taken up a brown mare. On August 14, 1810, the mare was given an appraised value of $12.
(2) William CRABTREE, near Drake's Lick, has taken up a sorrel mare. On July 21, 1810, the mare was given an appraised value of $25.
(3) William NEAL, on Hickman's Creek, has taken up a yellow sorrel mare. On July 21, 1810, the mare was appraised at a value of $11.50.

(4) Walter BRADLEY, on Cedar Creek, has taken up a bay horse. On July 31, 1810, the horse's value is $35. The following persons have reported estrays in Bedford County, per Howel DAWDY, r. b. c.:
(1) John ELLISON, on Rock Creek, has taken up a horse.
(2) William CRAWFORD, Garrison Fork, took up a mare.
(3) Amos M'ADAMS, Falling Creek, has taken up a filly. Reward $100. On Sunday the 2nd, Archibald RUTHERFORD broke jail. He was lately apprehended on the Duck River for horse stealing. He is 35 years old, 5 ft., 11 in. tall and has fair skin with dark hair. Charles B. HARVEY, Gordon's Ferry on the Duck River.

September 14, 1810, Vol. III, No. CXXXVIII
Williamson County, Tennessee, September term,1810. Samuel COX, collector, reports that taxes remain due for the years of 1807, 1808, 1809, and 1810 on the following lots.

Reputed Owners	Years	Lot No.
ALLEN & BURTON	1807	165, 156
Thomas CONNELY	1807	12
ALLEN & BURTON	1808	165, 156
ALLEN & BURTON	1809	165, 156
Samuel BELL	1809	141, 155
Wm. C. C. CLAIBORNE	1809	67
Samuel CHAPMAN	1809	96
Nath. EWEN	1809	175
Zebulon HASSEL	1809	24, 40, 42
James HUMER	1809	43, 53
Benj. BRADSHAW	1810	155, 141
ALLEN & BURTON	1810	156
Wm. C. C. CLAIBORNE	1810	167
Jos. COWAN	1810	77
Thos. CRUTCHER	1810	117
Thos. CONNLEY	1810	157
Zebulon HASSEL	1810	40, 42, 24
John MITCHELL	1810	93
John NICHOLS	1810	78
Daniel PERKINS	1810	90
John PAGE	1810	120
Thos. SHANNON	1810	101, 54, 126, 133, 134, 136, 144, 158

Open, for the business of millinary and mantua-making. Mary LACY.

September 21, 1810, Vol. III, No. CXXIX
On the 13th of October in the town of Nashville, there will be a public sale directed by the court of the District of West Tennessee of 200 acres, that is the property of Samuel SUGG. The property is occuppied by Squire HANNAN in

142

Wilson County, Warrant No. 1514. Also for sale, are 400 acres adjoining Logue LAW, William WARAN, and David FOSTER and 400 acres in Wilson County, that is occuppied by Blake RUTLAND. The properties were taken at the influence of Abigns (sic) SUGGS against Lemuel SUGG. John CHILDRESS.

Stewart County, Tennessee, August Sessions, 1810. Abner PEARCE, collector, reports that the following tracts still have unpaid taxes for 1809 and are liable for a double tax. The properties will be sold in the town of Dover on the first Monday in November next. John ALLEN.

Reputed Owners	Acres	Situation	Warr. No.
John SMITH	60	Tennessee River	140
James M'MURTEE	109	Blue Creek	133
Alex. MABANE	130	Blue Creek	251
John WILLIAMS	40	Richland Creek	4
Thos. E. SUMNER	209	White Oak Creek	278
Goodwin THOMPSON's heirs	213	Ran. 21, Sec. 6	4428
Wm. BRATHER	640	White Oak Creek	2446
John CASEY	640	Trace Creek	
James M. and William			
M. T. LEWIS	640		3090
Wm. BECK	640	Blue Creek	514
John WALKER	700	Blue Creek	240
Capt. Robert FENNER	1920	Duck River	333
Jesse WILLIAMS, jr.	320	Trace Creek	4113
Richard COOK	640	Richland Creek	5037
Isaiah WATKINS	213	Ran. 3, Sec. 21	109
Edwin GWIN	320	White Oak Creek	4231
John MASSEY	50	Trace Creek	5032
Saml. CROCKET	150		
Jackson HULL's heirs	250	White Oak Creek	88
Hillary MORRISS	50	White Oak Creek	4198
Edward KING's heirs	213	Trace Creek	3814
Thos. M'KISSICK	114		200
Edwin GWIN	136		423
Wm. HILL	320	White Oak Creek	772
Jacob GARRISON	640		4179
Moses ELLISON	285	Richland	
Wm. PACOCK	320	Blue Creek	
Phillip DUFF	320	Blue Creek	
Michael DICKSON	360	Blue Creek	
Richard SIMMONS	150	North Blue Creek	
Hezekiah JOHNSTON	204	Hurricane Creek	
Richard BROWN	106	Hurricane Creek	
Joel LEWIS	640	Tennessee River	272
Jos. TILMON	640		1094
W. WILLIAMS	1000	White Oak Creek	2627
Thomas BERRY	247	Tennessee River	1397

(Continued on following page)

143

(Stewart County delinquent tax list continued)

Jas. RICHARD's heirs	247	N. Tennessee River	2029
Martin ARMSTRONG	640	Richland Creek	924
Betsey BARROW	640	Porterfield Creek	774
Abel MUSLANDER	2560	Tennessee River	851
W. WILLIAMS	274	Tennessee River	1321
Jas. LEWIS	640	Trace Creek	
James TUCKER	640	Tennessee River	
James COGHLIN	640		3258
John CASEY	640		1069
Thomas BLOUNT	640		1874
Geo. DOHERTY	640	Tennessee River	434
Robert BROOMFIELD	1000		780
Jos. TILMON	1000		434
John ALLEN	640	Tennessee River	377
Hiram TRAYLOR (sic)	160	Tumblin Creek	
Wm. BROWN	100	Brown Branch	
Wm. GIBSON	150	Blue Creek	
John HUNTER	300	Hurricane Creek	
James GWIN	281	Hurricane Creek	
Preston NUNOC	125	Hurricane Creek	
John WHITE	192	Hurricane Creek	
Richard WHITE	300	Hurricane Creek	
James WILSON	77	Richland Creek	241
Q. H. HAIL	1000	Hurricane Creek	
Benj. SHEPERD	460		
Edmond YARBOROUGH	3860	Saline Creek	
Ezekiel HUTSON's heirs	220	Sec. 4, Ran. 23,	
		Loc. 472, Hurricane	97
Jackson HULL's heirs	140	Leatherwood Creek	88
Nathaniel SKINNER	50		4662
Evan GARKILE	50		4642
James DIXON	108	Richland Creek	241
James MURRAY	100	White Oak Creek	229
Joseph ROBBINS	15	White Oak Creek	4366
Lewis POWERS	100	Blue Creek	4295
Drury OLIVER	40	White Oak Creek	5931
James Cole MONTFLORENCE	640	Trace Creek	223
Jessee WILLIAMS, jr.	325	Trace Creek	413

Wanted, a blacksmith. Thomas E. SUMNER.
  I shall apply to the Commissioner of West Tennessee for a
certificate for 1168 acres, that is part of Grant No. 2555,
dated March 17, 1776, issued to Stockley DONELSON and
William TYRELL as assignees of Llew. John VANEE from North
Carolina. The land conveyed to me by John B. CHEATHAM,
sheriff of Robertson County. Jos. CASTLEBURY.
  On the 27th of October in the town of Nashville, there
will be a public sale directed by the Circuit Court of West
Tennessee of 640 acres, that is the property of Thomas E.

WAGGMAN. The land was orginally granted to William OVERALL, and then was purchased by Thomas WAGGMAN from John LOVE. The property was attached by Marcus HEYLAND, Richardson GALT, Jesse ECHLEBURGER, Thomas DEADERICK, and Isaac SITLER. J. CHILDRESS.

Bledsoe County, Tennessee, August Sessions, 1810. Peter LOONEY reports that the following tracts of land still have unpaid taxes for the years 1809 and 1810. The tracts will be sold on the first Monday in November next at Phillip THURMAN's. Samuel TERRY, c. b. c.

Reputed Owners	Acres
Robert MAITLAND	Lot No. 5, 6, 11
John ARMSTRONG	600
Hensam UMPHRIES	300
Richard H. LOVE	Lot No. 7
Charles I. LOVE and Thomas LYNN	4000
John M'IVER and Wm. I. LOVE	5000
Thomas SWANN and John M'IVER	5000
William D. NEILSON	178
Robert CARTER's heirs	500

The following persons have reported estrays in Wilson County, per Edmund CRUTCHER, d. r. w. c.:

(1) John JAMES, on Spencer's Creek, has taken up an iron grey mare. On August 10, 1810, the mare was given an appraised value of $30.
(2) Leonard H. SIMS, on Fall Creek, has taken up a bay mare. On August 24, 1810, the mare's value is $17.
(3) James CAMPBELL, on Smith's Fork, took up a horse. On August 20, 1810, the horse was valued at $25.
(4) Joseph COLE has taken up a sorrel roan mare. The mare was valued at $50 on September 1, 1810.
(5) William ADAMSON, on Purtie Creek, has taken up an iron grey mare. On August 17, 1810, the mare was appraised at $12.
(6) James THOMPSON, sen., on Smith's Fork, has taken up bay mare. On August 24, 1810, the mare was given an appraised value of $30.
(7) Edmund PARSONS, on Purtie's Creek, took up a horse. The horse's value was $30 on September 2, 1810.
(8) Benjamin CASTLEMAN, on Barton's Creek, has taken up horse. On August 29, 1810, the horse's value is $25.
(9) Samuel HARRIS, on Barton's Creek, took up a mare. On September 10, 1810, the mare's value is $10.
(10) William STACY, on Hancan Creek, has taken up a mare. On September 5, 1810, the mare's value is $50.

October 5, 1810, Vol. ?, No. ?

The following is a list of letters remaining at the post office in Franklin, per Gurdon SQUIRER, a. p. m.: Wm. PEACH,

Dav. P. ANDERSON, Charles ANDERSON, Abner AIKEW, John BURNS, Joseph BURKE, Thomas BERRY, Jennett BLAKELY, Samuel BRADEN, Michael BUNAS, John BARLOW, Bartlet BARHAM, Kinder BAUCEON, Duncan BROWN, Samuel BULL, Stephen BROOKS, John BOWMAN, Wm. CAPLE, James COX, Alex. CLARK, Andrew CUFF, John CHAMP, Wm. M'LAIN, John CHAMP, Julia COLEMAN, Randolph DAVIS, Samuel E. ENGLAND, John DAVIDSON, James DODSON, Samuel EDMONDSON, Wm. M'CLELLAN, Edward ELAM, Arthur FULGHUM, James GRAHAM, Nancy HARTWELL, Clarrisa GRAHAM, John W. HEWLETT, John HANKS, John Jos. LONG, David JONES, Josiah KNIGHT, Allen LEEPER, Donald M'DONALD, Benj. LANCASTER, Nath. LEARD, Joseph MEADOW, John MILLER, Nelly M'MULLEN, Saml. MERRIT, Allen M'LAIN, Isabella MORRES, John MATTHEW, Dav. M'CLELLAN, Jas. NEELY, jr., Isham O'NEAL, Wiley O'NEAL, Richard ORR, Col. Robert PURDY, Jacob PATTON, James PENNEY, Mordiori (sic) PILLOW, Charles SMITH, John PORTER, Fred. PEEBLES, Saml. PERKINS, Benj. RYE, Edward STAPLETON, Absalom RYE, Maj. Gilbert C. RUSSEL, John REID, Joel RIGGS, Dav. RUSSELL, Perren SMITH, Mr. STANLEY, John SHEPERD, Lucy SAUNDERSON, Charles SIMPSON, Jos. TAYLOR, Wm. N. WADDILE, Heydon TILMAN, Leonard TARRANT, John WEBB, O. T. WATKINS, James TURNER, Thos. VANDYKE, John WEBB, Samuel D. WADDILE, John WITHERSPOON, Unit. (sic) WILSON, Gilbert C. WASHINGTON.

The following persons in Bedford County have reported estrays, per Howel DAWDY, r. b. c.:

(1) Levi HORN, near Warner's Ferry, has taken up mare. On August 9, 1810, the mare's value is $18.

(2) Samuel B. HARRIS, on Weakley's Creek, has taken up a brown mare. On August 3, 1810, the mare is given an appraised value of $45.

(3) James HARBISON, on Rock Creek, has taken up a mare. On August 31, 1810, the mare's value is $20.

(4) John LEIPER, on the west fork of Rock Creek, has taken up a bay mare. The mare was appraised at $23 on September 12, 1810.

(5) John SEATT, on the west fork of Rock Creek, took up a bay mare. The appraised value of the mare was placed at $25 on September 10, 1810.

(6) James NEIL, on Rock Creek, has taken up a mare. The mare was valued at $22 on September 12, 1810.

(7) John NEAL, on Rock Creek, has taken up a bay mare. On September 16, 1810, the mare's value was $25.

Norfolk, September 5th. Yesterday Capt. HAYNES commanding the sailing ship Woodrop Sims arrived thirty-five days from Lisbon.

For sale, fancy chairs. Charles M'KERAHAN.

On the 2nd of October, a negro man calling himself SAM was committed to the jail of Davidson County. He says that he belongs Richard BUTLER in Orleans. He is about 18 or 19 years old and was taken up in the Chicksaw Nation. E. D. HOBB, jailor.

On Monday last, Benjamin J. BRADFORD was elected Mayor of Nashville. Felix ROBERTSON, Joseph T. ELLISTON, William EASTIN, Ro. B. CURREY, Jo. DICKENSON and Alex. PORTER were elected as Aldermen.

The following persons have reported estrays in Lincoln County, per Brice M. GARNER for Phillip KOONCE:

(1) Samuel ISAACS, on Mulberry Creek, has taken up a a sorrel mare. On August 16, 1810, the mare was appraised at $25.

(2) Isaac MERONEY, on Nerris' Creek about two miles from Fayetteville, has taken up a bay horse. On September 5, 1810, the horse was valued at $30.

(3) James WILLIAMS, on the Elk River, has taken up a sorrel mare. On September 15, 1810, the mare was appraised at a value of $65.

(4) Caswell BIBEY, on the Elk River, has taken up a bay mare, that was valued at $9.

(5) Joseph DEAM, on the Flint River, has taken up a bay mare. On September 15, 1810, the appraised value of the mare was $30.

I want to forewarn the public against trading for a note in the amount of $25, that was given to Camel DOKE. George W. ROPER.

October 12, 1810, Vol. III, No. CXLII

Maury County, March term, 1810. John SPENCER, sheriff and collector, reports that the following tracts of land still have unpaid taxes for 1809. Joseph B. PORTER.

Reputed Owners	Acres	Situation
John BLAIR	300	Fountain Creek
James CONNER	600	Richland Creek
Martin ARMSTRONG	5000	Grant No. 72
Francis CHILD's heirs	3000	Elk River
John HAYWOOD & Jas. TURNER	600	
John NELSON	5000	Richland Creek
Mch. CAMPBELL & P. PHILLIPS	640	Rutherford Creek
William WALLACE	1800	Fountain Creek

Maury County, Tennessee, March term, 1810. John SPENCER, sheriff and collector, reports that the following tracts of land still have unpaid taxes for 1808 and 1809. The tracts are liable for a double tax.

Reputed Owners	Acres	Situation
John IRWIN	440	
Legt. Henry DICKSON	1500	Duck River
John DICKSON	1000	
Thomas HARRIS	5000	Duck River

(Continued on following page)

147

(Maury County delinquent tax list continued)

Mathew M'CULLY	3200	Rice's Creek
Simon ELLIOTT	1000	
Elizabeth BARROW	640	Porterfield's Creek
David ROSS	600	Duck River
Edmond KIRBY	300	1808 and 1809
Simon ELLIOT's heirs	1000	1808 and 1809
Alexander M'CALL	320	Leiper's Lick
James LEWIS	1400	

October 19, 1810, Vol. III, No. CXLIII
    Caution to the public. Martin PATTERSON, John PATTERSON,
and John BUCHANON, brothers and brother-in-law to my wife,
came in a friendly manner and said that they had lost their
home. Robert PATTERSON, jr. armed with a firelock came to
my house and concealed himself behind a corner, then induced
my wife Jemima to break open my trunk. She left with my
black mare and many other things. I will not pay her debts.
Elisha GOWER.
    The following persons have reported estrays in Maury
County, per Joseph BROWN, r. m. c.:
    (1) John L. WOOD, about fourteen miles above Columbia,
        took up a sorrel mare.
    (2) Robert CAMPBELL, on Rutherford Creek, has taken up
        a bay horse.
    On the 19th, a black horse was stolen from the subscriber
in Mercer County, Kentucky. I believe that the horse was
stolen by Andrew RUNTON. John MEAUX.

October 26, 1810, Vol. III, No. CXLIV
    I will do blue dying. Michael SPAKE.
    Open, a segar (sic) factory. Peter PETROE.
    For sale, a coache. Mr. GOODE.
    The following is a list of letters remining at the post
office in Columbia, per -- B. ESTES, a. p.: Jos. BRUNSTON,
Wm. BREAKIN, Nat. G. BURGEN, Max. BUCHANON, John ATKINSON,
John BARTLET, Alx. BARREN, Duncan BROWN, Ed. J. BERLAY, Jo.
A. CHAPMAN, Jane COOPER, Hugh CAMPBELL, Samuel BEVY, Gabriel
BUTLER, John BLACK, James BRANDON, James BIGHAM, Wm. MARTIN,
Daniel BEELAR, Isham CHRISTIAN, David CAMPBELL, John DRAKE,
Leah DOBBINS, Moses DRIVER, Robt. DONALDSON, James DOBBINS,
Alex. DUGGAR, Alex. DARTON, Nat. DUGLASS, Wm. R. DAVIS, Job
DILL, David DOBINS, Capt. Jo. DRAKE, W. & J. EMERSON, Wm.
FRIERSON, Wm. FULLERTON, Abraham FALLIS, Martha FULTON, John
GREEN, Brice M. GARNER, James GRIMES, John GRIFFIN, Samuel
KRILER, Mead HAIL, Jos. HUEINGSON, Peter HARREL, James MAY,
John HENDERSON, William HOUSE, David HUDSPETH, Wm. JOHNSTON,
Hob. J. HOLLAND, M. HUNNEYCUTT, Jos. JOHNSTON, William KIRK,
John KING, Jos. KIRKPATRICK, Lemuel LINDSEY, Benjamin LOVEL,

Wm. LEWIS, Charles A. LEWIS, Jacob LINDSEY, Robt. LANGFORD,
German LEITER, Richard MILLER, Wm. MASSEY, Jas. MONTGOMERY.
Charles MILLER, Saml. M'COLLUM, Seb. MILLWRIGHT, James REED,
John J. MEKELL, John MEDRICK, James MOORE, Jos. M'LSKEY, Jo.
MONTGOMERY, Robert MATHEWS, Henry NORMAN, Andrew NEELY, Amb.
POWELL, William PHILLIPS, Thomas PARKER, Abner PARTEE, David
PARKER, Hugh PARK, Greenb (sic) ROGERS, Lt. T. RAMSEY, Col.
William SIMS, James SPEER, Reverend J. RECORD, William SIMS,
James STUART, Major Robert STEEL, Cornelius STATER, Thomas
TAYLOR, Captain Robert SCOTT, Theo. TERREY, William THOMAS,
Benj. WARE, W. WARRINGTON, E. S. WHITWORTH, J. and S. WHITE,
Jos. WHITWORTH, S. WITHERSPOON, Peter VISSERY.

I forewarn all persons from signing my name to anything.
Robert RENFROE.

A sorrel horse was found on my plantation on the Upper
Ferry, Nashville. A. H. HARRIS.

In order to do justice to an unfortunate young man's
memory, we the subscribers heard John E. COOK express his
intention to see a certain married woman and we are certain
that the woman was his only object. Samuel S. HALL and
Henry CASTLE, October 15, 1810.

I certify that John E. COOK told me on Monday proceeding
the 3rd, that he was at the house of Mr. DODSON. As he was
going to the house, he spoke to Mrs. DODSON and went into
the house to wait for her return. It was an hour before she
returned. He told me that he was at the same house on
Tuesday evening and did not stay, as there was a young man
with Mrs. DODSON. He gave me to understand several times,
that he thought that from her conduct, that she wanted him
to try her virtue. He had no doubt, that he could succeed.
George MARTIN.

The following persons have reported estrays in Wilson
County, per Edmund CRUTCHER, d. r.:

(1) John BARLOW, on Bradley's Creek, has taken up a
sorrel mare. On September 25, 1810, the mare was
valued at $6.

(2) Peter GRISHAM has taken up a bay mare. The mare
was valued at $15 on October 1, 1810.

(3) W. H. WHITE has taken up a sorrel mare. The mare
was appraised at $15 on October 13, 1810.

(4) Edward DILLARD has taken up a sorrel filly. The
filly was valued at $10 on October 11, 1810.

(5) Wm. CLARK, living at Hart's Ferry on the Cumberland
River, has taken up a brown mare. The mare had a
value of $27.50 on October 6, 1810.

Open for business, a boatyard. W. BARROW.

Owners of stock in the Sumner County cotton factory are
requested to come forward. Henry COOK, cashier.

On the 29th, an invoice of merchandise, that belongs to

149

the late firm of VANCE, KING, & BRADLEY in Montgomey Co., Palmyra, Tennessee. Those interested need to see Samuel VANCE. George SIMPSON, attorney for William TRIGG, exr.

On the 3rd of November, an invoice of merchandise is for sale in Eddyville, Caldwell County, Kentucky. The property belongs to the late firm of VANCE, KING & BRADLEY. Those interested make application to John BRADLEY. Geo. SIMPSON.

November 2, 1810, Vol. III, No. CXLV

New York, September 29th. Yesterday the ship Frances under the command of Capt. TAYLOR arrived twenty-seven days from Grenock.

Rueben PAYNE, on Tuesday evening last, married Cinaarilla BLACKMORE. They are both of this county.

Married on Thursday, T. K. HARRIS to Miss Polly MOORE, the daughter of Rev. MOORE of this county.

Miss Elizabeth E. KENNEDY, the daughter of Robert KENNEDY of Lincoln County, married on Tuesday to Vance GREER.

On the 18th, Daniel M'KISSICK, the clerk of the Circuit Court, married Miss Polly GREER. She is the daughter of the late Andrew GREER of Bedford County.

On Wednesday the 24th, Patton ANDERSON was shot at the Bedford County court house. Perry Green MAGNESS and his sons, Jonathan MAGNESS and David MAGNESS, were apprehended for the homicide. They objected to being tried in Bedford County and the judge ordered that Williamson County be the place of holding trial. Mr. ANDERSON was descended from one of the most respectable families of Virginia.

Henry WARREN, on Mulberry Creek, Lincoln County, has taken up a bay horse, that was valued on October 3, 1810 at $20. Brice N. GARNER, for Phillip KOONCE, ranger.

The following persons have reported estrays in Giles County, per Lewis CLARK:
(1) John FRAISURE, on Blue Creek, has taken up a filly. The filly was appraised at $15 on October 10, 1810.
(2) Isaac REYNOLDS, on Richland Creek, has taken up a horse. The value of the horse was appraised at $75 on October 22, 1810.
(3) Joseph RILEY, Buchannon's Creek, has taken up a bay horse. On October 15, 1810, the horse was given an appraised value of $20.

For rent, a farm. Ellis MADDOX.

MINOR & BOTTS vs. David ROSS, Bedford County. David ROSS is ordered to appear in court on the fourth Monday in April next. Jas. M'KISSICK.

On the 15th of December in the town of Columbia, there will be public sale directed by the court of Maury County of 200 acres, that is the property of Wm. THOMPSON. The land is part of a grant issued on Warrant No. 1053, by the state of North Carolina to Elijah ROBERTSON. The land was taken at the influence of Alexander MONTGOMERY. William BRADSHAW.

November 30, 1810, Vol. III, No. CXLIX
Will all those indebted to Thomas INGRAM, dec., please come forward and settle their accounts. Charles CABINESS.
For sale, assorted merchandise. Addison CARRICK.
Will all those indebted please come forward and settle their accounts. Robert STAINBECK.
On the 12th of January next in the town of Franklin, there will be a public sale directed by the Williamson Co. court of two lots. The property was taken at the influence of Elizabeth WRIGHT, admnx. of John WRIGHT, dec. Wm. HULME.
The barge Lark that is bound for Natchez and New Orleans will take passengers. The barge is to sail between the 15th and 20th of December. Those interested to Richard RAPIER.

December 7, 1810, Vol. III, No. CL
On the 15th of November, John PETTY married Miss Polly BOOTHE. They are both of Hickman County.
On the 29th, Col. Thomas CLINTON died at Dover.
Died in a drunken fit, William HAYS of this county.
Died lately in Kentucky, Mrs. WILLIAMSON, consort of Capt. John S. WILLIAMSON of this town.
On the 19th of January next in the town of Nashville, there will be a public sale directed by the Davidson County court of four town lots and the 60 acres where John BOYD, dec. resided before his death. The property belongs to John BOYD, Harrison BOYD, Richard BOYD, William L. BOYD, George W. BOYD, Jeremiah HINTON and his wife Sally, John L. YOUNG and his wife Nancy. The property was taken at the influence of James HENNEN and William DICKSON. M. C. DUNN, sheriff.
On the fourth Monday in December next, there will be a public sale in the town of Shelbyville, directed by the court of Rutherford County, of 640 acres, that belong to Francis R. NASH, dec. The property was taken by William P. ANDERSON and John STROTHER against Peter LEGRAND, admn. Benjamin BRADFORD, shff.
On the 19th of January next in the town of Nashville, there will be a public sale directed by the Davidson County court of 320 acres, that belong to Frederick PINKLEY. The property was attached by DEADERICK & SOMERVILLE. M.C. DUNN.
On the 19th of January in the town of Nashville, there will be a public sale directed by the Davidson County court of lot no. 34, that is occupied and owned by Bennet SEARCY. The property was taken at the influence of OGDEN & BRUNSON and BUSTARD & EASTIN, John HARRISON, Geo. HOFFMAN against SEARCY as security of Nath. G. CHILDRESS. M. C. DUNN.
Mr. BRADFORD, on the 11th of October, an account of the

151

death of John E. COOK was published. It did not happen as you stated in your article. On the previous Sunday night after I put my children and my two sisters to bed, I went to have a conversation with my sister, that lives 120 yards from my house. After staying at my sister's for about an hour, I returned to find him at my house. On Tuesday, John E. COOK came in and said there was so much company at home, that he had started to go to Mr. JOHNSTON's to stay all night. I told him that Mr. DODSON was not home and that he could not stay here with no man at home. He left. Then on Wednesday night, he came back after I went to bed. He came in the house and I caught holt (sic) of a large smooth bore gun and fired. He cried out and fell. I ran to my sister's and Mr. JOHNSTON's family. Elizabeth DODSON.

Achilles COX did on the 14th make a deed of gift to his two sons John COX and James H. COX of his two negro girls MOURNING and AGGY and a number of livestock.

December 14, 1810, Vol. III, No. CLI

Four sheep strayed October last. Joseph ENGLEMAN.

Jacob SILVERTOOTH, on Mulberry Creek, Lincoln County, has taken up a sorrel horse. Brice M. GARNER for Philip KOONCE, ranger.

On the 19th of January next in the town of Nashville, there will be a public sale directed by the Davidson County court of 160 acres, that is the property of Isaac CURRY. The property adjoins James BRADLEY and Samuel M'MURRY. M. C. DUNN, sheriff.

On the 19th of January next in the town of Nashville, there will be a public sale directed by the Davidson County court of 640 acres, that is the property of Benjamin SEWELL. The land is occuppied by Benjamin SEWELL and Thomas SEWELL. The property was taken at the influence of Elishu S. HALL & Co. John C. HALL, de. shff.

December 21, 1810, Vol. III, No. CLII

The following persons have reported estrays in Wilson County, per Edmund CRUTCHER, d. r.:
    (1) Ezekiel LINDSEY, living on M'Neely's Bend, has taken up a brown mare. On October 15, 1810, the mare was valued at $20.
    (2) William STACEY, on Hurricane Creek, has taken up a bay horse. On October 22, 1810, the horse was appraised at a value of $10.
    (3) Thomas CYPRET has taken up a bay mare. The mare was valued at $1250 on October 30, 1810.
    (4) Thomas CARVER, near Cedar Lick, has taken up a chesnut sorrel mare. The mare was appraised at a value of $12 on November 7, 1810.

(5) Seth HARRISON has taken up a sorrel mare. The mare was valued at $45 on November 19, 1810.

(6) Henry CARSON, on Cedar Creek, has taken up a bay mare. On November 21, 1810, the mare was appraised in the amount of $60.

(7) William DOANL, on Spring Creek, has taken up a bay horse. On November 16, 1810, the horse was valued in the amount of $25.

(8) Thomas BLACK, on Bradley's Creek, has taken up a bay horse. On November 21, 1810, the horse was appraised at a value of $8.

(9) John HILL, on Spring Creek, took up a bay horse. On November 19, 1810, the horse was valued at $5.

(10) Jeremiah TUCKER, on Spring Creek, has taken up a sorrel horse. The horse was given an appraised value of $10 on December 12, 1810.

On the 10th, a negro man was committed to the Nashville jail. He was taken up on the Tennessee Ridge, Chickasaw Nation. He says that his name is GEORGE and that he is the property of Lewis CABELL near Greenville in the Mississippi territory.

I purchased 150 acres from Hugh STEPHENSON for $1000. The land was less than the amount that he said. I forewarn all persons from trading or taking assignments on a note in the amount of $500, payable on the 25th of December, for said property. Henry FEATHERSTONE, sen.

December 28, 1810, Vol. III, No. CLIII

Married on Sunday the 16th, Ferdinand Rionman TURNER to Miss Susanna RULE. They are both of this county.

Died on Sunday last, John CHILDRESS, sen., a citizen of this county.

The following persons have reported estrays in Lincoln County, per Brice M. GARNER for Phillip KOONCE, ranger:

(1) Joseph GARDNER, on Swan Creek, has taken up a bay mare. On November 27, 1810, the mare was appraised in the amount of $25.

(2) John WHITAKER, jr., on Mulberry Creek, has taken up sorrel mare. On November 27, 1810, the mare was appraised at a value of $25.

(3) Jacob BUCKLY, on Richland Creek, has taken up a bay mare. On November 18, 1810, the mare was given an appraised value of $25.

(4) Richard WYATT, on Swan Creek, has taken up a horse. On December 3, 1810, the horse was valued at $25.

(5) Matthew BARBA, on the south side of the Elk River, has taken up a grey mare. On December 3, 1810, the mare was given an appraised value of $30.

(6) Joseph SUMNER, on Cane Creek, has taken up a sorrel

horse. The horse was appraised on November 30, 1810 at a value of $30.
(7) Joseph DUMROLE, on Hannah's Ford, has taken up a colt. On December 17, 1810, the colt's value is $8.

January 4, 1811, Vol. III, No. CLIV
    The following is a list of letters remaining at the post office in Franklin, per Gurdon SQUIRER, a. p. m.: And. CUFF, Joseph ANTHONY, James BLAKELY, Wm. BLAKELY, Bartlet BASHAM, Eliza BRUFF, Jeremiah BURNES, Frederic BROWDER, Benj. BROWN, Adam BOYET, Edward BEVILL, Joshua CANNON, David CARTER, Joel CASEY, Joseph CARSON, Alex. CLARK, And. CUFF, John DEPRIEST, John DOAK, Moses CURNEY, Nelson CHAPMAN, Thos. EVANS, John GHOLSON, George ELIOTT, Elizabeth GOWER, Samuel GLASS, Thos. GILLESPIE, James HOURS, Hardy HIGHTOWER, Wm. HESS, John HILL or John AUSTIN, Jos. HUTCHINSON, Stephen HARGAVE, William JOHNSON, Francis HALL, Thos. H. JENKINS, Ezekiah INNAN, And. KEIGLER, Charles JOHNSON, David JONES, Sally KIRLEY, Henry LESTER, Nath. LAIRD, Elizabeth LAKE, Kinchen MASSENGALE, Wm. THOMPSON, Sally MERRITT, John M'MEEN, James MANS, Pallace NEELY, James NEELY, James NEELY, jr., Peter PINKERTON, Henry PETTEY, Joseph POTTS, Alex. ROGERS, John RUSSEL, Ann WILSON, Thos. E. SUMNER, Turner SAUNDERS, Richard SAMPSON, Benjamin STOKES, Geo. SIMPSON, Saml. SHELBURNE, Isaac TARKINTON, Jas. WILSON, Harden TILMON, Elijah TABER, Phineas THOMAS, Johnson WOOD, John WATSON, Isaac WRIGHT, Richd. WALKER, John WEST, Wm. WADDLE.
    Married on Tuesday last, Ruben BIGGS to Miss Betsy VICK. They are both of this county.
    Died on Friday the 28th, William Thomas TUNSTAIL, age 7. He was the son of James TUNSTAIL of Robertson County.
    Francis JOHNSON, attorney at law, has removed to the town of Nashville.
    Open a house of private entertainment. Joseph WALLACE, Sumner County.
    The following persons have reported estrays in Rutherford County, per N. B. ROSE, d. r. r. c.:
    (1) Joseph DUNKIN, on Bradley's Fork, has taken up a black mare. On December 4, 1810, the mare's value was appraised at $8.
    (2) Clarissa ROSHAUND, in Jefferson, has taken up a sorrel mare. On December 15, 1810, the mare had a value of $25.
    (3) Richard STEPHENS, on Bradley's Fork, has taken up a sorrel horse. On December 10, 1810, the horse was appraised at $20.
    (4) David CORDEN, on the west fork of the Stones River, has taken up a bay mare. On December 3, 1810, the mare was appraised at a value of $12.

(5) Isaac BENSHAW, near Ready's Mill, has taken up a
bay mare. On December 19, 1810, the mare was given
an appraised value of $10.
(6) Thomas GORDEN, near Burnett's Mill, has taken up a
bay mare. On November 19, 1810, the mare was given
an appraised value at $10.
(7) William UMPHRIES, on the west fork of the Stones
River, has taken up a sorrel horse. The horse was
appraised at $10 on November 19, 1810.
(8) Joshua ZACHARY, on the Stones River, has taken up
sorrel mare. On November 10, 1810, the mare was
appraised at $30.
(9) John BROTHERS, near Miller's Mill, has taken up a
chesnut sorrel mare. On December 10, 1810, the
mare was appraised at a value of $24.
(10) John WALDEN, junr., on Hurricane Creek, has taken
up a sorrel mare. On November 24, 1810, the mare
was appraised at $25.

On the 23th of February in Fayetteville, there will be a
public sale directed by the court of Smith County of 2260
acres, that is the property of John SWAN. The property was
taken at the influence of Daniel ALEXANDER. Cornelius
SLATER, sheriff.

On the 25th of February in Fayetteville, there will be a
public sale directed by the Jackson County court of 5000
acres, that is the property of Spencer GRIFFIN. The land
was granted under the name of PEDDY. The property was taken
at the influence of Samuel TERRY. Cornelius SLATER, shff.

On the 25th of February in Fayetteville, there will be a
public sale directed by the court of Lincoln County of 100
acres, that is the property of Thomas TROTTER. The property
was taken at the influence of John R. BEDFORD. Cornelius
SLATER, sheriff.

The following persons have reported estrays in Bedford
County, per Howel DAWDY, r. b. c.:
(1) Robert MUGHES, at Noah's Fork, has taken up a bay
horse, that was valued at $27.
(2) John FRAZER, on Scull Camp, has taken up a sorrel
mare. On November 10, 1810, the mare was appraised
at a value of $30.
(3) ---- GARNER has taken up a sorrel horse.
(4) Joseph BOYD, on the Duck River, has taken up a bay
mare, that was valued at $9.50.

Wanted, an apprentice for the blacksmith business. James
PORTERFIELD.

For sale or rent, the house I occuppy. S. CANTRELL, jr.

January 11, 1811, Vol. III, No. CLV
Wanted, salt petre. Wilkins TANNEHILL.

Two negro men ranaway from William EDWARD, York District, South Carolina. They are ADAM, 23 or 24 years and CATO, 20 or 21 years old. They are making for Black Fox Camp or the Indiana Territory.

The horse Young Diomede will stand this season at Robert HEWITT's. Jesse WESTMORELAND.

The following persons have reported estrays in Bedford County, per (no ranger given):

    (1) Sion RECORD, on Rock Creek, has taken up a blue dapple horse. On December 17, 1810, the horse was appraised at $13.

    (2) Richard MARTAIN, on Powel's Creek, has taken up a sorrel mare. On December 13, 1810, the mare was appraised at $30.

    (3) Abraham BYLER, on the Duck River, has taken up a black filly. On December 22, 1810, the filly was appraised at $13.

There was a letter to the editor from Tom RAKISH.

I want to forewarn the public from trading for two notes given to James CURTIS on July 24, 1810. Wm. ROREX.

I want to forewarn the public from trading for or taking assignments against an obligation given to James WARRICK sometime in January or February, 1807, for a barrel of whiskey. John EUBANKS.

A saddler's shop is opened for business in the house formerly occuppied by Ellis MADDOX. Thomas WILLIAMSON.

January 25, 1811, Vol. III, No. CLVII

    Cash for tallow. Joseph ENGLEMAN.

    For rent, 100 acres. John M'NAIRY.

    For sale, an assortment of merchandise. Addison CARRICK.

    For sale, a tract of land adjoining Capt. J. HOOGGET, near Clover Bottom. Frederick STUMP, White Creek.

February 1, 1811, Vol. III, No. CLVIII

    Wanted, cotton to be delivered in Nashville. Wm. CARROLL.

    The Legislature of Georgia has granted to Zachariah SIM a loan in the amount of $3000 to complete his paper mill.

The following persons have reported estrays in Lincoln County, per Brice M. GARNER for Philip KOONCE, ranger:

    (1) John BLAND, on the Coldwater, has taken up a bay horse colt. On December 29, 1810, the colt's value was appraised at $6.

    (2) Samuel VANCE, on Snow Creek, has taken up a brown bay horse. On January 2, 1811, the horse was given an appraised value of $11.

    (3) George PARKS, on Loss Creek, has taken up a filly. On Janaury 15, 1811, the filly was valued at $20.

Married at Hendersonville by Reverd. Thomas B. CRAIGHEAD,

Col. Albert RUSSEL, of Williamson County, to Mrs. Lockey HENDERSON, of Sumner County.

February 8, 1811, Vol. III, No. CLVII

Baltimore, December 15th. Capt. CHILD, of the schooner Sarah Lansden, arrived here from Lisbon.

For sale, pork. John HARDEMAN, Williamson County.

Married on the 13th, Miss Eliza CHILDRESS, the daughter of Stephen CHILDRESS in Williamson County, to William HULME, sheriff of the same county.

Married on the 31st, Thomas HITER, of Franklin, to Miss Sally M'CRORY. She is the daughter of Col. Thomas M'CRORY, of Williamson County.

For sale, a flatbottom boat. C. M'DANIEL.

The following persons have reported estrays in Wilson County, per Edmund CRUTCHER, d. r.:

(1) James THOMAS, on Smith's Fork, has taken up a mare. On November 27, 1810, the mare was valued at $20.

(2) Phillip HOWELL, on Cedar Lick, has taken up a black horse. On December 17, 1810, the horse was valued in the amount of $22.

(3) George SMITH, on Drake's Lick, has taken up a bay mare. On December 22, 1810, the mare was appraised at a value of $10.

(4) William CRABTREEE, on Drake's Creek, has taken up a horse. On December 22, 1810, the horse was valued in the amount of $20.

(5) William M'NEELY, on the Cumberland River, has taken up a sorrel mare. On December 27, 1810, the mare was appraised at a value of $30.

(6) John GOODLOE, on Cedar Creek, has taken up a sorrel mare. On January 7, 1811, the mare was given an appraised value of $25.

For sale, appels (sic), cider, beer, and glasses. Samuel HAMILTON.

On the 16th of March next, there will be a public sale directed by the court of Rutherford County of 121 acres, that is the property of James CLEMENT and Thomas CLEMENT. The land was taken at the influence of John ANDERSON. Wm. SMITH, d. shff.

For sale, 640 acres. Isaac SHELBY.

We the undersigned living in Boteourt (sic) County, Va. do declare, that the stud horse Volunteer has stood as a covering horse in our neighborhood. The horse is the property of Ralph CRABB, which he purchased from John TAYLOR of Mt. Airy. Jas. LOCKHART; And. HAMILTON; Thos. M. FANNIN; Jas. KYLE; Jas. ROWLAND; Gen. HANCOCK; Jas. BRECKENRIDGE; H. BOYER; Jas. MITCHELL; Matt. HARVEY; Matthew WILSON; William LEWIS; Sam. LEWIS; Saml. WILSON; T. V. S. BURWELL.

Baltimore, December 15th. The schooner Washington under the command of Capt. NOYES arrived 40 days from Lisbon.

The following is a list of letters remaining at the post office in Jefferson: David ABBOTT, Francis ALEXANDER, James BURGE, Frederick BARFIELD, Nancy BEAVERS, John BANKHEAD, Wm. BRICHEATI, Thomas BEAVERS, Beel BISHOP, Joseph BOWMAN, John DAVIDSON, Frederick BARFIELD, Archibald BAYN, Alx. CARMIKLE, Theophlius A. CANNON, Charles CAMPBELL, Geo. BRAWNING, David B. CARNS, David CLARK, John DAVIDSON, Henry DAVIS, Wm. DUKE, James DENARE, Daniel DAVALT, Thos. DUNN, Thos. ESERIDGE, Wm. GOWEN, Daniel ELANE, John FLEMING, Absalom FRY, John FAGINS, Elizabeth FAIRFAX, George GRAY, Wm. GRIFFIN, Edward GREGORY, Pleasant HENDERSON, George W. HENDERSON, Jonathan HAMPTON, Thomas HOPKINS, Joseph HASTINGS, Dibba HATTEN, Elijah HILL, James HARRISON, David IRWIN, Edward JOHNSTON, Thomas JOYCE, Joshua JOHNSTON, David JONES, Wm. KROWELL, Wilson KERR, Levy LAWLER, Dr. Charles KAVENAUGH, Jos. M'REYNOLDS, Thomas REDY, James MONTGOMERY, Jos. M'LAUGHLIN, Jos. M'CLESKY, Humphrey NELSON, Wm. MOORE, Dav. M'CRORY, George MOORE, John PEACOCK, Charles READY,John RABUCK, John RANDOLPH, Thomas RUCKER, Wm. RANSOM, Sam. RICHARDSON, Timothy ROOK, Thomas REDY, Andrew RENOLD, Peter READE, Benj. SHEPLEY, Wm. THRET, Thomas TABB, Daniel TRAVERS, Benj. TALIAFERRO, Jacob VANRAN, John WADDEL, Jacob VANZANT, Wm. WHITE, Jos. WHITSETT, Saml. WILSON, John WALLACE.

The following persons have reported estrays in Bedford County, per Howel DAWDY, r. b. c.:

(1) Thomas GREER, on Sugar Creek, has taken up a grey horse. On January 11, 1811, the horse was given an appraised value of $45.

(2) Christopher SHAW, on the Duck River near Pharr's Mill, has taken up a bay horse. The horse was given an appraised value of $20.

(3) Baxter RAGSDALE, on War Trace, has taken up a stud colt. On January 27, 1811, the colt was given an appraised value of $15.50.

(4) David YEARY, on Noah's Fork, has taken up a mare. On January 29, 1811, the mare was valued at $12.50.

(5) James CHENAULT, on Noah's Fork, has taken up a sorrel mare. On January 22, 1811, the mare's value was appraised at $20.

(6) Timothy CARREL, on the Duck River, has taken up a sorrel mare. On January 26, 1811, the mare's value was appraised at $20.

In Shelbyville, there will be a public sale on the 23rd of March of 500 acres, that is the property of John DRAKE. The property was taken at the influence of SINDENBERGER and HENRY. John SINGLETON, deputy sheriff.

The partnership of E. BENOIT and Henry WYAND is hereby dissolved by mutual consent. E. BENOIT and Henry WYAND.

A negro man called ABRAHAM ranaway from the subscriber on Mill Creek, Davidson County. He is 28 or 29 years old, and 5 ft. tall. He has worked the town of Nashville and at the nailing business for three years. He will aim for Natchez, as Jas. RUSSEL took a woman, that he called a wife. John TOPP.

On the 2nd of February in the town of Lebanon, there will be a public sale directed by the court of Wilson County of 200 acres, that is the property of Thomas MITCHELL. The land is north of Alx. M'CULLOCK and west of Jno. R. ERWIN. The tract was granted to Harrison PARSONS. The land was taken at the instance of John WALLACE. Wm. SMITH, d. s.

Reward $20. Ranaway from the subscriber in Williamson County on the 2nd of February, a negro man called PETRO. He is about 23 years old and is 5 ft., 6 or 7 in. tall. The reward will be paid by Moses CHAMBERS or the subscriber. Joseph HARDEWAY.

For rent, the Stone Tavern. Jno. GORDON.

The Talbot Hotel is open in Nashville. Clayton TALBOT.

For sale, good pork. John HARDEMAN, Williamson County.

I will petition the Court of Pleas and Quarter Sessions in Columbia, Maury County on the third Monday in September next for a partition of a tract on the Tombigby. The land was granted by North Carolina to MARTIN, by him devised to Pleasant HENDERSON, Thomas SEARCY, Alexander MARTIN and myself. A. M. ROGER.

February 22, 1811, Vol. III, No. CLVX
On the 15th, Le-- PERKINS, daughter of Major Jo-- PERKINS of Williamson County, died. She was 13 years old.

Maj. Abram MAURY will run for public office.

On the fourth Monday in March next, there will be sale directed by the Rutherford County of 140 acres, that is the property of Anderson POWELL. The land was attached by Jesse GEORGE. Benj. BRADFORD, sheriff.

On the 6th of April in the town of Franklin, there will be a public sale directed by the court of Williamson County of 87 acres, that is the property of Nathan CHAMBERLIN and William M'COY. Wm. HULME, sheriff.

On the 6th of April next in the town of Franklin, there will be a public sale directed by the court of Williamson county of 3840 acres, that is the property of John PARKER. The land was conveyed by D. STEWART to said PARKER, warrant no. 4151. The land was attached by Tho. GIBSON. Wm. HULME.

There is a reward offered for PETER, that ranaway from the subscriber in Willimson County. He is about 30 years old and is 5 ft., 10 in. tall. Michael SCALES.

March 1, 1811, Vol. III, No. CLVXI
The following persons have reported estrays in Rutherford County, per N. B. ROSE, d. r. c.:
(1) Samuel BELL, near Wright's Mill, took up a mare.
(2) Anderson BRUCE, near Fox Camp, took up a filly.
(3) Mathy BRUCE, near Fox Camp, took up a sorrel horse.
(4) Isreal GABLE, near Fox Camp, took up a bay mare.
(5) Samuel M'BRIDE, on the Stones River, has taken up a sorrel horse.
(6) Richard BARGE, on the Stones River, took up a mare.
(7) Hance HAMILTON has taken up a black mare.
(8) Adam RAMER, near Ready's Mill, took up a horse.
(9) Wilson KARE, on the Stones River above Jefferson, has taken up a black mare.
(10) Anderson NUNNLEY, near Bradley's Mill, has taken up sorrel yearling colt.
(11) John NEAL, Hurricane Creek, took up a sorrel mare.
(12) Thomas NOX, near Bradley's Mill, took up a filly.
(13) John MERIDY, near Bradley's Mill, took up a mare.
(14) Isaac RENSHAW, near Ready's Mill, has taken up a grey mare.
(15) Thomas CHAMBERLAIN, Stones River, took up a horse.
(16) John CLAXTON, near Fox Camp, took up a bay mare.
(17) Samuel CAMPBELL, Stones River, took up a mare.
The Grand Jury at Washington indicted John RANDOLPH for assaulting Mr. ALSTON.
For hire, several negroes. Christopher STUMP or Lemuel T. TURNER.
The following persons were mentioned in the Treasurer's Report in Nashville: J. DEATHERAGE, D. MOORE, Henry GUTHRIE, C. STUMP, Josiah MULLEN, I. METCALF, W. RUTHERFORD, James A. STURGES, Moses EAKIN, John HARRISON, Edward D. HOBBS.
The following persons were members of the Knox County Grand Jury of the Circuit Court: Jeremiah JACK, Foreman; Asa CHAPMAN; William BELL; John WEBB; Julian FRAZIER; William John HUBBS; Joseph ROGERS; Beriah FRAZIER; John MEEK; David AYRES; John BAYTERS; Mor. YARNELL.

March 8, 1811, Vol. III, No. CLVXII
The Princess Charlotte Packet was involved in a battle with a French Privateer. The following persons were aboard: Mr. ILLIS; Rev. CORREA, portugese priest; W. DUKE; W. CADE; Capt. STISTED, 13th Dragoons; M. MACOMB; John DUPEN; John JOHNS; J. DREWLY.
On the 28th on Thursday night, Randal M'GAVOCK married Miss ROGERS.
Married on Wednesday last, James S. CLEM, of Franklin, married Miss Mary Ann Caroline DEADERICK, daughter of Thomas DEADERICK of this town.

For rent, 100 acres near Geo. ROBERTSON's. John M'NAIRY.
Benjamin PARRY, on New Hope, Bucks County, Pennsylvania,
has invented a machine for drying corn.

March 15, 1811, Vol. III, No. CLVXIII
Will all those indebted to the estate of William CORBIT,
dec., please come forward. David BEATY, adm.
Reward $10. A grey mare strayed or was stolen from the
subscriber on Richland Creek, tweleve miles above Pulaski.
Stephen ANDERSON, Giles County.
Williamson County, Tennessee, January Sessions, 1811. Wm.
HULME, sheriff and collector, reports that the following
tracts of land still have unpaid taxes for 1810. The land
will be sold in Franklin on the first Monday in November
next. N. P. HARDEMAN, clerk.

Reputed Owners	Acres	Situation
John DAVIS	362	
Thomas BLOUNT	3642	Arrington's Creek
John GILLISPIE	323	
John CRAWFORD	137	Big Harpeth
ALLEN & BURTON	lot	Two
Nathaniel ARMSTRONG	160	
William ALLEN	lot	Two
William HESS	lot	1 white & black
James D. MIAM	lot	Two
Samuel RYAN	120	
Samuel JACKSON	662	
Guilford D. READ	1844	
Thomas H. JONES	1028	

The following persons of Nashville have attested to the
pedigree of the celebrated horse Royalist: Robert C. FOSTER,
John BRADLEY, Wm. W. SEARCY, Anderson SEARCY, John GRIFFIN,
Wm. A. SUBLETT, Alexander CARMICHAL, Mark MITCHELL, James
PHILLIPS, John COFFEE, Blackman COLEMAN, James BRIGHT, John
STROTHER, John B. HOGG, James L. ARMSTRONG, Robert B. CURRY,
Benjamin JOSTIN, Thos. A. CLAIBORNE, Anthony FOSTER, Joseph
GREEN, Alexander HUNTER, John BRAHAN, Wm. RICKARD, Joseph
PARK, Wm. T. LEWIS, John SHUTE, Thomas TALBOT, Francis MAY,
Elihu S. HALL, Wm. LYTLE, jr., Isaac SITTLER, Howel TATUM,
Wm. SMITH, Alexander EWING, James JACKSON, James HOOD, Wm.
NASH, Washington JACKSON, Donalson CAFFERY, Bennit SEARCY,
George M. DEADERICK, Stephen CANTRELL, junr., Robert SEARCY,
George BELL, John CHILDRESS, Isaac SHELBY, Alexander PORTER,
John B. CRAGHEAD, Isaac TAYLOR, junr., John M'NAIRY, John W.
CLAY, John BAIRD, Willis R. SMITH, Samuel FINNEY, Wm. POLK,
James HART, John HOGGATT, John M. GOODLOE, Andrew JACKSON,
R. W. HART, Thomas OVERTON, Wm. DICKSON.
The celebrated running horse Wonder will stand this
season at my stable in Franklin. David DUNN.

I have opened a house of private entertainment. Ephraim PARHAM, Fayetteville.

Reward $20. Two apprentice boys have runaway from the subscriber. John FORD is 17 years old, slender made and is 5 ft., 11 in. tall. John MARTIN is 21 years old, stout made, and is 5 ft., 8 or 9 in. tall. Moses EAKIN.

The public is forewarned against buying 5000 acres, that was entered in the name of Martin ARMSTRONG in the office of J. ARMSTRONG. The land issued on warrant no. 1202 belongs to William and Charles POLK and the heirs of George DOHERTY. William CHRISTMAS does not have permission to divide this land into small warrants.

The following persons are attesting to the pedigree of the running horse Collection: Lemuel KENNEDY, j. p.; John W. CLAY, Davidson County; John HAYWOOD; Wm. CARNAL, Capt. of Cavalery; Luk CROSS, j. p.; John SPELL, Pitt County, North Carolina; James JOHNSTON, Pitt County, North Carolina; John CALLAND, Tarborough, North Carolina; Robt. WILLIAMS, N. C.

March 22, 1811, Vol. III, No. CLVXIV

A patent for a washing machine is held by E. F. HILL, of New York. G. POYZER.

My wife Polly THURMOND, formerly Polly SIMPSON (divorce), and primarily Polly HOWELL, has left my bed with out just cause. She is the daughter of Josiah HOWELL of Smith Co. I will not pay her debts. John G. THURMOND, March 7, 1811.

My wife Martha has left my bed with out just cause. John MUNHELD.

Reward $4. A sorrel mare on September 30, 1809 strayed or was stolen in Nashville. J. BRYSON.

The following persons have reported estrays in Bedford County, per H. DAWDY:
  (1) Thomas PATTON has taken up a sorrel filly. The filly was valued at $18 on February 2, 1811.
  (2) Isaac BRINCE, on Garrison Fork, has taken up a bay horse. On February 2, 1811, the horse was given an appraised value of $3.
  (3) John ROSS has taken up a chesnut sorrel mare. The mare was valued at $16 on February 2, 1811.
  (4) Timothy SUG, on War Trace, has taken up a filly. On February 3, 1811, the filly's value was $15.

I will teach the art of dancing. Charles GUDRAIN.

Rosanna M'INTOSH made a statement concerning her joining the Shakers at their town in Warren County, Kentucky.

March 29, 1811, Vol. III, No. CLVXV

For sale, a new gig. William WALLACE.

On the first Monday in April next, Rev. Gideon BLACKBURN will open Harpeth Academy. John H, EASON, sec.

For sale, land in Williamson County. Thos. E. SUMNER.
Open for business, a boatyard. James VANCE.
The following persons have reported estrays in Lincoln
County, per (no ranger given):
  (1) David HOWELL, on Stewart's Creek, has taken up a
       brown horse. On February 1, 1811, the horse was
       appraised at a value of $20.
  (2) Jacob GILHAM, on Swan Creek, has taken up a sorrel
       mare. On January 11, 1811, the mare was given an
       appraised value of $14.

April 2, 1811, Vol. III, No. CLXVI
  The following is a list of Acts passed at the 3rd Session
of the 11th Congress:
  (1) An Act for the relief of George ARMROUD.
  (2) An Act to change the name of Lewis GRANT to Lewis
       Grant DAVIDSON.
  (3) An Act to compensate John Eugene LEITSEDORFER for
       service at Tripoli.
  (4) An Act to discharge Nathaniel FOSDICK from prison.
  (5) An Act for the relief of John MACNAMARA.
I want to purchase a negro woman. Rueben PAYNE.

April 9, 1811, III, No. CLXVII
  The following is a list of letters remaining at the post
office in Franklin on April 1, 1811, per Gurdon SQUIER, a.
p. m.: Nath. ALDERIDGE, John ALEXANDER, James ALLISAN, Adam
BOYER, Fredk. BRAWDER, Fairfield BARNES, Joseph BURNES, John
BLYTHE, William BYRNE, Bartlet BASHAM, Thos. BARNET, Samuel
BITTICK, Duncan BROWN, Samuel BARKER, Moses CHAMBERS, James
CLEM, Robert C. CRAWFORD, Thos. CUMMINS, James CAVENDER, Jo.
K. CAMPBELL, Alexander CLARK, John DUNN, Thos. DAVIS, James
DEFRIESE, John P. ELLIOTT, Steph. ELAM, Sampson EDWARD, Joel
FITZ, Thomas EVANS, Samuel EASTIS, Peter FULKERSON, Neilson
FIELDS, John GHANON, Benj. GOLSAN, James GRIER, John HILL,
John GRAY, John GRIFFITH, James GARDINER, D. GEREMIAN, Thos.
A. HARRIS, Joseph HOWELL, Elijah HARLAN, Daniel HAMER, Thos.
A. JONES, George HUNT, Henry INMAN, Henry JACKSAN, Samuel
JACKSON, George KINNARD, Josiah KNIGHT, Richard LOCK, Martha
LITTLE, William LINSTER, Elizabeth LAKE, William LEWIS, John
M'SWAIN, Chas. KAVANAUGH, Moses LINDSEY, Jesse M'RAY, Saml.
MORTON, Jesse B. HORTON, Charles MURPHEY, Wm. M'KENRIE, And.
M'CORKLE, James M'QUIRE, Thos. MILLER, Mary Ann NEAL, James
PUGH, Wm. NALL, James PUGH, Wm. PRICE, Arch. PATTER, Horatio
PETTUS, Thos. POWEL, John POTTS, Daniel PATE, Benj. RUSSEL,
Geo. W. PARSONS, Aaron RUNNOLDS, Hen. RUTHERFORD, John REID,
Absalom RYE, Solomon ROBERTS, John RACHFORK, Osburn RIVERS,
Edward SCRUGGS, David SPOON, Stephen SMITH, Abram SCOTT, Wm.
WADOLE, James SHORTER, Henry SCALES, Geo. SIMPSON, Wm. WALL,

Joel SHERWOOD, Thos. SIMMONS, Thos. E. SUMNER, James TERRIL, Wm. THOMPSON, Josiah TAKINGTON, John TANKERSLEY, Wm. WADOLE, James WILLIAMSON, Robert WOLF, Samuel WILLIAMS, Langhorn T. WALTON, Lewis WOODARD, Jane L. WOODS, Elisha WILLIAMS.

I am open for the clock, watch-making, and silversmith business in Gallatin. D. H. WHIPPLE.

April 16, 1811, Vol. III, No. CLXVIII

Reward $30. There is a reward for the return of three Virginia Bank notes. David C. SNOW.

Rev. Finis EWING will preach at CASTLEMAN's on the 23rd.

Carthage, April 5th. Armstead STUBBLEFIELD and Carey BIBB were discharged fron the Circuit Court on the charge of forgery. Alexander HENDERSON was rebound to the next court. John LOONEY was rebound for an appearance. Robert W. ROBERTS and Adam DALE gave oaths at the trial.

The following persons have reported estrays in Wilson County, per Edmund CRUTCHER, d. r. w. c.:

(1) John FERRINGTON, on Spring Creek, has taken up a bay mare. On January 29, 1811, the mare was given an appraised value of $18.

(2) James HICKS has taken up a sorrel mare. The mare was valued at $15 on February 21, 1811.

(3) Jonathan DOWNEY, on the Cumberland River at Stewart Ferry, has taken up a sorrel horse. The horse was appraised at $15 on March 2, 1811.

(4) John CARRY has taken up a black horse. The horse was appraised at $2 on March 2, 1811.

(5) Joham (sic) WEBB has taken up a bay mare. The mare was appraised at $15 on March 2, 1811.

(6) William RICHARDS, on Smith Fork, has taken up a sorrel horse. On March 23, 1811, the horse's value was appraised at $18.50.

(7) William WARREN has taken up two fillies. They were valued at $20 each on March 24, 1811.

(8) Ezekiel LINDSEY, on the Cumberland River, has taken up a sorrel mare. On March 26, 1811, the mare was appraised at a value of $20.

(9) Joshua TAYLOR, on Round Lick, has taken up a sorrel horse. On March 30, 1811, the horse's value is $15.

I am open for the tayloring (sic) business. A.M. OSBURN.

George KEESEE states for the benefit of the public, that his consumptionwas cured by Dr. J. ALLEN of Sumner County.

Reward $13.50. There is a reward for the return of an order, that was lost on the 12th, that is on John WILLIAMSON as Judge Advocate for the 21st Regiment. Joseph WRIGHT.

In a letter from Mr. DEBROCOR, of Mobile, states that the Brig Salesby that was consigned to the house of John FORBES & Co. of Pensacola, was stopped by the British Fleet.

Jeremiah PERRY vs. Stephen BEST, in Equity. Stephen BEST is not an inhabitant of Tennessee. He is ordered to appear in court on the 3rd Monday in August next in McMinnville. J. HENDERSON, c. w. c.

April 30, 1811, Vol. III, No. CLXX
The following is a list of letters remaining at the post office in Jefferson on April 1, 1811, per J. SPENCE, p. m.: Wm. P. ANDERSON, John BANKHEAD, David BLALOCK, Wm. BUCKNER, Benj. BRADFORD, Abner CHAPPELL, John D. COOK, James CRAIG, John DAVIS, Tilmon DIXON, Dan. C. DIXON, Thos. DUNN, Luckett DAVIS, James DOREN, Henry DAIS, Mordi. EDWARDS, Wash. GREY, Thomas GREER, Peter GARRISON, Benj. HANCOCK, Jas. HARRISON, James HENDERSON, Pleasant HENDERSON, William HALL, Harrison HINSON, Charles HOLDEN, William LAW, Mordicai LILLARD, Miss LACK, Doct. LAWRENCE, Bird NANCE, Thos. NASH, Richard PRICE, David NARVILLE, John PEACOCK, Osborn RIVES, Gordon RIDEOUT, Wm. RANSAM, Daniel REEL, Roderick RAWLINGS, Benj. RIDDLE, J. STROTHER, Wm. SMITH, Miss B. SMITH, James SHARP, Col. John WINN, Absalom SMITH, John THOMPSON, William TODD, William WEBB, John TROUTT, Absalom WILLIAMS, Maj. Thomas WASHINGTON, Jacob WRIGHT.

The following persons have reported estrays in Bedford County, per Howel DAWDY, r. b. c.:
(1) Richard MORLAIN, on Powell Creek, has taken up a black mare. On March 2, 1811, the mare was given an appraised value of $30.
(2) Amos M'ADAMS, on Harricane Creek, took up a sorrel mare. On March 19, 1811, the mare's value was $4.
(3) Edward ZEAL, on Noah's Fork, has taken up a sorrel colt. On March 18, 1811, the colt's value is $20.
(4) Gabriel PRINCE has taken up a yellow sorrel horse. On March 16, 1811, the horse was valued at $45.
(5) John PATTERSON, on the Duck River, has taken up a bay horse. On March 11, 1811, the horse was given an appraised value of $30.
(6) Samuel KING, on Little Flat Creek, has taken up a brown horse. On March 26, 1811, the horse's value was appraised at $25.50.

My wife Polly has left me without just cause. Wm. ROPER.
For sale, apples. John SHREVE, jr.
For sale, a house and lots in Franklin. Abraham WALKER.
For sale, books and stationary. D. ROBERTSON.
William WALLACE, on Nashville, did on the 19th of April take benefit of the Gaming Act.
I want to forewarn the public against carrying away any timbers from the tract known as PURNEL's Premption, that is the property of William SLOAN. David M'EWIN, for Wm. SLOAN.
On the 8th of June next in the town of Nashville, there

will be a public sale directed by the West Tennessee Court of 5000 acres, that is the property of Thomas EASTLAND in Lincoln County. The property was taken at the influence of William HENRY and Thomas EASTLAND against James COOLEY and William THOMPSON. (sic?) J. CHILDRESS.

The following persons have reported estrays in Lincoln County, per Brice M. GARNER for the ranger of said county:

(1) Elijah RADFORD, below Brook's Mill, has taken up a bay horse. On February 22, 1811, the horse was given an appraised value of $3.

(2) Joseph PARISH, on Norris' Creek, has taken up an iron roan mare. On March 9, 1811, the mare's value was appraised at $35.

(3) John MOORE, on Bradshaw's Creek, has taken up a bay horse. On March 30, 1811, the horse was appraised at the value of $30.

(4) James SIMMS, on Elk River below Fayetteville, has taken up a grey horse. On April 3, 1811, the horse was appraised at $9.

May 7, 1811, Vol. III, No. CLXX
Died on Saturday the 28th, Peter JONES, an inhabitant of this city.

Reward $10. On the 5th, my negro man, JACK, ranaway from the undersigned. John P. WIGGINS, Nashville.

Open for the business of sign painting. H. EVANS.

The following persons have reported estrays in Wilson County, per Edmund CRUTCHER, d. r. w. c.:

(1) Alexander BEARD, on Jinning's Fork, has taken up a small horse. On April 11, 1811, the horse's value was appraised at $5.

(2) Elijah GARR, on the Cumberland River, has taken up a bay horse. On April 13, 1811, the horse's value was appraised at $12.

(3) Samuel CALHOUN, on Cedar Creek, took up a chesnut sorrel mare. On April 26, 1811, the mare's value was appraised at $8.

(4) Jacob LASSETER, on Fall Creek, has taken up a bay mare. On April 26, 1811, the mare was appraised at a value of $5.

May 14, 1811, Vol. III, No. CLXXII
I have lost a pocket book with notes on Edward MITCHELL, Turner BESHARS, George STRAMLER, and James SWANSON. Terry BRIDGES.

On the 24th of June next in Nashville, there will be a public sale directed by the Davidson County court of a tract of land on Bull Creek, that is owned and occuppied by Robert GOWER. The land was attached by Thomas HICKMAN. M.C. DUNN.

Sumner County, Tennessee, March term, 1811. William HALL
reports that the following lots have unpaid taxes and are
liable for a double tax. David SHELBY.

Reputed Owners	Lots	Location
Heirs of Gilver SMITH	3	Cairo
William DICKSON	3	Cairo
William MORGAN	4	Cairo
Thomas CAMPBELL	1	Cairo
Edwin SMITH	1	Cairo
John LAWRENCE	1	Cairo
George REESE	1	Cairo
James SIMPSON	1	Cairo
William DENNIS	-	500 acres
Edward HUDSON	1	Cairo
John PEARSON	1	Cairo

The following persons have reported estrays in Bedford
County, per Howel DAWDY, r. b. c.:
  (1) Daniel BARDNAST, on Sinking Creek, has taken up a
       bay horse. On April 11, 1811, the horse was given
       an appraised value of $25.
  (2) John WILSON, on Mill Creek, has taken up a brown
       mare. On April 22, 1811, the mare's value is $30.
  (3) Samuel B. HARRIS, on Weakley's Creek, has taken up
       a brown bay horse. On March 25, 1811, the horse's
       value was appraised at $40.
  (4) Jonathan PHARR, on Garrison Fork, has taken up a
       sorrel filly. On April 15, 1811, the filly,s value
       was appraised at $20.

Lincoln County, Tennessee, February term, 1811. On the
first Monday in Novmber next, Cornelius SLATER reports that
the following tracts of land have unpaid taxes for 1810.
Brice M. GARNER, c. l. c..

Reputed Owners	Acres	Situation
H. RUTHERFORD	320	Swan Creek
John BRAHAN	500	
W. ROSEBROUGH	590	FLINT & STROTHER
Wm. T. LEWIS	5000	Entered in the name
		E. W. LEWIS.
H. RUTHERFORD	320	Richland Creek
David PHILLIPS	640	Cane Creek
John GORDON	640	Cold Water
Stephen CLOYD	150	Coffee Creek
Isaac VARN	180	Kelley's Creek
Evant WRITTEN	50	
John BRAHER	500	Mulberry
William BROWN	460	Cane Creek
Robert BIGHAM	640	North Side Elk
J. CLADENNING	2406	Bradshaw's creek

(Continued on following page)

167

(Lincoln County delinquent tax list continued)

R. COOK	640	PILLOW, agant.
And. GREER's heirs	2140	VANCE, agent
Nathan ORR	1200	North Side Elk
A. PEDDY and COBB	5000	Mulberry
Wm. TOMMERSON	150	Mulberry
Abraham NOBLET	400	
Thos. HICKMAN	50	Mulberry
John COBB	30	Duke's Creek
James WINCHESTER	640	William WALKER, agt
Robert WALKER	1200	Clemment CANNON,agt
CHERRY & STUBBLEFIELD	640	Mulberry
Mathew PATTERSON	300	Swan Creek
Thomas S. SCOTT	40	Swan Creek
William DOUGLAS	640	Mulberry
NOBLET & MERIDETH	400	Elk River
Amos DAVIS	150	Swan Creek
A. NELSON's heirs	4200	Bradshaw's Creek
CAMPBELL & PILLOW	200	
Charles POLK	5000	
GRAY & STUBBLEFIELD	640	Farris Creek
A. and W. STUBBLEFIELD	640	Norris Creek
Adam ALLISON	50	Swan Creek
Martin ARMSTRONG	5000	South Side Elk
John ALCORN	200	Bradshaw's Creek
Wallace ALEXANDER	1000	Elk River
Andrew BOYD	1100	Elk River
Lewis BAIRD	400	Elk River
George DOHERTY	881	
Henry MONTFORD	500	Elk River

Lincoln County, Tennessee, February term, 1811. On the first Monday in November next, the following tracts of land were reported by Cornelius SLATER, sheriff, as properties that are to be sold to satisfy the unpaid taxes for 1811. Brice M. GARNER, c. 1. c.

Reputed Owners	Acres	Situation
Hugh ALEXANDER	300	Middle Fk. Cane Cr.
Adley ALEXANDER	400	Norris Creek
Mat. ARMSTRONG	6	Kelley's Creek
William ADAMS	74	Keer's Creek
J. ALLISON and T. COX	40	Bradshaw's Creek
John ALCORN	160	Swan Creek
James ANDREW	649	Elk River
Henry BLAGRAVES	50	Mulberry Creek
Sumner BOOTH	640	Elk River
George BELL	640	Elk River
William BOWEN	640	Cane Creek
Geo. BELL's heirs	640	Cane Creek

(Continued on following page)

168

(Lincoln County delinquent tax list continued)

Abraham BYLER	308	
---oab BUCKLEY	50	Richland Creek
Thomas R. BUTLER	454	
Thomas N. CLARK	150	Kelley's Creek
John COBB	40	Duke's Creek
John COCKS	50	Cold Water
Isaac CROW	100	
Aa. CUNNINGHAM	640	Mulberry Creek
David CARSON	1280	Adj. EDMISTON
Mich. CAMPBELL	227	
Wm. CUMMINGHAM	50	Swan Creek
Samuel DOBBINS	100	Cane Creek
Eph. DAVIDSON	1000	Tucker's Creek
Geo. DOHERTY, dec.	1000	Noris Creek
James DAVIS	213	Mulberry Creek
John DAVIDSON	50	Leatherwood Creek
Wm. FREEMAN	60	Swan Creek
Anthony FOSTER	640	
Mathew GWINN	40	Short Creek
Daniel GILLISPIE	620	Flint River
Joseph GRAHAM	613	North Side Elk
John GORDON	300	Cumberland River
Joseph GRAY	80	Bradshaw's Creek
GARLAND & ROBERTSON	220	Kerr's Creek
Jonathan GRAVES	228	West Kerr's Creek
John HARDEMAN	106	Bradshaw's Creek
John HAYWOOD	100	Duke's Creek
Thomas HOPKINS	100	M'Cullough's Creek
Tm. HUNTER's heirs	640	
Joel HOBB's heirs	640	
HENRY & EASTLAND	2575	Mulberry
Wm. HENDERSON	900	Mulberry
Thomas HICKMAN	400	Mulberry
Thomas HALL	3000	
Thomas JONES	106	Cold Water
Amos JOHNSTON	640	Mulberry
Alexander JOICE	440	Cane Creek
Moses KINDALL	100	Bradshaw's Creek
Wm. LITTLE	640	Sinking Creek
Jacob LOCK	25	Cold Water
Saml. LOCKEHART	238	Cold Water
Jos. LAURENCE's heirs	640	
Wm. T. LEWIS	2000	
John LAURANCE	100	Norris Creek
David M'GAVOCK	1000	Kerr's Creek
John M'CORCLE	41	Swan Creek
Mic. MUCKLEROY	400	Cane Creek

(Continued on following page)

169

(Lincoln County delinquent tax list continued)

Har. MURFREY	300	Mulberry
James MACKY	640	
Benj. M'CULLOCK	50	Bradshaw's Creek
Henry MONTFORD	100	Mulberry Creek
Jos. M'DONALD	70	Bradshaw's Creek
John MORRIS	100	Nettle Patch
Alexander MARTIN	40	Swan Creek
Alex. M'DONALD	20	Bradshaw's Creek
John NEWMAN	1150	Moss Tract
Thos. H. PERKINS	76	Swan Creek
PHILLIPS & CAMPBELL	640	Elk
Thomas PERSONS	960	Elk
Elijah PATTON	250	Mulberry Creek
Francis PATTON	640	
John RECORD	220	Flint River
David ROSS	100	Flint River
Mordecai PILLOW	60	Mulberry
James ROBERTSON	90	Elk
Samuel RICHARDS	50	Old Town Creek
ROLING & LOFTIN	274	Swan Creek
Benj. FITZRANDOLPH	540	Mulberry Creek
Lavina ROBERTSON	640	
Geo. RUTLEDGE	1675	Swan Creek
R. B. SAPPINGTON	160	Richland
Jo. T. SMITH	1000	Mulberry
David SHANNON	100	Mulberry
Jas. SHIVER's heirs	274	Mulberry
Dav. SHELBY	123	Sinking Creek
J. TESLEY's heirs	100	Limestone
Tipton LEWIS	1500	
Miles THRIFT's heirs	640	
Robt. THOMPSON	640	Cane Creek
Steph. HOLBERT	50	
Oliver WILLIAMS or WILSON	140	Elk
Hadon WELLS	640	Elk
Joseph ALLIS	1200	Little River
M. WATSON's heirs	150	Duke's Creek
Dav. WILSON	20	Kelly's Creek
Mic. WARD's heirs	640	Cane Creek
Jos. WILLIAMS	640	
Jos. and Jno. WILLIAMS	646	
Wm. WILSON	76	Swan Creek
Jno. J. WILLIAMS	640	Cane Creek
Mich. WARD	640	Cane Creek
Jas. WINCHESTER	580	Mulberry
Robt. M. WHITE	80	Bradshaw's Creek
John WILSON	31	Kelly's Creek

(Continued on following page)

170

(Lincoln County delinquent tax list continued)

Wm. YOUNG	60	Kelly's Creek
John YOUNG	375	
Wright WILLIAMS	70	Cane Creek
James GREENLEE	100	

For sale, assorted goods. John INSTONE & Co.

John TERRY, on the Elk River, three miles from Whitaker's Mill, Lincoln County, has taken up a sorrel mare. The mare was appraised at $20 on April 6, 1811. Brice M. GARNER.

Samuel JOHNSTON vs. Abraham PRICE, Stewart Co., February, 1811, Original Attachment. It is ordered that a dedimus potestatum be issued to take the depositions of Robert OATS; James GOODWIN; James EVANS, Wayne County, Kentucky; Hannah MULKA, Pulaski County, Kentucky; James MONTGOMERY, Pulaski County, Kentucky; and John SUTTON, Garrard County, Kentucky. R. COOPER, clerk.

The persons are members of the Grand Jury, April term, 1811, Twickingham, Madison County, Mississippi Territory: John BUNCH, foreman; J. KIRKSEY; Thomas COUCH; Spencer BALL; jacob BROTTES; Joseph MATTHEWS; Robert DAVIS; Joseph ACKLIN; William SIMPSON; Jacob PREWETT; Andrew SWILTY; Hugh ROGERS; Alford MASSENGALL; John CONNELLY; John BYRD.

May 21, 1811, Vol. III, No. CLXXIII

Married on Thursday evening the 16th by Rev. CRAIGHEAD, Doct. Wm. BUTKER to Miss Patsy HAYS.

Married on the same evening, Stokley D. HAYS to Lydia BUTLER.

The following persons have reported estrays in Rutherford County, per N. B. ROSE, d. r. r. c.:

(1) Goldsmith W. HART, on the west fork of the Stones River, has taken up a sorrel mare.
(2) Robert MILLER, near Miller's Mill, has taken up a sorrel mare.
(3) James CROWDER, on the road from Jefferson, took up a black mare.
(4) Elizabeth RUCKER, on the west fork of the Stones River, has taken up a bay horse.
(5) Thomas BROETHES, on Long Creek, took up a bay mare.
(6) Joseph GOWEN, on Cripple Creek, took up a mare.
(7) George WALLICE, on Fox Camp, took up a bay filly.
(8) Thomas GARRETT, on Overall's Creek, has taken up a sorrel colt.
(9) Lewis BATON, on Hurricane Creek, took up a mare.
(10) Moses M'CONNEL, on the west fork of the Stones River, has taken up an iron grey horse.
(11) Cornelius DABNEY, on the west fork of the Stones Rlver, has taken up a bay mare.
(12) Thomas BERRY, Ready's Mill, took up a black mare.

(13) Daniel MARSBEL, on the west fork of the Stones
River, has taken up a roan sorrel horse.
(14) William CARNEY, on the road from Jefferson, took up
a brown by horse.
I thought Henry GROS was a gentleman and I am sorry, that
I was disappointed. Wm. WALLACE.

May 28, 1811, Vol. III, No. CLXXIII

Col. Jesse DENSON is a candidate for the Senate for the
Robertson District.
Adam DALE is a candidate for the Senate for the district
of Winchester.
Humphreys County, Tennessee, January Session, 1811. David
BURTON, collector, reports that the following tracts of land
have unpaid taxes for 1810. the property will be sold at
the house of Samuel PARKER, jr. in November next. Dawsey
HUDSON, clerk.

Reputed Owners	Acres	Situation
John SHEPARD	640	Tennessee River
John Baptist ASHE	4457	Tennessee River
Peter BECOTE	3840	Duck River
James IVIS	640	Tennessee River
James TUCKER	640	Trace Creek
John CASEY	1000	Tennessee River
Wm. BECK	350	Duck River
Joel LEWIS	640	Tennessee River
Simon SMITH	274	Tennessee River
Thomas TAUNT	640	Richland Creek
John ALLEN	640	Tennessee River
Joseph TILMON	640	Tennessee River
Alexander BREVARD	3840	Tennessee River
Elijah MOORE	3840	Duck River
Nicholas LONG	640	Tennessee River
Jesse COBB	640	Duck River
Richard FENNER	640	Duck River
Daniel WILLIAMS	500	Duck River
James GLASGOW	571	Duck River
Martin ARMSTRONG	640	Duck River
Berry LENSE	2560	Duck River
Robert FENNER	3840	Duck River
Thomas DAVIS	640	Blue Creek
John PATRICK	640	Tennessee River
James COGLIN	640	Tennessee River
Betsey BARROW	640	Tennessee River
John BLAIMER	640	Buffaloe Creek
Mathew BARROW	640	Buffaloe Creek
Keedar PHILLIPS	1000	Buffaloe creek
James KING's heirs	640	Buffaloe Creek

(Continued on following page)

(Hunphreys County delinquent tax list continued)

Robt. BROOMFIELD	1000	Buffaloe Creek
Martin ARMSTRONG	640	Buffaloe Creek
James COGLIN	1000	Buffaloe Creek
Geo. DOHERTY	640	Buffaloe Creek
Henry JOHNSTON	640	Tennessee River
J. M. and W. T. LEWIS	640	Tennessee River
Heirs of J. RICHLAND	640	Tennessee River
Thos. ANGELL	274	Tennessee River
Amos WARD	274	Tennessee River
James ROBERTSON	640	Tennessee River
John MORGAN	274	Duck River
Archibald MAHAN	400	Duck River
Wm. HILL	320	Tennessee River
Edward GWIN	320	Tennessee River
Jac. WHORTON's heirs	480	Tennessee River
John HARVEY	640	Duck River
John DUNNING	320	Ran. 19, Sec. 9
Adam RABY	480	Tennessee River
John GWIN	320	Duck River
Jesse WILLIAMS	274	Duck River
Howel TATUM	320	Tennessee River
Wm. WHITE	1097	Turkey Creek
John ALSTON	228	Tennessee River
Alex. MABANE	640	Tennessee River
Wm. MURY	320	Tennessee River
J. BLANCHARD's heirs	480	Tennessee River
Wm. WHITE	210	Tennessee River
J. and D. LATIMORE	100	Richland Creek
Edward TURNER	50	Turkey Creek
Robert YOUNG	50	White Oak Creek
John WRIGHT	127	Hurricane Creek
Nath. SKINNER	5	Tennessee River
Robt. NELSON	320	Tennessee River
John GWIN	300	Richland Creek
Henry PICKARD	400	Richland Creek
J. BLANCHARD's heirs	100	Richland Creek
Dan. LATIMER	150	Richland Creek
Joseph TILL	226	Tennessee River
Edward GWIN	100	Blue Creek
John G. BLOUNT	100	Trace Creek
John HENDRICK	160	Blue Creek
Henry BATE	100	Tennessee River
James DICKSON	90	Tennessee River
Robert PRINCE	90	Tennessee River
Robert NELSON	180	Tennessee River
Ad. RABEY's heirs	160	Ran. 22, Sec. 6
J. WHORTON's heirs	100	Tennessee River

(Continued on following page)

173

(Humphreys County delinquent tax list continued)

John PRICE	320	Duck River
Thos. M'KISSICK	213	Tennessee River
James ROBERTSON	166	Tennessee River
Ed. TURNER	50	Tennessee River
Wm. DENNIS	100	Duck River
John ARCHER	200	Duck River
John DOHERTY	640	Richland
Wm. WILLIAMS	640	
Wm. MURRY	107	Tennessee River
James MEAKINS	1090	Buffaloe
J. PORTERFIELD's heirs	500	White Oak Creek
John ELLIOTT	640	Duck River
James LEE	274	Duck River
Abraham THRIFT	640	Reasons Creek
Hugh WILLIAMS	228	Duck River
Daniel WILLIAMS	640	Duck River
Wm. WILLIAMS	3840	Duck River
John CASEY	640	Tennessee River
Wm. ALFORD	640	Tennessee River
Heirs of R. ROCESTER	1000	Duck River
Heirs of E. HARRIS	640	Duck River
Thos. BLOUNT	640	Tennessee River
James ARANDALL	640	Duck River
Wm. MOORE	1000	Duck River
Heirs of Jao. BLACK	640	Warr. 1598
R. and J. BOWLAND	428	Duck River
Robt. NELSON	274	Trace Creek
Wm. WHITE	360	Tennessee River
Abraham DAVIDSON	178	Ran. 21, Sec. 8
Sterling MAY	220	Hurricane Creek
James DICKSON	180	Duck River
James TUCKER	640	Trace Creek
James MORROW	228	Richland
John MASSEY	50	Trace Creek
Ed. GAMBLE	274	Tennessee River
Thos. ASKEN	640	White Oak Creek
Thos. BERRY	274	N. S. Tennessee
Abel MOSLANDER	2560	N. S. Tennessee
Bryt. WHITEFIELD	640	Tennessee River
Charles GARRARD	320	Trace Creek
John WILLIAMS	40	Richland Creek
James COGHLIN	640	Trace Creek
Thos. E. SUMNER	200	Halls Creek
Robert PRINCE	150	Spring Creek
Martin HARDIN	33	Richland Creek
Josiah HORTON	640	Tennessee River
Sterling MAY	100	Hurricane Creek

(Continued on following page)

174

(Lincoln County delinquent tax list continued)

Elijah WALKER	400	Tennessee River
Isaac HUDSON	200	Tennessee River
Wm. BURNETT	640	Tennessee River
Eliz. W. LEWIS	500	Tennessee River
Alx. MABANE	220	Tennessee River
Thomas WIGGINS	640	Tennessee River
Daniel ANDERSON	250	Tennessee River
Jas. BLANCHARD's heirs	100	Trace Creek
Enoch DOUGE	160	Hurricane
Spillesby TRIBBLE	200	Duck River
Saml. M'CULLOCK	4500	Tennessee River
C. H. HAIL	793	Hurricane Creek

For sale, ready made cloathes. (sic) Wm. Y. PROBART.

On the 8th of June next, I will apply to the Commissioner of West Tennessee for a certificate on Grant No. 1391, dated December 20, 1791, for 640 acres, that was issued to Sarah HAYS. I claim the land by deed received from the sheriff of Montgomery County. Robert SEARCY.

On the 11th of July next in the town of Nashville, there will be a public sale directed by the Davidson County court of 314 acres on the Big Harpeth, that belong to George WADE. The property was taken at the influence of Benjamin ANDREWS, Alexander RICHARDSON, James REEVES, & Co., and Wm. GRIMES. M. C. DUNN, shff.

On the 11th of July next in the town of Nashville, there will be a public sale directed by the Davidson County court of 100 acres in two tracts, that is the property of Thomas SIMPKINS and Noel WATKINS. The land was attached by Thomas HICKMAN. M. C. DUNN, shff.

In the town of Franklin on the 6th of July next, there will be a public sale directed by the court of Williamson County of 60 acres, that belongs to Thomas SPRATT. The land adjoins Thomas and James HERRON. The property was taken at the influence of James GORDON & Co. Wm. HULME, sheriff of Williamson County.

The subscriber, lately from England and an inhabitant of Nashville, is open for the sign painting business. Those interested, please see Charles M'KARAHAN. H. EVANS.

The following persons have reported estrays in Franklin County, per James THOMPSON, r. f. c.:

(1) Elijah ARNOLD, on Bradley's Creek, has taken up a black stud colt.
(2) Henry RUSSELL, on Boiling Fork, took up a bay mare.
(3) James BRANDON, on Parraria Creek, has taken up a bay mare.
(4) John WOODS, on Spring Creek, took up a bay mare.
(5) Barbee COLLINS has taken up a bay mare.
(6) Anthony J. KERD has taken up a brown bay horse.

175

The following persons have reported estrays in Lincoln County, per Brice M. GARNER, for Philip KOONCE, ranger:
(1) William HENDERICKS, on the Elk River about one mile above Fayetteville, has taken up black horse. The horse was valued at $9 on April 29, 1811.
(2) Joel MECRENY, on the Elk River three miles above Fayetteville, has taken up a bay horse. The horse was appraised at $28 on April 24, 1811.
(3) John H. MOORE, on Cane Creek, has taken up a roan horse. On May 4, 1811, the horse's value is $27.
(4) John GREER, on Cane Creek, has taken up a brown horse. On May 8, 1811, the horse's value is $10.
(5) William DYE, on the Elk River, has taken up a black horse. On April 30, 1811, the horse was appraised at a value of $30.
(6) Stephen ALEXANDER, on the Elk River, has taken up a sorrel mare. On April 18, 1811, the horse was appraised at a value $15.
(7) Daniel WARREN, on Mulberry Creek, has taken up a horse. On May 7, 1811, the horse's value is $20.

June 4, 1811, Vol. III, No. CLXXIV
On the 29th of June next in the town of Jefferson, there will be a public sale directed by the court of Rutherford County of the rights to a tract of land lying on the Stones River, one and a half miles below Barton's Ford, that is the property of Richard W. SCRUGGS. The land was taken at the influence of Gabriel VEST, the guardian of Robert VEST; Wm. HUGGINS; and James CLEMET. Wm. SMITH, d. shff.
On the 29th of June next in the town of Jefferson, there will be a public sale directed by Rutherford County court of 520 acres, that is property of and formerly owned by John FLEMING. The land was attached by William SMITH. Wm. SMITH.
The following persons have reported estrays in Lincoln County, per Brice M. GARNER, for Philip KOONCE:
(1) James SLATS, on Swan Creek, took up a black mare. On May 13, 1811, the mare was appraised at $33.
(2) Ephraim DRAKE, on Swan Creek, has taken up a sorrel horse. On May 2, 1811, the horse's value is $20.
(3) James GARRET, on the west fork of Richland Creek, has taken up a sorrel mare. On April 17, 1811, the horse was appraised at $20.
(4) Joseph GARNER, on Swan Creek, has taken up a horse. On May 11, 1811, the horse was appraised at $20.
(5) Morris FRIEL, on Swan Creek, has taken up a horse. On May 12, 1811, the horse was valued at $126.
(6) William BRUMLEE has taken up a horse.
(7) Glound (sic) CLAYTON, on Kerr's Creek, has taken up a mare, that was valued at $20 on May 9, 1811.

The following persons have reported estrays in Bedford County, per Howel DAWDY, r. b. c.:
(1) Spencer GLASCOCK, near Old Garrison, has taken up a bay horse. On April 21, 1811, the horse was given an appraised value of $3.
(2) Joel CRAINE, on Flat Creek, has taken up a yellow bay mare. On April 23, 1811, the horse was given an appraised value of $33.
(3) Richard MARTIN, on Powels Creek, took up a sorrel horse. On April 23, 1811, the horse's value is $5.
(4) Henry BINGAMAN, on Garrison Fork, has taken up a stud colt. On April 29, 1811, the colt was given an appraised value of $25.
(5) Timothy SUGS, on War Trace Fork, has taken up a horse. On April 22, 1811, the horse was appraised in the amount of $30.
(6) James MEEK, on the Duck River, has taken up a mare. On April 25, 1811, the mare was valued at $3.
(7) Rubin CLARITON, on Wilson's Creek, has taken up a sorrel mare. On April 26, 1811, the mare was given an appraised value of $24.

On the 13th of July next in the town of Nashville, there will be a public sale directed by the Davidson County court of 500 acres, that is owned and occuppied by Absalom PAGE. The property was taken at the influence of Snederick CAYCE to satisfy his security for Allen SCRUGGS and Finch SCRUGGS. I. A. PARKER, d. s.

June 14, 1811, Vol. III, No. CLXXV
On the 13th of July next in the town of Nashville, there will be a public sale directed by the Davidson County court of the rights to 54 acres, Warrant No. 380, that David HUNT has to a certificate assigned by Willie BARROW, admin. of Micajah BARROW, dec. The property was taken at the influence of Aaron LAMBERT. I. A. PARKER, d. s.

On the 13th of July next in the town of Nashville, there will be a public sale directed by the Davidson County court of 100 acres, that is the property of Daniel ROSS. The land adjoins Widow BROWN and the tract of land that was possessed by Mark B. SAPPINGTON at the time of his death. The land was taken at the influence of Alexander RICHARD and Owen T. WATKINS. I. A. PARKER, d. s.

On Saturday the 27th, Robert ANDERSON, age 27, died very suddenly at his farm near Gallatin.

The following persons have reported estrays in Wilson County, per Edmund CRUCTHER, d. r. w. c.:
(1) Joseph WRIGHT, on Barton's Creek, has taken up a bay horse. On April 25, 1811, the horse was given an appraised value in the amount of $45.

(2) John HILL, on Spring Creek, has taken up a mare. On April 21, 1811, the horse was appraised at $20.
(3) John BOATE, Cedar Lick, has taken up a bay mare. On April 22, 1811, the mare was appraised at $14.
(4) Aaron EDWARDS, Fall Creek, has taken up a bay mare. On April 27, 1811, the mare was appraised at $10.
(5) Edward BROWN, on Hendrick's Ferry, has taken up a sorrel mare. On April 30, 1811, the mare was given an appraised value of $20.
(6) Meredith DAVIS, on Barton's Creek, has taken up a horse. On May 1, 1811, the horse's value is $32.
(7) Wm. WOODARD, on Bradley's Creek, has taken up a bay horse. On May 13, 1811, the horse's value is $20.
(8) Richard DRAKE has taken up a bay horse. The value of the horse was given at $20 on May 12, 1811.
(9) John BONNER, on Beasley Bend, has taken up a bay horse. On May 21, 1811, the horse's value is $30.
(10) Jeremiah BROWN, on Jennings Fork, has taken up a bay horse. On May 27, 1811, the horse was given an appraised value of $20.
(11) Anthony WINSTON, sen., on Sander's Ferry, took up yellow bay horse. On May 17, 1811, the horse was appraised at $30.
(12) Benjamin GRAVES, on Stones Creek, has taken up a mare. On may 18, 1811, the mare's value is $30.

Giles County, Tennessee, February Sessions, 1811. Charles NEELY, sheriff and collector, will be sold to satisfy the unpaid taxes for 1810 on the first Monday in November next. German LESTER, clerk.

Reputed Owners	Acres	Situation
Joseph BROWN	1000	Richland Creek
Alfred M. CARTER	4000	Richland Creek
Joseph GREEN	1000	Buchanan Creek
John M'NAIRY	5000	Buchanan Creek
Abraham WALKER	150	Robertson Fork
John WILSON	5000	Big and Blue C.
Wm. P. ANDERSON	400	Elk River
John M'IVER	5000	Big Creek
Thomas POLK	5000	Richland Creek

The following tracts are liable for a double tax:

Reputed Owners	Acres	Situation
Richard COOK	726	Richland Creek
James CONNER	600	Richland Creek
Francis CHILDS	3000	Elk River
Micajah P. LEWIS	5000	Richland Creek
Henry MONTFORD	5000	Richland Creek
John NELSON	5000	Richland Creek
Edward KERLEY	300	Haywood Creek

(Continued on following page)

178

(Giles County delinquent tax list continued)

Benjamin M'CULLOCK	640	Elk River
John ERWIN	440	
Robert LANIER	500	
Devisees of geo. DOHERTY	1000	
William ERWIN	640	Warr. 2067
Thomas GREEN	1000	Warr. 592
Elijah WILLIMS	400	Warr. 643
Thomas GREEN	2000	Warr. 805
Thomas GREEN	1655	Warr. 1098
Charles REESE	640	Big Creek
Simon ELLIOTT	700	Warr. 95
James LEWIS	1400	Elk & Richland
Isaac L. WATERS	50	Big Creek
Wm. WALKER	740	

On the 5th at lat. 38 long. 52, Hallet HAMBLIN, a native of Barnstable, Massachuetts was pressed from the schooner Eagles Hawes.

I will apply to the Commissioner of West Tennessee on the 13th of July next for a certificate in conveyance of Grant No. 2300, dated May 20, 1793, for 640 acres, that was issued to Joshua DAVIS. Joshua DAVIS conveyed said land to Joshua John LEE.

June 18, 1811, Vol. III, No. CLXXVI

On Friday morning last, Mrs. CONDON, consort of James CONDEN, died. She leaves several small children.

On Tuesday last, Mrs. PLUMMER died.

The following persons signed a letter to the editor about the court system: Samuel MORTON, Nelson FIELDS, Benj. KEDD, Jacob MORTON, Benjamin HUMPHREYS, James WILLIAMS, William ANTHONY, John COCHRAN, Henry WISENOR, John LOVEL, sen., Jas. TURNER, Charles JOHNSON, Joseph DIXON, Thos. SIMMONS, Anslem NOLEN, William NOLEN, Joseph MAJOR, Moses CURREY, J. KNIGHT, Wm. M. SIMPSON, Thomas TAYLOR, Joseph ANTHONY, Gresham HUNT, W. KIDD, John WINSTEAD, Ambrose OWEN, Allen RICHARDSON, John SMITH, Herbet OWEN, Joshua CUTCHEN, David BOWEN, Jonathan THORN, Samuel MORTON, sen.

Married on Sunday last, Bernard M. KERNAN to Miss Mary A. WATERS, both of this county.

July 2, 1811, Vol. III, No. CLXXVIII

On the 11th of August next in Nashville, there will be a public sale directed by the court of Davidson County of 198 acres, that is the property of Thomas G. WATKINS and Thomas HARNEY. The land adjoins Henry JACKSON, Mathew P. WALKER, John WALKER and Samuel JACKSON. The land was taken at the influence of Moses READ. I. A. PARKER, d. s. d. c.

Reward $15. In February last, a negro man called, JERRY

ranaway from the subscriber in Twickingham, Madison County. Robert GALLASPIE.

July 9, 1811, Vol. III, No. CLXXIX
On Saturday the 1st of June, Gen. William EATON died at Brimfield, Massachuetts.

The following is a list of letters remaining at the post office in Franklin on July 1, 1811, per Gurdon SQUIER, a. p. m.: Geo. H. ALLEN, Polly ATKINSON, Henry ATKINSON, Etheldred BOYET, Polly ALEXANDER, Hiram ALEXANDER, Isreal ARCHER, Alx. BENNET, Thomas BRADLEY, Nancy BAKER, Turb. BARNES, William BATES, Wm. G. BAYED, William BAILEY, George BENNETT, James BEASLEY, Jonathan BETTS, Terry BRIDGES, John BLYTHE, William BARKER, John BURGESS, James BLACK, David BARKER, John COOKE, Drury BENNET, James BRUFF, John COVEY, John CHESTER, Andrew CUFF, James CARRELL, Thos. CAPEHART, Newton CANNON, Dempsey DEAN, Abner CRAWSBY, David CAMPBELL, James CROCKET, Joseph DAVISON, Isaac CROW, David CRAIG, Reps (sic) CHILDRESS, Wm. DICKEY, Col. David CRAIG, Andrew H. DAVIS, Zech DRAKE, Rev. Wm. B. ELGIN, William DEAN, Robert DAVIS, John FINEH, Thos. EDINGTON, Etheldred EVANS, Susannah FAVER, Robert FINNEY, John GLOVER, Wm. GARNER, George GANTER, Samuel GLASSS, John GHOLSON, George GENTRY, Eliz. GRAYSON, John GRAY, John HILL, Allen GATES, John GEERY, John HOOKS, James HALBERT, Thomas HARDEMAN, Mark HARDISON, Horras HARDEN, Richd. W. HYDE, Wm. LANDERS, Archd. LYTLE, Henry LESTER, Jessee JACKSON, Sally JACKSON, Andw. JAMESON, James JOHNSON, Jno. MONTGOMERY, Bird A. MILES, Andr. M'GRADY, Sherwood MILLS, David M'CORD, Jas. M'RUNNALDS, George W. L. MARR, Wm. MARSHAL, Daniel M'COLLUM, John MATTHEWS, Saml. M'CRACKEN, William MOORE, John M'SWAIN, Alex. M'COWN, David M'EWEN, Jas. M'CUTCHEN, William NOLIN, Wm. M'CALPIN, Chls. B. NEILSON, Wm. NEELEY, Glen OWEN, John PAUL, Morda. PILLOW, Drury PULUM, John PATTON, Thomas PAGE, Jeremiah PRIMM, Turner PINKSTON, Solomon ROBERTS, Richard SMITH, James SCOTT, Thos. REYNOLDS, Geo. REYNOLDS, Sampson SAWYERS, Geo. STRAMLER, Saml. SHELBOURNE, John SIMMONS, Tho. SIMMONS, Benja. SIMMONS, James STEWART, Robert SHARPE, Nath. SPENCER, ---- TANKERSLEY (sic), Christr. TENNISON, Jonathan WOOD, Geo. TREMBLE, John TABER, Phins. THOMAS, Polly TEMPLE, John VAUGHTEN, Js. WILLIAMSON, August WILLIS, Thomas WELLS, Ruben WALKER, Joel WALKER or David CARTER, John WALL, John C. WORMLEY, William WILSON.

On the 22nd, a negro man called TOM, between 35 and 40, ranaway from the subscriber living in Davidson County about ten or eleven miles east of Nashville. Henry SEAT.

Reward $20. There is a reward for the return of a negro man called JACK, age 35, who ranaway from the subscriber living near Nashville. His right hand is crippled. He is headed toward North Carolina. John D. GARRETT.

Reward $50. Two men took off on Monday on the 1st July. John WILSON, a chunky Irishman, black hair and 35 years old. The other is Andrew WATSON, Irish, 40 years old and he has black hair that is getting gray.

Jesse RIGSS, on Garrison Fork, Bedford County, has taken up a brown horse. On December 25, 1810, the horse's value was appraised at $25.15. H. DAWDY, r. b. c.

The following persons were mentioned in a certificate and other information on the racehorse Young Knowsley: William GAINES, Isaac H. COLE of Virginia, Peter SINGLETON, Martin HANCOCK, General PARKER, Sir Peter TEASLE, Mr. PIERCE, Sir H. T. VANE, Mr. FIELD, Mr. FLETCHER, G. CROMPTON, William GRAYSON, Mr. GARFORTH, Robert PORTERFIELD, Charles LEWIS, John SNAPP, Triplet T. ESTES, Sr. C. WILLIAMSON, T. WOODSON John GILLUM, Jonathan BARKSDALE, Richard WALLACE, William RAMSEY, Cliften RODES, Rice GARLAND, P. GILLUM, Samuel CARR, Jos. MONTGOMERY, Stephen MOORE, Nicholas FAGE, James BRADEN Andrew HART, Saml. CARR, Marshall DARRETT, Abraham MARTIN, James BARBOUR, Hugh NELSON.

July 16, 1811, Vol. III, No. CLXXX

Ephraim PARHAM, jailor, Lincoln County, has made an oath before me, that John MACLIN, who was in jail on a case to satisfy John BOYD, did forcibly on the night of the 27th break out of jail. Robert HIGGINS.

We have commenced the brickmaking business one mile south of Nashville. Tarranoe BURNS and John BOYD.

The following is a list of letters remaining at the post office in Jefferson on July 1, 1811, per John SPENCE, p. m.: W. P. ANDERSON, Carter ABBOTT, Wm. ARRONTON, David BLALOCK, Joseph AKE, Moses BELLAH, John BRADLEY, John BOWMAN, Abner CHAPPEL, Jessee CHEEK, Wm. CHILDRESS, Henry CONWAY, Charles COLIER, Daniel DODD, Peter DANIEL, George DEMPSEY, Richard FIELDS, Mordi. EDWARDS, Capt. Michael FISHER, Wm. GANAWAY, Eliz. GIBBONS, Susanna GAMBLE, Jonathan GRAVES, John HALL, Rubin HORTIS, John N. S. JONES, Robert JARRET, Wilson KERR, Wm. KELTON, Penny KING, Phillips S. LOE, William LOVE, Wm. LINDSEY, Andrew LUSK, Ezekiel MURPHY, Thomas MASON, Robert MAJORS, Wm. MORRER, James MEADOR, Wm. MARTIN, John MARSHALL, John M'PIKE, John MIDISON, Bird NANCE, Joseph PHILIPS, John PURKEN, Stephen PANKY, Samuel PEPPER, Abraham PALLET, George RUNICAN, Fredk. REPLOGLE (sic), John RHEAR, Benjamin RIDDLE, John RAGSDALE, Benjamin RUSSLE, John H. ROOSE, Thomas REAY, Daniel REEL, William STILL, Isaac SANDERS, M. B. STEOHENS, Shereard (sic) STROUD, Maj. Isc. SHELBY, John TARPLEY, Amos THIGPEN, Osole (sic) SLOULALTT, Wm. THWEATT, Capt. Valentine VANHOOSE, Alexr. VINCENT, Surril WHITE, Abn. WEATHERLY, Maj. Thomas WASHINGTON, J. G. WASHINGTON, Robert W. WASHINGTON, John WADDLE, Samuel WILSON, Samuel S. WASHBUM, Eliza WEST,

Lewis WATTSON (sic), Joseph WHITSETT.
The following persons have reported estrays in Rutherford
County, per N. B. ROSE, d. r. r. c.:
   (1)   William M'NIGHT, on the east fork of the Stones
         River, has taken up a bay horse.
   (2)   John HOOVER, on the west fork of the Stones River,
         has taken up a sorrel mare.
   (3)   --- MULKEY, on Cripple Creek, has taken up a horse.
   (4)   Daniel WEBB, on the east fork of the Stones River,
         has taken up a bay horse.
   (5)   Thomas DUNN, on the Stones River, has taken up a
         black horse, that is valued at $50.
   (6)   Arthor PIERCE, on Dry Creek, has taken up a horse.
   (7)   James NORMAN, on the west fork of the Stones River,
         has taken up a strawberry roan mare.
   (8)   Joseph M'LAUGHLIN, on the west fork of the Stones
         River, has taken up a horse.
   (9)   James JONES, near M'Coy's Mill, took up a horse.
  (10)   Abner DEMENT, near Jefferson on the east fork of
         the Stones River, has taken up a sorrel mare.
  (11)   Caleb ZACHERY, on Hurricane Creek, has taken up a
         sorrel mare, that is valued at $15.
  (12)   John PIGG, on Overall's Creek, took up a mare.
  (13)   Micajah PEACOCK, on Stewart's Creek, has taken up
         a horse, that is valued at $4.
  (14)   Richard W. CUMMINS, near Abott's Mill, has taken up
         a bay mare, that is valued at $13.
The following persons have reported estrays in Bedford
county, per Howel DAWDY, r. b. c.:
   (1)   Beady BROWNIN, on Powel's Creek, has taken up a bay
         brown mare. On June 5, 1811, the mare was given an
         appraised value of $15.
   (2)   Alexander RODES, on Rhyley's Creek, has taken up a
         bay mare. On May 21, 1811, the mare's value is $1.
July 16th, Tuesday, Nashville. Stewart W. THORNTON and
Jacob PICKERING were executed on Saturday for the murder of
Elisha GARNER.

July 23, 1811, Vol. III, No. CLXXXI
The following persons have reported estrays in Lincoln
County, per Brice M. GARNER, for Philip KOONCE, ranger:
   (1)   John CROSLAND, one mile from Fayetteville, took up
         a bay mare. On June 15, 1811, the mare was valued
         in the amount of $6.
   (2)   George WHITE, at Mulberry old courthouse, has taken
         a black horse. On June 18, 1811, the horse was
         appraised at a value of $20.
   (3)   David FERREL, near Mulberry old courthouse, has
         taken up a horse valued at $35 on June 5, 1811.

(4) Levi MIZELL, by permission of William DICKSON, has
taken up a brown filly. The appraised value of the
filly was $9 on June 15, 1811.

(5) William WILSON, one mile from Swan Creek, has taken
up a bay horse. On June 15, 1811, the horse was
appraised at a value of $20.

The followining persons were mentioned in an article
concerning the Cumberland College: John ERWIN, John SCOTT,
William PRIESTLY, John A. CHEATHAM, Ephraim FOSTER, Charles
PERKINS, Constance PERKINS, William GRAHAM, John POPE.

On the 17th, Wm. WAITSETT of Logan County, Kentucky, age
40, died.

The following persons have reported estrays in Wilson
County, per Edmund CRUTCHER, d. r.:

(1) James RAINSEY, on Harricane Creek, has taken up a
bay horse. On May 27, 1811, the horse was given an
appraised value of $40.

(2) Nathan WHEELER, on the third fork of Round Lick,
has taken up a strawberry roan horse. The horse
was valued at $20 on May 23, 1811.

(3) Samuel NAIL, on Fall Creek, has taken up a chesnut
sorrel roan mare. On June 1, 1811, the mare was
appraised at a value of $20.

(4) Alexander D. GAROLOR, on the Cumberland River, has
taken up a bay mare. On June 7, 1811, the mare was
appraised at a value of $51.

(5) John CARTERIGHT, on Round Lick, has taken up a bay
mare, that was valued at $11.

(6) John B. WALKER has taken up a bay horse. The horse
was valued at $15 on June 6, 1811.

(7) John LAURENCE, on Round Lick, has taken up a bay
horse. On May 28, 1811, the horse was appraised at
a value of $17.

(8) David HANKS, on Round Lick, has taken up a white
mare. On June 16, 1811, the mare was appraised at
a value of $12.

(9) Harvey YOUNG, on Sanders Fork, has taken up a mare.
On June 19, 1811, the mare was valued at $15.

(10) Aaron LAMBERT, jun., on Spring Creek, has taken up
a black mare. On July 6, 1811, the mare was valued
at $10.

(11) Samuel W. SHERRILL, on Barton's Creek, has taken up
bay mare. On July 3, 1811, the mare was appraised
at a value of $15.

(12) Joshua TAYLOR, on Round Lick, has taken up a brown
horse. On June 25, 1811, the horse's value is $25.

Reward 25 cents. On the 27th of June, an apprentice
named Thomas YOUNG, age 12, ranaway. Sumner HARPER.

Will all those indebted please pay. John S. WILLIAMSON.

183

August 4, 1811, Vol. III, CLXXXII
The following persons have reported estrays in Bedford County, per Howel DAWDY, r. b. c.:
(1) Beady BROWNING, on Powel's Creek, has taken up a bay mare. On June 5, 1811, the mare's value is $15.
(2) James M'CUESTION, on Harricane Creek, has taken up chesnut bay horse. On May 25, 1811, the horse was appraised at a value of 415.
(3) Alexander RHODES, on Ryley's Creek, has taken up a bay mare. On May 28, 1811, the mare was appraised at a value of $15.
(4) Daniel DAWDY, on Thompson's Creek near Dawdy Mill, has taken up a brwon bay horse. The horse's value was appraised at $16 on June 15, 1811.
(5) James CARREL, on the Duck River, has taken up a black mare. On May 27, 1811, the mare was valued in the amount of $12.
(6) George BEARD, on War Trace, has taken up a bay mare colt. On June 15, 1811, the colt's value is $1.
(7) Thomas PUCKKINGS, on Barren Fork, has taken up a black mare. On June 11, 1811, the mare's value was given in the amount of $20.
(8) John DAVIDSON, on Barren Fork, has taken up a bay mare. On June 11, 1811, the mare's value is $20.
(9) William ADAMS, on the Duck River, has taken up a sorrel filly. On May 29, 1811, the filly was given an appraised value of $20.

August 13, 1811, Vol. III, No. CLXXIV
Jackson County, Tennessee, February Sessions, 1811. James COOK reports that the following tracts of land will be sold on the first Monday in November next to satisfy the unpaid taxes for 1810 in the town of Williamsburg. John BOWEN.

Reputed Owners	Acres	Situation
Benjamin BLACKBURN	1095	Different tracts
John DARVAN	100	1 pole
Wilson CAGE	51	Indian Creek
Edward FITZPATRICK	100	Walton Road
Joshua GEORGE	150	Mill Creek
Orson MARTIN	640	Cumberland River
David MITCHELL	50	Nob Creek
John MARTIN	640	Line Creek
Hardy MURFREE's heirs	1536	Salt Lick Creek
Robert BROOKS	120	Brooks Bent
Isaac MOORE's heirs	2106	
Thomas PAYTON	201	Jinning's Creek
Daniel CHERRY	274	Watson Road
Solomon PRIEST's heirs	640	
Stokley DONELSON	640	Grant No. 2814

184

On the 8th, a negro man called ELIJAH ranaway from the subscriber near Franklin, Williamson County. He is about 5 ft., 10 or 11 in. tall. Nicholas T. PERKINS.

On the 21st of September next in the town of Nashville, there will be a public sale directed by the Davidson County court of 630 acres on Marrow Bone Creek, that belong to Bennet SEARCY. The property adjoins Frederick FISHER. Also for sale, are two tracts, that adjoins John GOWEN and Jenkin WHITESIDE. The property was taken at the influence of E. S. HALL & Co, Thomas G. WAKINS, and John P. DAVIS. M. C. DUNN.

On the 21st of September next in the town of Nashville, there will be a public sale directed by the Davidson County court of 40 acres on Big Marrow Bone Creek, that belong to Jacob DICKART. Also for sale, is the place known as Edward BLACKBURN's. The land was taken at the influence of Thomas HICKMAN and John STUMP. M. C. DUNN, shff., d. c.

On the 29th of August next in Nashville, there will be a public sale directed by the court of Davidson County of the tights, title, claim and interest, that Thomas G. WATKINS and Thomas HARNEY have to an entry made in William CRISMAS' land office for 190 acres. The land adjoins Henry JACKSON, Mathew WALKER, John WALKER, and Samuel JACKSON. The land was taken at the influence of Moses READ. I. A. PARKER.

On the night of the 8th, a negro named CUPID eloped from a boat above Clarksville. He is between 25 to 30 years old and is 5 ft., 6 or 8 in. tall. Benj. P. HOWARD, Nashville.

On the 10th, a negro man who says that his name is CHARLES was committed to jail. He says that he belongs to Edward BRADSHAW of Christian County, Kentucky. He is 19 or 20 years old and is 5 ft., 10 or 11 in. tall. E. D. HOBBS.

Smith County, Tennessee, March term, 1811. John BAKER, collector, reports that the following tracts of land will be sold in the town of Carthage on the first Monday in November next to satisfy the unpaid taxes for 1810. Joseph W. ALLEN.

Reputed Owners	Acres	Situation
Robert BANKS	182	
Rueben YARBURY	357	
Samuel HOAZRD	lot	Two in Carthage
Wm. P. LAWRENCE	lot	Three in Carthage
Robert BROWN	426	
John HUSTON	100	1 white poll
James M'QUISTEN's heirs	640	
Anthony HART's heirs	640	
John M'NAIRY	1020	
Gidean and Wm. PILLOW	594	Caney Fork
Henry CHANDLER	196	1 white & 6 black
John W. NICKLES	122	1 white & 1 black
Stephen MONTGOMERY	237	Goose Creek

(Continued on following page)

(Smith County delinguent tax list continued)
Stephen MONTGOMERY   237   Goose Creek, 1809
The following tracts are liable for a double tax for the
years of 1807 and 1808:

Reputed Owners	Acres	Situation
Washington L. HANNUM	640	Hylton's Creek
James ABERCORMY	1560	Round Lick

The following are liable for a double tax for 1809:

Reputed Owners	Acres	Situation
Washington L. HANNUM	640	Hylton's Creek
James ABERCORMY	1560	Round Lick
Robert FENNER	1280	Caney Fork
Thomas PARSONS' heirs	4800	Caney Fork

The following are liable for a double tax for 1810:

Reputed Owners	Acres	Situation
Washington L. HANNUM	640	Hylton's Creek
James ABERCORMY	1560	Round Lick Creek
Robert FENNER	1210	Caney Fork
Thomas PARSONS' heirs	4800	Caney Fork

August 20, 1811, Vol. III, No. CLXXXV

Elisha WILLIAMS died very suddenly on Saturday morning
last at his home in Haysborough. He was an old inhabitant
of this county.

The following persons have reported estrays in Bedford
County, per H. DAWDY, r. b. c.:

(1) John C. DUNN has taken up a sorrel filly. The filly
    was appraised at $15 on July 4, 1811.
(2) John NEIL, on Big Spring Creek, took up a mare. The
    mare was valued at $25 on July 6, 1811.
(4) Jesse HUGHES, on Rock Creek, has taken up a filly.
    The filly was valued at $10 on July 15, 1811.
(5) Josiah WILLIAMS, on the Duck River, has taken up a
    sorrel mare. On July 8, 1811, the mare was given
    an appraised value of $20.
(6) John BYCER, on Weakley'Creek, took up a horse. The
    horse was valued at $3 on July 8, 1811.

There is a handsome reward for the return of a negro man
named FEBRUARY, who ranaway from the subscriber on the 23th
of July. He may be W. B. ROBERTSON's plantation as he has a
negro wife there. To collect the reward deliver him to the
jail or to Jasper SUTTON. Rogal FARGUSSON. (sic)

Stewart County, Tennessee, February Sessions, 1811. John
ALLEN, sheriff, reports that the following tracts are liable
for a double tax for the year 1809. Robert COOPER, c. s. c.

Reputed Owners	Acres	War.	Situation
James M'MURTREE	109	132	Blue Creek
James MORROW	228	4448	Richland Creek

(Continued on following page)

186

(Stewart County delinquent tax list continued)

Joel LEWIS	640	272	Tennessee River
Joseph TILMAN	640	109	Tennessee River
Willoughby WILLIAMS	1000	2623	Richland Creek
Willoughby WILLIAMS	1000	2627	White Oak Creek
James RICHARD's heirs	640	2029	Blount Creek
Abel MOSTANDER	2560	851	Tennessee River
James IVIS	640	----	Trace Creek
James COGHLIN	1000	2626	Trace Creek
James TUCKER	640	----	Trace Creek
Thomas BLOUNT	640	1354	Tennessee River
George DOHERTY	640	424	Tennessee River
Robert BROOMFIELD	1000	780	Tennessee River
James KING's heirs	640	545	Tennessee River
Joseph TILMAN	1000	434	Tennessee River
John ALLEN	640	377	Tennessee River
John BLAIMER	640	1024	Tennessee River
Bryant WHITFIELD	640	----	Tennessee River
Richard BROWN	100	Occp	Hurricane Creek
Edward KING's heirs	114	3814	Blue Creek
William PEACOCK	100	Occp	
Hezekiah JOHNSTON	204	Occp	Hurricane Creek
Richard WHITE	120	Occp	Hurricane Creek
James GWIN	281	Occp	Hurricane Creek
Preston NUNOR	125	Occp	Hurricane Creek
John WHITE	300	Occp	Hurricane Creek
Ezekiel HUTSON's heirs	240	97	
Nathaniel SKINNER	50	4662	
Nathaniel SKINNER	15	4682	
James MURRAY	100	229	White Oak Creek
Asa WALKER	45	----	Tumblin Creek
Jesse WILLIAMS	274	4116	Tumblin Creek
John DUNING	320	774	Hurricane Creek
Robert DUNING	640	113	Hurricane Creek
Henry PICKARD	640	----	Hurricane Creek
Jesse WILLIAMS	274	4106	Duck River
John GWIN	228	4171	Duck River
John GWIN	340	904	Duck River
John M'NAIRY	228	4106	Duck River
John GWIN	320	2445	Blue Creek
Hugh WILLIAMS	228	----	Duck River
Micail SANTEE	200	48	Duck River
Sterling MAY	220	6947	Hurricane Creek
James DICKSON	180	241	Hurricane Creek
Bartholomew SMITH	228	4760	Hurricane Creek
Andrew SIMPSON	250	474	Hurricane Creek
John PRICE	320	3647	Hurricane Creek
Richard WHITE	320	5284	Hurricane Creek

(Continued on following page)

187

(Stewart County delinquent tax list continued)

John WRIGHT	127	4047	Hurricane Creek
John WRIGHT	93	4074	Hurricane Creek
Thomas M'KISSICK	213	----	Richland Creek
Michael BULLEN	240	648	Camp Creek
Philip CAKE	240	647	Blue creek
John H. ARCHER	200	2349	Blue Creek
William DENNIS	100	5	Blue Creek
BRACKEN & ANDERSON	333	----	Hurricane Creek

Stewart County, Tennessee, February Sessions, 1811. John ALLEN, sheriff, reports that the following tracts are liable for a double tax for the year 1810. Robert COOPER, c. s. c.

Reputed Owners	Acres	Warr.	Situation
Willoughby WILLIAMS	274	1321	Tennessee River
John CASEY	640	842	Tennessee River
Green HILL	640	1070	Tennessee River
Joel LEWIS	640	272	Tennessee River
Joseph TILMON	640	1094	Tennessee River
John SHEPERD	640	2690	Tennessee River
Mann PHILLIPS	640	2289	Tennessee River
Mann PHILLIPS	640	2258	Tennessee River
Willoughby WILLIAMS	1000	2633	Tennessee River
Nancy SHEPERD	640	2086	Tennessee River
John SHEPERD	640	2643	Tennessee River
John PATRICK	640	1275	Tennessee River
Jesse COBB	640	1176	Tennessee River
Jesse COBB	640	1175	Tennessee River
Jesse COBB	640	1092	Tennessee River
Jesse COBB	640	1128	Tennessee River
RICE and RICETON	640	1767	Tennessee River
Benjamin SHEPARD	1000	2318	Indian Creek
Jas. M. and Wm. T. LEWIS	640	309	Hurricane Creek
Benjamin SHEPARD	1000	2318	Indian Creek
Betsey BARROW	640	2774	Porterfield Cr.
Thomas ASKEN	640	1342	White Oak Creek
Willoughby WILLIAMS	1000	2617	White Oak Creek
Christopher GOODWIN	3840	959	White Oak Creek
John PATRICK	640	1280	Elliot's Creek
J. M'NAIRY and R. NELSON	640	149	Tennessee River
Jacob WHEATON	160	132	Tennessee River
John P. WIGGINS	320	4149	Tennessee River
William HILL	320	772	Tennessee River
Abner CLARK	640	5106	Tennessee River
John M'NAIRY	640	14	Tennessee River
Bartholomew SMITH	228	476	White Oak Creek
John P. WIGGINS	320	4163	Cane Creek
Jackson HULL's heirs	100	88	Leatherwood
Emanuel DAVIDSON's heirs	440	4229	Tennessee River

(Continued on following page)

188

(Stewart County delinquent tax list continued)

John WILLIAMS	50	109	Tennessee River
Ezekiel HUSON's heirs	30	97	Tennessee River
Jethro SUMNER	909	278	Tennessee River
Adam RABY	160	567	Tennessee River
Andrew SIMPSON	250	774	White Oak Creek
Hillary MORRISS	50	4195	White Oak Creek
Abner CLARK	320	5106	Hurricane Creek
Ezekiel HUTSON's heirs	240	97	Hurricane Creek
Samuel LEWIS	200	5146	White Oak Creek
James ROSS	200	Occp	Lewis Branch
Thomas D. WIGGINS	320	4276	White Oak Creek
John DAVIDSON	100	4534	White Oak Creek
James MILLS	400	546	Tennessee River
William MURRY	60	77	White Oak Creek
Isaac KITRELL	350	2402	White Oak Creek
James MURRY	100	320	White Oak Creek
Good. THOMPSON's heirs	55	4420	White Oak Creek
Good. THOMPSON's heirs	45	4420	White Oak Creek
James YOUNG	274	4430	White Oak Creek
William CLARK	22	1699	White Oak Creek
James COPPAGE's heirs	40	5203	Tennessee Ridge
Thomas ARNOLD	640	772	Tennessee Ridge
Huziekiah NOBLE	228	4468	Tennessee Ridge
Green HILL	640	3095	To Robt. NELSON
James SCOTT	620	3095	To Robt. NELSON
William HILL	320	772	Tennessee Ridge
Joseph COLSON	80	91	White Oak Creek
John PATRICK	274	1235	Tennessee River

Stewart County, Tennessee, February Sessions, 1811. John ALLEN, sheriff, reports that the following tracts of land will be sold on the first Monday in November next to satisfy the unpaid taxes for 1810. Robert COOPER.

Reputed Owners	Acres	Situation
William CARR	400	Clem. LANIER's
Major FREEMAN	1070	
Nicholas LONG	7680	Nine tracts
William MARSHALL	400	Clement LANIER
M'CLELAND's heirs	400	Clement LANIER
William NEELY	700	Cumberland Riv.
William TYRRELL	1000	Saline Creek
Edward YARBOROUGH	3840	In the Barrens
Thomas BERRY	914	Leatherwood Cr.
Hardy BRYAN	640	Leatherwood Cr.
Wm. MOORE and Jas. LYON	560	Cumberland Riv.
Curtis GRAY	253	Cross Creek
Sherwood BARROW	640	
John C. M'LEMORE	469	

(Continued on following page)

189

(Stewart County delinquent tax list continued)

William CHRISTAMS	637
Robert FENNER	2560
James FLETCHER	347
James DUNN	200

For sale, assorted merchandise. Calvin STRATTON.

For sale, prime whiskey. Martha TURNER.

The following persons have reported estrays in Bedford County, per H. DAWDY, r. b. c.:

(1) John C. DUNN, on Spring Creek, took up a filly. The filly is valued at $15 on July 4, 1811.

(2) John NEEL, on Big Spring, has taken up a sorrel mare. On July 6, 1811, the mare's value is $25.

(3) Jesse HUGH, on the west fork of Rock Creek, took up a bay filly. On July 15, 1811, the filly was given an appraised value of $30.

(4) Josiah WILLIAMS, on Duck Creek, took up a sorrel mare. On July 11, 1811, the mare's value is $29.

(5) John BYER, on Weakley's Creek, took up a chesnut sorrel horse. On July 8, 1811, the horse was given an appraised value of $8.

August 27, 1811, Vol. III, No. CLXXXVI

Found, a ladies gold sleeve clasp. John A. S. ANDERSON.

Reward $100. Two negroes ranaway from the subscriber on Sunday the 18th. JOHN is about 24 years old and is 5 ft., 6 or 7 in. tall. ABRAHAM is 22 years old, 5 ft., 6 or 7 in. tall and reads English. George M. DEADERICK.

Reward one cent. An apprentice named William WILLIAMS, age 20, ranaway from me on the Red River, Sumner County. Samuel PIPER.

Died after a short illness in this town on Thursday evening last at an advance age, Abner PECK. He was an early settler in Nashville. He leaves behind a widow and several children.

September 3, 1811, Vol. III, No. CLXXXVII

Russelville, August 23th. We were informed by a man from Christian County, that a child about 3 years old, the son of Edward BRADSHAW, surveyor, was killed by one of his negro women.

On Sunday the 11th, William LOGGINS was found dead near Bowling Green, Kentucky. He was on a visit to purchase land.

On the 11th of October next in Franklin, there will be a public sale directed by the Williamson County court of 3840 acres on the south Harpeth, that belong to John PARK. The property was taken at the influence of Thomas GIBSON. Wm. HULME, sheriff of Williamson County.

The following persons have reported estrays in Bedford
County, per Howel DAWDY, r. b. c.:
  (1) Nathaniel DRYDEN, on Dryden's Fork, has taken up a
      brown horse. On July 31, 1811, the horse was given
      an appraised value of $35.
  (2) Thompson THOMPSON, near Thompson Ford, has taken up
      a bay mare. On July 31, 1811, the mare was given
      an appraised value of $20.
  (3) John DEZASH, on Rock Creek, has taken up a sorrel
      mare. On July 27, 1811, the mare's value is $18.

September 10, 1811, Vol. III, No. CLXXXVIII
      On the 19th of October next in Nashville, there will be a
public sale directed by the court of Davidson County of 153
acres, that is the property of Charles CABANESS. The land
is occupied by Abraham STANDEFER. The property was taken
at the influence of Fanny INGRAM. M. C. DUNN, shff.
      On the 18th of October next in the town of Fayetteville,
there will be a public sale directed by the Davidson County
court of 400 acres in Lincoln County, that is the property
of John MACLEN. The land was taken at the influence of John
BOYD. Thos. M'BRIDE, d. s. l. c.
      The following persons have reported estrays in Lincoln
County, per (no ranger):
  (1) George DARNAL, on the Elk River, has taken up a
      chesnut sorrel horse. The appraised value of the
      horse is $15 on August 28, 1811.
  (2) John M'WHERTER, on Mulberry Creek, has taken up a
      mare. On August 26, 1811, the mare's value is $12.
  (3) Thomas Herrey, on Richland Creek, took up a mare.
      On August 24, 1811, the mare's value was $15.
  (4) Eli GARRETT, on Swan Creek, has taken up a sorrel
      mare. On August 27, 1811, the mare's value is $18.
  (5) James DENNIS has taken up a black horse. The horse
      was be valued at $18 on August 27, 1811.
  (6) William DAVIS, on Bradshaw's Creek, has taken up a
      mare. On August 19, 1811, the mare's value is $20.
      Bledsoe County, Tennessee, August Ssssions, 1811. Peter
LOONEY, collector, reports the following tracts of land will
be sold on the first Monday in November next in Madison to
satisfy the unpaid taxes for 1811. Samuel TERRY.

Reputed Owners	Acres
John M'IVER, Joseph JAMES and	
William PARKS	5000
John M'IVER and Thos. SWAIN	5000
CARTER's heirs	5000
Richd. H. LOVE and Hen. J. LOVE	5000
John C. HAILEY	100
Benjamin Grayson ORR	5000

Jeremiah PERRY vs. Stephen BEST, August term, 1811, In Equity. Stephen BEST is not an inhabitant of Tennessee and he is ordered to appear in court on the third Monday in February next. P. HENDERSON, c. c. r. w. c.

On the 19th of October in the town of Nashville, there will be a public sale directed by the Davidson County court of 314 acres on Big Harpeth, that is the property of George WADE. The land was taken at the influence of William GRIMES. M. C. DUNN, shff.

On the 19th of October in the town of Nashville, there will be a public sale directed by the Davidson County court of 80 acres on Pond Creek, that is the property of James LOVELL. The land was formerly occuppied by Charles STEWART. The land was attached by Wm. HOOPER. M. C. DUNN, shff.

On the 18th of October in the town of Fayetteville, there will be a public sale directed in the Davidson County court of 400 acres in Lincoln County on Cane Creek, that is the property of John MACLEN. The land was attached by John BOYD. Thos. M'BRIDE, d. s. l. c.

On the 19th of October next in Nashville, there will be a public sale directed by the court of Davidson County of 150 acres, that is owned and occuppied by William RUSSEL. The land was taken at the influence of Roland RICE. M. C. DUNN.

On the 19th of October next in Nashville, there will be a public sale directed by the court of Davidson County of 505 acres, that is owned and occuppied by John GORDON. The land was conveyed to John GORDON by James HOGGAT and James BOSLEY by a deed bearing a date of January 30, 1798 in Book D in the Registrar's Office on pages 432-433, dated June 1, 1798. The land was attached by Tho. G. WATKINS against John GORDON as security for Bennet SEARCY. There were other attachments by John B. CRAIGHEAD and John ANDERSON. M. C. DUNN.

September 24, 1811, Vol. III, No. CXC

The imported stud horse Dragon will be sold on the third of October at the Nashville Turf. R. WEAKLY.

For sale, 300 acres. Alexander WALKER.

The following persons have reported estrays in Bedford County, per Howel DAWDY, r. b. c.:

(1) Nathan HOOKER, near Fishing Ford, has taken up a sorrel mare. On August 25, 1811, the mare's value was appraised at $15.

(2) William NEAL took up a yellow bay mare. The mare was appraised at $15 on August 8, 1811.

(3) Benjamin LITTLE, on Wilson Creek, took up a mare. On August 10, 1811, the mare's value is $10.

(4) Job COOPER, on Clem Creek, has taken up a bay mare. On August 17, 1811, the mare's value is $10.

(5) John TUCK, on Caney Spring Creek, took up a sorrel

mare. On August 21, 1811, the mare's value is $25.

(6) William ALDFED, on Rock Creek near Leeper's Mill, has taken up a brown mare. The mare was given an appraised value of $10 on August 6, 1811.

(7) Clement CANNON, near Shelbyville, has taken up a sorrel horse. On August 24, 1811, the horse's value was appraised at $15.

A mulatto man named BILL ranaway from Soldier's Rest. He is about 21 years old. Thomas OVERTON.

The copartnership of John and William PAYTON is dissolved by mutual consent on September 18, 1811. John and William PAYTON.

On the 18th, Miss Polly HAMPTON and Mrs. Jane FORTE died of a fever.

The subscriber informs the public that his boatyard will continue at Sanders Ferry. Francis SANDERS.

On Tuesday, John COXETTER, Greenham Mills, Newbury, had two sheep shorn at his factory at 5 am. By evening Sir John THORKMORTON was wearing the coat.

October 8, 1811, Vol. III, No. CXCII

By virtue of twenty-eight alias writs, there will be a public sale directed by the court of Dickson County in the town of Charlotte of the following tracts of land to satisfy the taxes for 1807. Edward PERSALL, shff.

Reputed Owners	Acres	Warr.	Situation
Martin ARMSTRONG	5000	253	Duck River
James ARANDALE	640	2494	Duck River
John BLACK's heirs	640	1598	Duck River
Jesse COBB	640	1119	Duck River
John ELLEOTT	640	263	Duck River
Elisha HARRIS	640	3052	Duck River
John HURLY	640	243	Duck River
James LEE	640	1939	Duck River
William MOORE	640	3419	Duck River
David PENDERGRASS	225	1293	Paine River
Thomas PARSON's heirs	640	1488	Duck River
Thomas PARSON's heirs	640	1387	Duck River
William POLK	640	172	
Robert & John ROWLIN	274	580	Duck River
Robert & John ROWLIN	428	581	Duck River
Oliver SMITH	274	3717	Pine River
Oliver SMITH	640	1906	Pine River
Willis SMITH	640	964	Bushes Meet
Lt. Daniel SHAW	2560	1794	Duck River
George A. SUGG	640	2474	Pine River
George A. SUGG	640	2030	Pine River
Daniel WILLIAMS	640	932	Duck River
Thomas PARSON's heirs	228	156	Duck River

Died in this town, Jesse WESTMORLAND of Giles County.
On the 23th, Patrick CAMPBELL died in Knoxville.
Dr. Elias PORTER, on the Elk River, died.
John CUNNIGHAM was hung in Beldsoe County for the murder
of his wife.
On the first Monday in November next in Charlotte, there
will be a public sale directed by the Dickson County court
to satisfy the unpaid taxes for 1809. Edward PEARSALL, shf.

Reputed Owners	Acres	Situation
James G. BEHAN	640	Yellow Creek
Alexander HUNTER	60	Cumberland River
Tapley IRBY	40	Turnbull Creek
John KIMBLE	1053	Harpeth
Ebenezar MOTT	640	Jones Creek
Benjamin T. WARREN	100	Pine River

October 13, 1811, Vol. III, No. CXCIII
The following is a list of letters remaining at the post
office in Franklin on October 1, 1811, per Gurdon SQUIRER,
a. p. m.: Samuel AKINS, Eleazer ANDREWS, Wm. ALEXANDER, Wm.
BROWN, John ANDREWS, John ADAMS, Samuel P. BLACK, Wm. LOGAN,
John ANDREWS, John ADAMS, Eliz. BAXTON, Charles BURNS, James
BLACK, Elisha BALEY, Sarah BERRY, John BRISCOE, John BURNS,
Fred. BRAWDER, George BENNETT, Thos. CUMMINS, Newton GANNON,
David CHRIESMAN, John COOR, James B. CARROL, Henry COOK, Wm.
HOUSTON, James CUMMINS, David CAMPBELL, Capt. Robt. CANNON,
J. J. and D. CAMPBELL, John CRENSHAW, Henry CHILDRESS, John
DUNNAGAN, John DURLEY, Samuel DAVIS, John DADNEY, John KERR,
Robert DAVIS, Joseph DAVISON, Eph. P. DICKSON, Geo. DICKEY,
James DRAKE, James DAVIS, Robert DANIEL, James DAWNING,
Elisha DOTSAN, Josiah ELLIOTT, John ELLISAN, Samuel ELAM,
Thomas EVANS, Joseph FARRAR, William SMITH, Thomas FURNAGE,
Enos FARMER, Jordan FIPPS, Joel FELTS, Polly FREEMAN, Sam.
FITZPATRICK, John GRIFFITH, Sally GARNER, John GASAGE, Moses
GORDON, John GRIGGS, Pamelia GRAY, John HANKS, Rbt. GUTHERIE
Benjamin HOOKER, An. HARDEMAN, James KINNARD, Wm. M. MARR,
Samuel HEMPHILL, David HOOKS, Walter HILL, J. HARDEMAN,
Polly JOHNSTON, Andrew JAMESON, James KELLEY, James MARTIN,
Chas. KAVANAUGH, Alexander M'CAWN, James MARTIN, Matt. S.
MURFREE, Fred. MAYBERRY, Go. W. MEDIARIS, G. L. NOLEN, Berry
NOLEN, Drury NOBLES, To. H. PERKINS, Alxr. PATTON, Hinchey
PETTAWAY, John SMITH, Hinchey B. PETTWAY, Peter PERKINS,
John WHEAT, Edward RAGSDALE, Wm. PHILIPS, Susanna RUSSELL,
Robert RICHARDS, Benj. RUSSELL, Alx. SIMMON, Thos. STEVENS,
James SWANSON, Polly STREET, Henry SISSONS, Nehemiah SMITH,
Joseph SUMNERS, Rheu. SIMMONS, Alxr. SMITH, Michael SHEFLER,
Stephen SMITH, Sampn. SAWYERS, To. E. SUMNER, James TAYLOR,
Edmund WELLS, Michael SMITH, Anthony SHARPE, Sarah WIER,
John TREMBLE, Mart. TRANTHAM, Richard TANNER, James TAYLOR,

Dixon VAUGHAN, John WHITE, Thos. WESTON, Christr. WOOD, John
C. WORMLEY, Thompson WOOD, Samuek WILLIAMS, James WEST, Geo.
WARD, Pleasant WATKINS, Jas. WILLIAMSON, Daniel YOUNG, Nich.
WILBURN.
     The following is a list of letters remaining at the post
office in Jefferson on October 1, 1811, per John SPENCE, p.
m.: James BOSLEY, Geo. BOOTH, William BENNET, John BULLARD,
David BLALOCK, Fred. E. BECKTON, James BARKLEY, Geo. DOGGED,
Geo. BRANDON, Phil. and E. CROWDER, Henry CONWAY, Benjamin
CARR, Newton CANNON, Joel CHILDRESS, Benjamin CARR, Thos. A.
CANNON, Washing. DUKE, Robt. H. DYER, Cors. DABNEY, Wiley J.
DAVIS, Dav. FLEMMING, Ezekiah FERIS, And. FERRICE, Wateman
GULLET, Jesse FEATHERTON, Hugh GRAHAM, Capt. Peter GRAY, Wm.
HALL, Mrs. Cat. GRAYSON, Jeremiah GRAVES, Oliver HARRIS, Wm.
HAMBLET, Thos. A. HARRIS, Pleasant HENDERSON, Wm. HOPE, Wm.
LOVE, John HALES, Edwd. JOHNSTON, Levis LOLLAR, Thos. LAND,
Alex. LEWRENCE, Henry LANGFORD, Benj. H. LEWIS, Col. Danl.
MARSHALL, David MACKEY, Jonathan MACKEY, Saml. MASSEY, Jacob
M'CLEROY, Obediah M'CLIN, Andw. M'CRORY, John M'CLURE, John
MADISON, Samuel M'CORMICK, James M'CAMPBELL, Humphrey MOUNT,
James MOORE, John M'PEAK, John M'GLOUGHLIN, James NEELY, Wm.
NICHOLS, James M'GILL, Mod'k. M'CRARY, James NEVINS, Thomas
NASH, James NORSWORTHY, Capt. JOhn PARKES, Thos. A. PEACOCK,
David PRICE, Nathaniel PERRIG, John H. RHODES, Benj. RANSOM,
Gordon RIDOUT, John REYNOLDS, Jesse ROBINSON, George WATSON,
Joseph D. SMITH, Hullet SULLIVAN, John M. TAYLOR, Col. James
WILSON, Ninion WHITTLE, Samuel WODLEY, Mrs. Celia WATSON, C.
WHITE, Benjamin WILSON.
     On the 23rd of November next in Nashville, there will be
a public sale directed by the Davidson County court of 1000
acres on the south side of the Cumberland River, that is the
property of William RICKARD in Stewart County. The land was
granted to Thomas and James ARMSTRONG on September 15, 1788.
Also for sale, is 640 acres in Hickman County granted to
James ARNOLD, December 20, 1791. The property was taken by
the United States Government. John CHILDRESS.
     Charleston September 11th. A tornado passed through
killing the following persons: Miss Margaret COZENS, age
24; Dr. CANTON, native of France; Mr. PETERSON, a native of
Germany; a negro man belonging to Mr. DENER.

October 22, 1811, Vol. III, No. CXCIII
     New York, September 25th. Capt. DOLLIVAR arrived at this
port from the Ship Remittance.
     Capt. HURD arrived yesterday from Oporto.
     Died a few days since, Mrs. HALL. She was the partner of
Maj. HALL, near Clover Bottom.
     Died on Tuesday, Mrs. WILLIAMS. She was the relict of
the late John WILLIAMS of Mill Creek.

On the 5th, a named PHILL ranaway from the subscriber. He has worked in the carpenter's trade. Burwell SNEED.

November 12, 1811, Vol. III, No. CXCVI

The following persons have reported estrays in Wilson County, per Edmund DRUTCHER, d. r. w. c.:

(1) John BRADLEY has taken up a bay mare. The mare was appraised at $20 on July 15, 1811.
(2) James HOOPER, near Drake's Lick, has taken up a bay mare. On July 20, 1811, the mare's value is $30.
(3) Henry FREEMAN, on Spencer's Creek, has taken up a colt. On August 1, 1811, the colt's value is $6.
(4) John BRADLEY, on Spring Creek, took up two fillies. On August 24, 1811, the fillies' value are $25.
(5) George MORTON, on Sugg's Creek, took up a filly. On August 19, 1811, the filly's value is $15.
(6) John RALLS, on Spring Creek, took up a bay filly. On August 23, 1811, the filly's value is $10.
(7) John M'NIGHT, on Sander's Fork, took up a bay mare. On September 23, 1811, the mare's value is $30.
(8) James RAMSEY, on Sander's Fork, took up a bay mare. On September 21, 1811, the mare's value is $15.
(9) Domeris ADAMSON, on Purtle Creek, has taken up a bay mare. On September 23, 1811, the mare's value was appraised at $15.
(10) Robert BURNETT, on Smith's Fork, took up a sorrel horse. On September 13, 1811, the horse's value was appraised at $20.
(11) Nathan WHEELER, on Round Lick Creek, has taken up a sorrel mare. On September 9, 1811, the mare was given an appraised value of $35.
(12) Isaac EASTLICK, on Bradley's Creek, has taken up a sorrel horse. On September 21, 1811, the horse was appraised in the amount of $30.
(13) John BURSELL, on Fall Creek, took up a bay mare. A value of $13 was given on September 13, 1811.
(14) William DILLARD, on Clendening Creek, took up a chesnut sorrel mare. The mare was appraised at a value of $25 on September 26, 1811.
(15) James M'DONALD has taken up a bay mare. The mare was appraised at $15 on September 9, 1811.
(16) John LUMPKIN, on Stones Creek near Cedar Lick, has taken up a bay mare. On September 25, 1811, the mare was appraised at $22.
(17) Edmund PERSONS, on Purtle Creek, took up a horse. On September 20, 1811, the horse's value is $4.50.
(18) John REATHERFORD has taken up a sorrel mare. The mare was appraised at $25 on September 27, 1811.
(19) William PORTERFIELD, on Smith's Fork, took up a bay

mare. The mare's value on October 3, 1811 is $30.
(20) James JONHSON, on Smith Fork, has taken up a sorrel
    filly. On September 27, 1811, the filly was given
    value of $12.50.
(21) William ELKINS, on Sinking Creek three miles south
    of Lebanon, has taken up a black mare. The mare was
    appraised at $22 on October 22, 1811.
(22) James LUCH, on Spring Creek, has taken up a sorrel
    mare. On October 3, 1811, the mare's value is $10.
Those indebted to the late John M'CONNLL in the hatting
business, please come forward. Ann M'CONNELL.
The following persons in Bedford County have reported
estrays, per Howel DAWDY, r. b. c.:
(1) Benjamin KING, on Big Flat Creek, has taken up a
    bay horse colt. On September 24, 1811, the colt
    was appraised at $6.
(2) Richard BURGESS, on Big Flat Creek, took up a bay
    filly. On September 16, 1811, the filly was given
    an appraised value of $16.
(3) George CATHEY, on Rock Creek, has taken up a horse.
    On September 16, 1811, the horse's value is $16.
(4) Ezekiah BILLINGSTON, at Warners Ferry on the Duck
    River, has taken up a sorrel mare. The mare's value
    was appraised at $20 on September 22, 1811.
(5) Timothy SUGS, on War Trace, took up a sorrel stud
    colt. The colt's value is $5 on September 25, 1811.
(6) John BURNES, on Fishing Ford, has taken up a horse.
    The horse's value is $15 on September 20, 1811.
(7) Charles MORRISS, on Fishing Ford, has taken up a
    horse. On September 30, 1811, the horse was given
    an appraised value of $5.
The following persons have reported estrays in Lincoln
County, per Brice M. GARNER, for Phillip KOONCE, ranger:
(1) John W. SMITH, by permission of his father, has
    taken up a sorrel horse. On October 5, 1811, the
    horse was appraised at $17.
(2) Samuel BUCHANNON took up a bay filly. The filly was
    appraised at $15 on October 7, 1811.
(3) Isaac CONGER, on Norris Creek, took up a bay mare.
    The mare was appraised at $12 on October 19, 1811.
(4) Ebineser M'EWIN, on Hannah's Ford, has taken up a
    bay filly. On October 5, 1811, the filly was given
    an appraised value of $60.
The following persons have reported estrays in Bedford
County, per H. DAWDY, r. b. c.:
(1) Philip BARROW, on Big Fall Creek, has taken up a
    black horse. On October 10, 1811, the horse was
    appraised at a value of $15.
(2) Starling TUCKER, on Fall Creek, took up a horse. An

appraised value of $6 on October 12, 1811.
(3) Stephen JOHNSON, on Weakley's Creek, has taken up a horse. On October 12, 1811, the horse was given an appraised value of $15.
Cash will be given for Louisanna and Natchez Bank notes at a discount. James and Washington JACKSON.

November 26, Vol. III, No. CXCVIII
The following persons have reported estrays in Wilson County, per Edmund CRUTCHER, d. r.:
(1) Wyatt BETTS, on Barton Creek, has taken up a black mare. On October 24, 1811, the mare's value is $16.
(2) Matthew CARTWRIGHT, on Cedar Creek, has taken up a bay horse. On November 2, 1811, the horse was given an appraised value of $1.
(3) Benjamin NICHOLS, on Pond Lick, has taken up a bay mare. On November 2, 1811, the horse was given an appraised value of $20.
(4) A sorrel horse was taken up on Spring Creek by John CARLIN. The horse was appraised at a value of $15 on November 1, 1811.
(5) Edward DREW took up a brown bay horse. The horse was appraised at $8 on November 4, 1811.
(6) William M'CULLEY, on Stone Creek, took up a horse. On November 5, 1811, the horse's value is $2.
(7) Howell PEARSON, on the Cumberland River at Pharr's
The following persons have reported estrays in Bedford County, per Howel DAWDY, c.:
(1) Benjamin LITTLE, on Wilson's Creek, has taken up a sorrel horse. On October 9, 1811, the horse was appraised at a value of $17.50.
(2) James CLINTON, on Wilson Creek, took up a filly. On October 25, 1811, the filly's value is $16.
Died on Sunday last, Mrs. Mary M. CAMP. She is the wife of James CAMP formerly of Madison County, Virginia.

December 9, 1811, III, No. CXCX
My wife Esther GAGE has absconded from my bed without just cause. John GAGE, sen.
New Orleans, November 15th. The following were members of the convention: J. VILLERE, Orleans; S. WINTER, Orleans; T. UREHART, Orleans; J. LIVAVARIS, Orleans; A. EBERT, Pointe Couppee; D. DELARONDE, Orleans; S. HENDERSON, Orleans; James BROWN, German Coast; Col. BELLECHASSE, Orleans; Wm. WIKOFF, Ibderville; M. GUCGARD, Orleans; J. BLANQIER, Orleans; Levi WELLS, Rapide; J. B. DORGENOIS, Orleans; H. S. THEBODEAUX, La Fouche; J. WATKINS, Orleans; B. MARIGNIG, Orleans; James DUNLAP, Concordia; L. L. DESTREHAN, German Coast; D. SATOON, Opelousas; Mr. LABRANCH, German Coast; T. F. OLIVER, Rapide;

198

Mr. CANTRELLE, Acadia; Mr. ROSSIN, Acadia; Alexander PORTER, Attakapas; Mr. SMITHFELL, Acadia, Mr. ROSSIN, Acadia, John THOMPSON, Opelousas; R. B. MAGRUDER, Opelousas; N. MEZZIAN, La Fouche; B. HUBBARD, La Fourche; A. GOFORTH, La Fourche; Mr. J. POYDRASS, Pointe Coupee; S. HEBIER, Pointe Coupee.

The following persons have reported estrays in Rutherford County, per N. B. ROSE, r. r. c.:

(1) Henry NORMAN, on the west fork of the Stone River, has taken up a bay horse.
(2) Samuel FULKS, near Browley's Mill, has taken up a bay horse, that is valued at $50.
(3) William LEWIS, on the west fork of the Stone River, has taken up a bay mare.
(4) Larkin JOHNSTON has taken up a black mare.
(5) Mathew JOHNSON, on Miller's Mill, took up a horse.
(6) Seth WEBB, near Wright's Mill, has taken up a black horse, that is valued at $3.
(7) Phillip DAVICE, on Horse Spring Fork, has taken up bay mare, that is valued at $25.
(8) James TUCKER, on the east fork of the Stone River, has taken up a sorrel stud colt.
(9) Lent BROWN has taken up a brown mare.
(10) Thomas THOMPSON, on the east fork of the Stone River, has taken up a sorrel mare.
(11) James JOHNSON, near Miller's Mill, has taken up a yellow bay mare, that is valued at $11.
(12) John WASSON, on Lock's Creek, has taken up a horse.
(13) Moses LOFTEN, on Miller's Mill, took up a filly.
(14) John BOWMAN, on the west fork of the Stone River, has taken up a white mare.
(15) James SULTFUE, on Locks Creek, took up a roan mare.
(16) Robert HENDERSON, on the west fork of the Stone River, has taken up a horse, that is valued at $10.

On the 18th of January next in the town of Fayetteville, there will be a public sale directed by the Davidson County court of several tracts of land, that are the property of Robert NEILSON, dec. The property consists of 182 acres, on Bradhsaw's Creek, Grant No. 2101, Warrant No. 196; 63 acres that is west of Robert NEILSON; 130 acres on the Elk River, Grant No. 2102, Warrant No. 840, adjoining Samuel LOCKHART. The land was taken by William TATE against Hugh F. BELL, admin. of Robert NEILSON, dec. Cornelius SLATER, shff.

For rent, a smith shop. Collin M'DANIEL.

On the 18th of Janaury next in the town of Nashville, there will be a public sale directed by the Davidson County court of 14-1/2 acres on the Big Harpeth, that belongs to James HARDING. The property was taken at the influence of Abraham DEMOSS. M. C. DUNN, shff.

On the 1st of February next in Columbia, there will be a

public sale directed by the Maury County court of a part of 5000 acres, that was entered in the name of Michael BACON and granted to Robert HILL. The land is occupied by Spencer GRIFFIN. The tract is the property of Spencer GRIFFITH and Ephraim MCLEON. The land was taken at the influence of William and Joseph MARTIN. William BRADSHAW.

The following persons have reported estrays in Lincoln County, per Brice M. GARNER, d. r. l. c.:

(1) Alexander GRAY, on M'Cullough's Creek, has taken up a sorrel mare. On November 13, 1811, the mare was given an appraised value of $25.

(2) Charles THROOP, by permission of Anthony HAMPTON on Cane Creek, has taken up a bay mare. The mare was valued at $14 on November 13, 1811.

(3) Robert M. WHITE, on Swan Creek, took up a sorrel horse. On November 23, 1811, the horse was given an appraised value of $38.

(4) Abner M'WHERTER, on Nicholas Old Mill, has taken up a bay horse. On November 24, 1811, the horse was appraised at $7.

(5) Jesse CRAWFORD, on Mulberry Creek, has taken up a sorrel mare. On November 23, 1811, the mare was valued at $10.

(6) Samuel BURKS, on Mulberry Creek, took up a horse. The horse was valued at $12.50 on November 23, 1811.

December 24, 1811, Vol. III, No. CCII

On the 16th Col. William CHRISTMAS died. He was the late Surveyor General and assisted in building the first log cabin in Kentucky by old Col. BOON.

On the 25th of January next in the town of Fayetteville, there will be a public sale directed by the Lincoln County court of 333 acres, that is the property of William M. GUNN. The land was taken at the influence of Joseph LAMASTER. Ethan WELLS, d. s. l. c.

On the 19th of January next in the town of Lebanon, there will be a public sale directed by the Davidson County court of several tracts of land, that is the property of Jonathan MAGNESS. The land was taken at the influence of John C. HAMILTON. Thomas BRADLEY, shff.

ARRONTON, 43 181
ARTHBURTHNOT, 96
ASDILL, 43
ASHBURN, 29
ASHE, 172
ASHLY, 106
ASKEN, 174 188
ATKINS, 16 106 118
ATKINSON, 127 148 180
AUDRAIN, 84
AULTON, 99
AUST, 7
AUSTAN, 10
AUSTIN, 75 79 127 139 154
AVENT, 72
AYERS, 44 51
AYRES, 21 139 160
BABBIT, 86
BACON, 51 132 200
BADGER, 1 7 11 17 75 114
BAILEY, 7 14 38 180
BAILY, 101 106 116
BAINS, 6
BAIRD, 95 107 131 161 168
BAKER, 10 22 28 64 74 81 86 92
    96 104 132-134 180 185
BAKLEY, 79
BALAYADA, 76
BALCH, 33 51 131
BALDRIDGE, 1 84
BALDWIN, 115
BALEY, 194
BALL, 38 39 171
BALLARD, 50 72
BALLEW, 93
BALLUS, 43
BALOTE, 73
BAMBRICK, 94
BANCROFT, 125
BANDY, 7 109
BANE, 106
BANKHEAD, 106 118 158 165
BANKS, 92 101 127 185
BARBA, 153
BARBOUR, 181
BARCLAY, 28
BARDLEY, 102
BARDNAST, 167
BAREGER, 43
BARFIELD, 158
BARGE, 160

BARGER, 65
BARHAM, 146
BARKER, 19 106 163 180
BARKLEY, 118 195
BARKSDALE, 181
BARLOW, 78 131 146 149
BARNAN, 127
BARNES, 64 69 70 163 180
BARNET, 163
BARNETT, 38 125
BARNHILL, 133
BARNS, 39 65 76
BARR, 28 127
BARREN, 148
BARRINGER, 38
BARRINGTON, 15
BARRON, 60
BARRONTON, 106 118
BARROW, 33 80 114 135 144 148
    149 172 177 188 189 197
BARRSLER, 22
BARRY, 25 82 109
BARTHOLMEW, 57
BARTHOLOMEW, 57
BARTLET, 148
BARTON, 116 117
BASHAM, 127 154 163
BASHAW, 91
BASKINS, 129
BASON, 7
BASS, 103 114 119 120 132
BASSEMULLER, 76
BASSINGER, 95
BASWELL, 99
BATE, 97 173
BATES, 14 99 180
BATON, 171
BAUCEON, 146
BAWERMAN, 52
BAXTON, 194
BAYARD, 62
BAYE, 50
BAYED, 180
BAYES, 20 63
BAYET, 127
BAYN, 158
BAYTERS, 160
BEALL, 27 28
BEALS, 44
BEAN, 11 43 49 76 118 134
BEARD, 15 49 166 184

BEARDEN, 28
BEARDING, 55 56
BEARDSLEY, 46
BEASELEY, 106
BEASLEY, 74 89 133 180
BEASLY, 65
BEATTY, 56
BEATY, 35 83 116 130 161
BEAVER, 15
BEAVERS, 101 158
BECK, 69 143 172
BECKET, 46
BECKOM, 11
BECKTON, 195
BECLER, 115
BECOTE, 172
BEDFORD, 8 106 118 122 155
BEEL, 100
BEELAR, 148
BEESLEY, 6
BEESLY, 11
BEHAN, 194
BELFORD, 137
BELFOUR, 54
BELL, 16 28 38 43 110 112 114
    122 139 142 160 161 199
BELLAH, 181
BELLECHASSE, 198
BELLENSLEY, 86
BELOTE, 97
BELSHER, 12
BELT, 132
BENGE, 17
BENHAM, 83
BENNET, 28 43 64 65 127 180
    195
BENNETT, 43 54 180 194
BENNIT, 1
BENOIT, 105 159
BENSHAW, 155
BENT, 10
BEREMON, 118
BERILE, 130
BERLAY, 148
BERMINGHAM, 112
BERRY, 30 54 103 130 140 143
    146 158 171 174 189 194
BERRYHILL, 130
BERRYMAN, 42
BESHARS, 166
BEST, 165 192

BETHEL, 11
BETTS, 102 180 198
BEVILL, 154
BEVIN, 65
BEVY, 148
BEYET, 101
BIBB, 164
BIBEY, 147
BIDDLE, 39
BIDDWELL, 44
BIDOLE, 29
BIERT, 125
BIGGS, 154
BIGHAM, 113 148 167
BIGLEY, 43
BILL, 193
BILLEW, 17
BILLINGSLEY, 65
BILLINGSTON, 197
BILYEY, 15
BINGAMAN, 177
BINNET, 51
BINNON, 14
BIRCHET, 84
BIRD, 46 94
BIRDWELL, 77
BIRK, 94
BISHOP, 16 158
BITTIC, 16
BITTICK, 163
BLACK, 28 91 101 103 139 148
    153 174 180 193 194
BLACKBURN, 6 10 23 86 87 91
    100 128 162 184 185
BLACKMAN, 55 133
BLACKMORE, 19 66 97 114 116
    123 133 150
BLACKON, 25
BLACKSAN, 22
BLACKWELL, 43 118
BLADWIN, 45
BLAGRAVES, 168
BLAIMER, 187
BLAIR, 10 17 56 61 106 112 134
    139 147
BLAKE, 106 130
BLAKELY, 146 154
BLALOCK, 165 181 195
BLANCHARD, 9 173 175
BLAND, 156
BLANKENSHIP, 95

BREVORT, 22
BREWER, 11 17 28 90 95
BRIANT, 15 38 43
BRICE, 17 38 43
BRICHEATI, 158
BRIDGES, 116 130 166 180
BRIDGET, 50
BRIDGEWATER, 1 16 101
BRIGANCE, 77
BRIGANN, 87
BRIGHT, 39 51 54 112 161
BRILES, 48
BRIMAGER, 103 136
BRIMIMAGER, 136
BRINCE, 162
BRINKLEY, 97 115
BRINSON, 127
BRISCOE, 194
BRISTOL, 46
BRITAIN, 38 60
BRITT, 28
BRITTAIN, 127
BRITTELL, 86
BRITTON, 1 5 52 65 76 121
BROADWAY, 130
BROCK, 133
BROCKET, 15
BROCKETT, 11
BROETHES, 171
BROILS, 54
BRON, 38
BROOK, 9
BROOKS, 7 18 19 28 38 50 54 82
    91 104 106 115 127 139 146
    184
BROOMFIELD, 144 173 187
BROOX, 137
BROTHERS, 133 155
BROTTES, 171
BROW, 77 96 108
BROWDER, 28 115 154
BROWN, 1 6 15 23 27 28 31 32
    36 38 42 43 45 49 51–56 59 61
    63 68 72 75 76 78 92, 95 96 98
    115 116 118 120 127 129 130
    135 140 143 144 146 148 154
    163 167 177 178 185 187 194
    198 199
BROWNFIELD, 1 17 76
BROWNIN, 182
BROWNING, 130 184

BROWS, 10
BRUCE, 17 38 79 114 160
BRUFF, 45 154 180
BRUFFY, 28
BRUMLEE, 176
BRUMLEY, 128
BRUNER, 54
BRUNSEN, 29
BRUNSON, 151
BRUNSTON, 148
BRUSH, 21 22
BRYAN, 31 38 40 42 104 139 189
BRYANCE, 97
BRYANT, 88 92 136
BRYD, 116
BRYLZE, 50
BRYSON, 39 162
BUCHANAN, 32
BUCHANNIN, 25
BUCHANNON, 71 103 197
BUCHANON, 31 123 148
BUCK, 36 46
BUCKINHANON, 79
BUCKLEY, 169
BUCKLY, 153
BUCKMAN, 121
BUCKNER, 43 165
BUCLEY, 76
BUDEN, 46
BUDWELL, 10
BUFORD, 2 14 75 93
BUGG, 116
BULL, 146
BULLARD, 49 106 124 133 141
    195
BULLEN, 188
BULLER, 59
BULLOCK, 70
BUMPASS, 115
BUNAS, 146
BUNCH, 171
BUNCOMB, 33
BUNDY, 10 16
BUNN, 28
BUNNELS, 12
BUNTING, 26
BURDETT, 130
BURDINE, 16 99
BURDS, 58
BURFORD, 90
BURGE, 106

BURGEN, 148
BURGESS, 11 127 180 197
BURGLAR, 51
BURGRESS, 101
BURKE, 6 146
BURKER, 7
BURKETT, 115
BURKS, 3 12 71 200
BURLET, 77
BURMINGHAM, 64
BURNES, 106 127 133 154 163
  197
BURNET, 53 76
BURNETT, 101 175 196
BURNEY, 127
BURNHAM, 46
BURNOM, 101 125
BURNS, 106 146 181 194
BURRIS, 15
BURROW, 10 14 130
BURSELL, 196
BURTON, 22 36 43 57 77 81 86
  89 90 94 134 142 161 172
BURWELL, 34 157
BUSH, 24 86 98
BUSSELL, 79
BUSTARD, 51 105 151
BUTKER, 171
BUTLER, 21 37 80 118 120 136
  140 146 148 169 171
BYCER, 186
BYER, 190
BYERS, 115
BYLER, 62 106 130 156 169
BYRAN, 38 140
BYRD, 171
BYRN, 77
BYRNE, 163
BYRNS, 110
CABANESS, 191
CABELL, 153
CABINESS, 151
CABOT, 112
CADE, 160
CAFFERY, 161
CAGE, 6 74 95 184
CAGLE, 78 109
CAINS, 98
CAKE, 188
CALBIRTH, 43
CALDWELL, 11 51 67

CALHOON, 119
CALHOUN, 7 166
CALIEN, 101
CALLAND, 162
CALLEWAY, 50
CALLINGHAM, 44
CALLOWAY, 14 43 90
CALLY, 27
CALVERT, 28 116
CAMAN, 5
CAMBIAN, 64
CAMERON, 43 112
CAMP, 198
CAMPBELL 1, 10 14 15 17 21 35
  38 43 44 46 48-50 57 60 61 73
  80 82 88 90 101 104 113 116
  127 129 131 137 145 147 148
  158 160 163 167-170 180 194
CAN, 43
CANADY, 90
CANAN, 121
CANNADAY, 14
CANNADY, 27
CANNAWAY, 16 64
CANNON, 38 67 101 103 114 116
  154 158 168 180 193-195
CANTON, 195
CANTREL, 102 123
CANTRELL, 21 155 161
CANTRELLE, 199
CAPEHART, 180
CAPLE, 116 146
CARDS, 50
CARDWELL, 68
CARLIN, 198
CARLOCK, 68 92
CARLTON, 134
CARMACK, 51
CARMAN, 74
CARMICHAEL, 57 125 161
CARMIKLE, 158
CARNAL, 162
CARNEY, 118 134 172
CARNS, 43 158
CARPENTER, 2 81
CARR, 24 52 97 133 181 189 195
CARRAWAY, 25
CARREL, 158 184
CARRELL, 180
CARRICK, 11 53 151 156
CARRIGER, 39

CLARK (continued)
154 158 163 169 189
CLARY, 50
CLASBY, 5
CLAXTON, 160
CLAY, 36 122 161 162
CLAYTON, 176
CLE, 15
CLEM, 160 163
CLEMENT, 157
CLEMET, 176
CLEMMONS, 129
CLENDENING, 32
CLERCK, 85
CLIFT, 43
CLIFTON, 132
CLINTON, 36 127 151 198
CLIPPER, 38 43
CLOPTON, 106 123
CLOUD, 38
CLOYD, 103 167
COARTS, 125
COATS, 9
COBB, 28 60 136 168 169 172 188
193
COBBINS, 5
COBELL, 115
COCHRAN, 179
COCK, 43 54 103
COCKBURN, 130
COCKE, 30 48
COCKERHAM, 53
COCKRELL, 137
COCKRIL, 111
COCKRILL, 140
COCKRUM, 11 76
COCKRUN, 130
COCKS, 169
CODWELL, 47
COE, 50
COEN, 43
COFFEE, 9 76 161
COFFERY, 26 106
COFMAN, 10
COGHLIN, 144 174 187
COGLIN, 172 173
COHE, 119
COKE, 38
COLDWELL, 38 55 106
COLE, 43 60 145
COLEMAN, 5 104 136 146 161

COLEVIN, 51
COLIER, 181
COLLIER, 79
COLLIN, 114
COLLINGS, 82
COLLINS, 18 55 82 100 175
COLSON, 189
COLVILLE, 7 17
COMMONS, 1
CONAWAY, 90 93
CONDON, 21 124 179
CONGER, 1 140 197
CONISON, 51
CONLY, 12
CONN, 29 39 42 44 52 58
CONNEL, 17
CONNELLY, 171
CONNELY, 142
CONNER, 16 113 140 147 178
CONNLEY, 142
CONNOWAY, 76 90
CONRAD, 26 103
CONUAIN, 39
CONWAY, 43 106 128 129 181
195
COO, 43
COOK, 1 5 16 47 51 63 64 85 86
91 94 100 104 112 116 118 143
149 152 165 168 178 184 194
COOKE, 21 57 180
COOL, 103
COOLEY, 166
COOPER, 13 24 38 39 65 80 89
95 105 148 171 186 189 192
COOR, 194
COPELAND, 29 39 42 43 68
COPLAND, 15 40 51
COPLE, 7
COPPAGE, 189
CORBIT, 161
CORDEL, 116
CORDEN, 154
CORDER, 65
CORMER, 43
CORMICK, 43 83
CORNELIUS, 7
CORNWALL, 90
CORNWELL, 64 84
CORREA, 160
COSBY, 13 14 48
COSSINEL, 38

COSSMAN, 39
COSTEGAN, 94
COTREL, 76
COTRELL, 6
COTTINGHAM, 95
COTTON, 23 83
COUCH, 61 62 171
COUDREA, 92
COULEY, 7
COULS, 25
COUNCIL, 43 59
COUNTS, 102
COUPLAND, 43
COURTNEY, 94
COVEY, 180
COVILLE, 125
COVINGTON, 57 134
COWAN, 29 30 34 36 54 142
COWELL, 43
COWLEY, 1
COX, 10 15 38 43 50 51 61 114
   139 142 146 152 168
COXETTER, 193
COZBY, 30
COZENS, 195
CRABB, 70 96 157
CRABTREE, 117 141 157
CRAGHEAD, 161
CRAIG, 38 140 165 180
CRAIGHEAD, 23 33 101 105 111
   125 156 171 192
CRAINE, 177
CRANE, 46 97 109
CRANK, 50
CRATCH, 32 56
CRAVENS, 127
CRAWFORD, 28 57 99 116 118
   127 134 135 142 161 163 200
CRAWSBY, 180
CREELEY, 16 54
CREESY, 16
CRENSHAW, 194
CRESS, 43
CREWS, 11
CREWSON, 18
CRIEN, 91
CRISMAN, 7
CRISMAS, 185
CRISPASS, 130
CROCK, 83
CROCKER, 135

CROCKET, 143 180
CROCKETTE, 69
CROFORD, 111
CROMPTON, 78 181
CROOKER, 92
CROSLAND, 182
CROSS, 14 17 18 29 53 56 162
CROUCH, 43
CROUGHTON, 66 123
CROW, 43 140 169 180
CROWDER, 1 43 171 195
CROWLEY, 60
CROWTEN, 66
CROZIER, 48
CRUCTHER, 108 177
CRUMB, 51
CRUTCHER 24, 87 105 111 117
   119 120 124 126 132 141 142
   145 149 152 157 164 166 183
   198
CRUTCHFIELD, 76 92 99
CUBBECK, 47
CUFF, 146 154 180
CUMMINGS, 17 66 72 108
CUMMINS, 123 163 182 194
CUNNIGHAM, 194
CUNNINGHAM, 38 50 91 116 130
   140 169
CUPID, 185
CURNEY, 154
CURREN, 11 132
CURRENT, 94
CURREY, 128 147 179
CURRIN, 102
CURRITHERS, 127
CURRY, 57 152 161
CURTIS, 70 156
CUTCHEN, 179
CYPRET, 152
DABNEY, 95 130 171 195
DADNEY, 194
DAGNER, 64
DAIS, 165
DALE, 2 16 80 90 164 172
DALES, 40
DALLAS, 86
DALZELL, 38 51
DAMERON, 40 41 49
DAMEWOOD, 28 115
DANDER, 19 82
DANIEL, 103 113 114 116 127

DANIEL (continued)
140 181 194
DARDIS, 13
DARIS, 41
DARMON, 128
DARNAL, 191
DARRETT, 181
DARTON, 148
DARVAN, 184
DAUGHERTY, 95
DAUGHTEN, 11
DAVALT, 158
DAVENPORT, 38
DAVICE, 199
DAVID, 17 34 60 77
DAVIDSON, 17 25 31 46 84 103
105 106 116 118 136 137 140
146 158 163 169 174 184 188
189
DAVIE, 31 109
DAVIS, 1 14 15 43 45 47 49 50 59
60 64 67 116 118 121 127 132-
134 140 146 148 158 161 163
165 168 169 171 172 178-180
185 191 194 195
DAVISON, 67 180 194
DAVY, 70
DAWDRY, 25
DAWDY, 69 101 108 122 125 127
131 133 135 142 146 155 158
162 165 167 177 181 182 184
186 190-192 197 198
DAWES, 39
DAWNING, 194
DAWSON, 37 52 59 64 130
DAY, 38 43 98
DAZELL, 43
DEADERICK, 48 54 56 105 114
145 151 160 161 190
DEADRICK, 113
DEAM, 147
DEAN, 28 47 101 116 180
DEATHERAGE, 21 110 160
DEBO, 2
DEBROCOR, 164
DEEK, 67
DEEKER, 51
DEES, 10
DEES, 14
DEFRIESE, 163
DELANDER, 22

DELAP, 28 40
DELARONDE, 198
DELASSUS, 80
DELOAH, 95
DELOCH, 130
DELOZENIER, 38
DEMENT, 11 123 182
DEMERON, 1
DEMOSS, 199
DEMPSEY, 181
DENARE, 158
DENER, 195
DENNESON, 106
DENNIS, 88 167 174 188 191
DENNISS, 128
DENNY, 14 92
DENSON, 172
DENTON, 40 42
DEPRIEST, 154
DERRYBERRY, 75
DESKINS, 27
DESTREHAN, 198
DEVINGTON, 6
DEVOE, 47
DEW, 24
DEWEL, 24
DEZASH, 191
DIAS, 76
DIBER, 130
DICE, 6
DICK, 125 134
DICKART, 185
DICKENS, 66 123
DICKENSON, 50 147
DICKERSON, 23 76
DICKEY, 106 129 180 194
DICKSON, 3 11 17 29 33 39 44 51
79 88 106 112 114 120 130 141
143 147 151 161 167 173 174
183 187 194
DICSON, 79
DIEL, 95
DIER, 76
DILL, 148
DILLAHUNTY, 104
DILLARD, 15 16 140 149 196
DILLIN, 92
DILLINHAM, 86
DILLON, 1 16 43 75
DITTO, 135
DIXON, 5 6 11 15 17 51 76 91 104

DIXON (continued)
144 165 179
DOAK, 154
DOANL, 153
DOBBIN, 2
DOBBINS, 106 114 140 148 169
DOBINS, 148
DOBKIN, 82 91
DOBS, 95
DOBY, 130
DOD, 126
DODD, 181
DODGE, 23
DODSON, 51 127 146 149 152
DOGAN, 76
DOGGED, 195
DOGGETT, 51 130
DOHERTY, 1 30 31 34 41 48 50
104 113 144 162 168 169 174
179 187
DOKE, 147
DOLE, 106
DOLEY, 94
DOLLIVAR, 195
DONALDSON, 27 72 148
DONALSON, 91
DONALSONKETH, 140
DONEL, 19
DONELSON, 5 27 36 49 83 108
128 133 134 144 184
DONOHO, 6
DONOHOO, 52
DONSON, 34
DOOBY, 111
DOOLEY, 67 99
DOOLY, 117
DORCAS, 102
DORE, 94
DOREN, 165
DORGENOIS, 198
DORRIS, 76
DOSER, 43
DOSS, 65 77
DOTSAN, 194
DOTY, 40 116
DOUGAN, 130
DOUGE, 175
DOUGHERTY, 11 39 70 79
DOUGLAS, 64 168
DOUGLASS, 6 50 64 66 67 77 83
98 112 140

DOUGLE, 38
DOW, 46
DOWELL, 43
DOWINING, 116
DOWLER, 38 49
DOWNEY, 164
DRACE, 44
DRAKE, 14 81 97 98 106 116 117
140 148 158 176 178 180 194
DRAPER, 16
DREAD, 141
DREW, 11 17 128 198
DREWLY, 160
DREWRY, 7
DRIGGS, 50
DRINCARD, 45
DRIVER, 89 116 148
DRUTCHER, 196
DRYDEN, 191
DRYDON, 84
DUBERRY, 127
DUDLEY, 66 123
DUFF, 143
DUFFIELD, 48
DUGGAR, 148
DUGGER, 44
DUGGIN, 50
DUGHERTY, 14
DUGLASS, 148
DUKE, 51 84 130 158 160 195
DULEY, 121
DUMROLE, 154
DUMVILL, 42
DUN, 39
DUNAWAY, 134
DUNCAN, 52
DUNHAM, 14 28
DUNING, 187
DUNKIN, 154
DUNLAP, 18 82 98 198
DUNLOP, 28 43 50
DUNN, 94 101 106 109 110 130
151 152 158 161 163 165 166
175 182 185 186 190 192 199
DUNNAGAN, 194
DUNNING, 173
DUNNINGHAM, 50
DUPEN, 160
DURHAM, 16
DURLEY, 194
DURNAL, 46

DURRIN, 50
DUTTON, 101
DWEHAN, 76
DYE, 176
DYER, 6 89 95 137 140 195
EAKIN, 120 160 162
EARLY, 74
EARWOOD, 106
EASLEY, 50
EASON, 162
EAST, 71
EASTIN, 105 147 151
EASTIS, 163
EASTLAND, 166 169
EASTLICK, 196
EASTON, 5
EATON, 31 76 87 180
EBERT, 198
ECHLEBURGER, 145
ECHOLS, 31 134
ECKFERD, 43
EDDY, 99
EDGAR, 58
EDINGTON, 180
EDMINSTON, 103 169
EDMISTON, 31 102 103
EDMONDSON, 146
EDMONSTON, 104
EDNEY, 127
EDWARD, 44 156 163
EDWARDS, 7 30 42 57 110 123
    127 165 178 181
ELAM, 43 93 146 163 194
ELANE, 158
ELCOTT, 33
ELDER, 134
ELGIN, 180
ELI, 15
ELIJAH, 185
ELIOTT, 114 154
ELKINS, 197
ELLEOTT, 193
ELLER, 106
ELLICOTT, 34 50
ELLIOT, 2 148
ELLIOTT, 82 83 148 163 174 179
    194
ELLIS, 26 38 43 51 67 109 121
ELLISAN, 194
ELLISON, 76 127 142 143
ELLISTON, 139 147

ELLUM, 19
ELM, 5
ELMORE, 47
ELSOD, 14
ELSTON, 84
ELTON, 86
ELUM, 125
EMERSON, 130 148
EMMERSON, 48
EMMETT, 135
ENCLE, 43
ENGLAND, 28 146
ENGLEMAN, 115 152 156
ENGLISH, 39 70 71 81 135
EPPENGER, 69
EPPERSON, 28 43
EPPS, 28 43 50
ERNEST, 39
ERWIN, 15 22 23 39 130 134 138
    159 179 183
ESERIDGE, 158
ESTE, 116
ESTES, 130 148 181
ESTICK, 120
ESTILL, 106
ESTIS, 34
ETHERAGE, 14 120
ETTES, 127
EUBANKS, 156
EVANS, 12 23 28 37 51 57 59 72
    73 89 154 163 166 171 175 180
    194
EVETTS, 15
EVITTS, 69
EWEL, 84 90
EWELL, 6 11
EWEN, 65 142
EWIL, 64
EWING, 11 23 31 61 102 109 110
    124 161 164
EWINGS, 14 76
EYCK, 47
EZETE, 130
FAGE, 181
FAGINS, 158
FAITNER, 127
FALEY, 76
FALING, 78
FALLIS, 148
FAMBROUGH, 31
FAN, 128

FANNIN, 157
FARAGOOD, 28
FARBY, 6
FARGUSSON, 186
FARIS, 106 130
FARLEY, 15
FARMER, 30 64 84 194
FARNSWORTH, 47 61
FARQUAHAR, 90
FARRAGOOD, 27
FARRAR, 194
FARRIS, 6 68
FARWELL, 85
FAVER, 180
FEAGELLY, 43
FEATHERSTONE, 153
FEATHERTON, 195
FEBRUARY, 186
FEEGARDER, 39
FELEN, 134
FELTS, 194
FENNER, 6 33 57 143 172 186
    190
FENWICK, 115
FERGUSON, 30 76 79 98 101
FERIS, 195
FERREL, 64 182
FERRICE, 195
FERRINGTON, 127 164
FEY, 106
FIELD, 181
FIELDS, 17 163 179 181
FIGURES, 43
FILSEY, 104
FINCH, 106
FINEH, 180
FINLAY, 38 67
FINLEY, 13 38 43
FINNEY, 106 161 180
FIPPS, 194
FISER, 26
FISHER, 140 181 185
FISK, 17 23 81 87
FITE, 16 64 81
FITLE, 94
FITTS, 70
FITXPATRICK, 116
FITZ, 163
FITZGERALD, 16 86
FITZPATRICK, 91 184 194
FITZRANDOLPH, 170

FIVEASH, 15
FIZRANDOLPH, 140
FIZZLE, 1 14
FLAKE, 109
FLANNAGIN, 136
FLEMING, 50 67 101 158 176
FLEMMING, 195
FLETCHER, 26 50 62 98 181 190
FLINNEN, 87
FLINT, 167
FLOWERS, 76 95
FLOYD, 38
FOLKES, 51
FONVILLE, 118
FORBES, 164
FORD, 6 51 96 162
FORD, 14 64 67 72 76
FORE, 48
FORGERY, 38
FORGY, 41
FORMAN, 14
FORMWALT, 27 52
FOROTS, 73
FORRESTER, 89
FORTE, 193
FORTNER, 30
FOSDICK, 84 163
FOSTER, 1 19 43 72 76 130 137
    140 143 161 169 183
FOUNTAIN, 100
FOURNIER, 126
FOURY, 130
FOUST, 28 38
FOWELER, 8
FOWLER, 85 90
FOX, 90
FRAILEY, 3
FRAISURE, 150
FRAKER, 128
FRANK, 102
FRANKLIN, 13 38 104 140
FRAZER, 155
FRAZIER, 39 118 160
FREEMAN, 103 169 189 194 196
FREY, 26
FRIERSON, 148
FRISBEY, 128
FRIZLE, 136
FRIZZEL, 76
FROTZE, 103
FRY, 127 158

FUDY, 50
FULGHUM, 146
FULKERSON, 75 163
FULKS, 1 84 199
FULLER, 22 106
FULLERTON, 148
FULTON, 48 106 148
FUQUA, 130
FURGESON, 79
FURGUSON, 43 122
FURNAGE, 194
GABLE, 160
GADDY, 6 67
GAGE, 47 198
GAINES, 7 62 181
GALAHER, 45
GALASPEY, 19
GALBREATH, 48
GALES, 95
GALISPIE, 136
GALLAGHER, 56
GALLASPIE, 180
GALLIGLY, 127
GALLIHER, 53
GALLION, 43
GALLOWAY, 56
GALT, 145
GAMBLE, 39 72 86 107 174 181
GANAWAY, 181
GANN, 28 62
GANNON, 194
GANSEVOORT, 24
GANT, 48
GANTER, 107 180
GAORE, 82
GARDENDENSHIRE, 44
GARDENIER, 35
GARDINAR, 2
GARDINER, 42 53-55 163
GARDNER, 101 141 153
GARFORTH, 181
GARKILE, 144
GARLAND, 169 181
GARNDER, 5
GARNER, 87 101 105 107 109
    119-120 122 133 147 148 150
    152 153 155 156 166 167 168
    171 176 180 182 194 197 200
GARNETT, 37
GAROLOR, 183
GARR, 166

GARRARD, 174
GARRET, 76 176
GARRETT, 111 133 171 180 191
GARRISON, 1 143 165
GARSON, 69
GASAGE, 194
GASS, 48
GAST, 28
GASTON, 44
GATES, 47 180
GATITS, 92
GAY, 102
GAYLES, 80
GEERY, 180
GENAERY, 122
GENTRY, 180
GEORGE, 96 137 153 159 184
GEREMIAN, 163
GERMAN, 1
GHANON, 163
GHOLSON, 154 180
GIBBONS, 38 43 95 181
GIBBS, 28 119
GIBSON, 3 10 16 24 35 38 116
    138 144 159 190
GILBERT, 33 94 114 135 137
GILBREATH, 28 103
GILCHRIST, 22 32 107 134
GILCREASE, 115
GILCREST, 14
GILDART, 95
GILE, 130
GILES, 59 137
GILHAM, 50 163
GILL, 23 90
GILLAM, 51
GILLESPIE, 5 28 33 50 57 134
    154
GILLESPY, 43
GILLESS, 17
GILLIAM, 88
GILLIESPIE, 17
GILLIHAN, 36
GILLISPIE, 104 114 134 137 161
    169
GILLS, 37
GILLUM, 181
GILMON, 109
GILMORE, 31 114 137
GILPIN, 28
GILSPIE, 113

GIMMEL, 53
GIMPSEY, 130
GIN, 114
GION, 44
GISS, 17
GIST, 100
GIVEN, 11 65
GIVENS, 30 107
GLASCOCK, 177
GLASCOW, 96
GLASGOW, 55 172
GLASS, 62 116 128 154
GLASSS, 180
GLEASON, 121
GLEN, 11 123
GLENN, 3 13 15 17 66
GLOVER, 29 180
GOARD, 74
GOARE, 5 87
GODMAN, 75
GOFF, 101
GOFORTH, 199
GOHERN, 97
GOLAHER, 38
GOLSAN, 163
GOODALL, 11 16
GOODE, 118 148
GOODING, 88
GOODKNIGHT, 116
GOODLOE, 124 132 135 157 161
GOODMAN, 17 107
GOODPASTER, 81
GOODSON, 90
GOODWIN, 171 188
GOOR, 82
GOORE, 16 82
GORDAN, 116
GORDEN, 155
GORDON, 27 33 36 39 54 64 80
   84 90 96 105 121 130 137 159
   167 169 175 192 194
GORE, 11 91
GORMAN, 11
GORSON, 67
GOSUT, 20
GOWEN, 158 171 185
GOWER, 109 148 154 166
GOZA, 45
GRACEY, 31
GRAGG, 39
GRAHAM, 2 39 40 48 82 94 95

GRAHAM (continued)
   105 116 137 138 146 169 183
   195
GRAMEIN, 38
GRANDOE, 15
GRANT, 37 40 44 51 84 163
GRARY, 11
GRAVES, 19 105 126 169 178 181
   195
GRAY, 11 15 22 23 28 36 51 54
   130 131 163 169 180 189 194
   195 200
GRAYSON, 50 180 181 195
GREAN, 118
GREEN, 1 11 15 28 38 45 70 107
   118 148 161 178 179
GREENE, 30 54
GREENLEAF, 86
GREENLEE, 32 171
GREER, 11 29 37 40 41 52 59 87
   107 126 150 158 165 168 176
GREGG, 51
GREGGORY, 54
GREGORY, 17
GREGRY, 127
GRENIER, 128
GREY, 1 117 165
GRIER, 118 163
GRIFFEN, 155
GRIFFIN, 14 105 107 116 127 129
   132 148 155 161 200
GRIFFING, 76
GRIFFISS, 14
GRIFFITH, 91 127 163 194 200
GRIGGS, 194
GRIMES, 63 111 148 175 192
GRINDALL, 141
GRISHAM, 16 107 149
GRISSEL, 38
GRISWOLD, 70 124
GROSON, 106
GROVE, 44
GROVER, 88
GROVES, 38 50
GRUNDY, 23
GUCGARD, 198
GUDRAIN, 162
GUIN, 36 125
GULLET, 114 195
GULLY, 44
GUNN, 200

GUNTER, 71 78 87 127
GURDON, 36
GUSOT, 63
GUTHERIE, 194
GUTHRIE, 160
GUZZARD, 133
GWIN, 37 66 123 143 144 173 187
GWINN, 59 169
GYSTEN, 1
HACKETT, 44
HADGES, 43
HADLEY, 5 19 33 138
HADLY, 37
HAGON, 38
HAGOOD, 38 43 51
HAIL, 65 90 144 148 175
HAILEY, 191
HAINS, 43 57
HALBERT, 180
HALES, 195
HALEY, 28
HALIMAN, 127
HALL, 6 25 38 44 47 50 54 84 88
    98 107 111 112 115 119 127
    149 152 154 165 167 169 181
    185 195
HALLIS, 127
HALNEY, 130
HAM, 38 50
HAMBLET, 110 195
HAMBLETON, 28 34 36 38 51 78
HAMBLIN, 179
HAMBLTON, 38
HAMER, 101 163
HAMIL, 16
HAMILTON, 10 14 48 66 67 107
    110 116 121 124 138 157 160
    200
HAMMOCK, 16
HAMONS, 15
HAMPTON, 11 25 47 53 56 72 77
    158 193 200
HANA, 72
HANCOCK, 11 35 93 157 165 181
HANEY, 9 11 76
HANKER, 44
HANKINS, 84
HANKS, 1 111 114 146 183 194
HANNA, 23 130
HANNAN, 142
HANNER, 28

HANNUM, 186
HANNUN, 32
HANSFORD, 28
HANUM, 93
HAR--, 102
HARBISON, 146
HARBOUR, 7
HARDEMAN, 101 111 113 116
    123 133 134 157 159 161 169
    180 194
HARDEN, 23 101 119 180
HARDEUSOLE, 116
HARDEWAY, 159
HARDIMAN, 31
HARDIN, 116 130 174
HARDING, 119 199
HARDISON, 180
HARDMAN, 66
HARDY, 60
HARELSON, 107
HARELY, 38
HARGAVE, 154
HARISON, 107
HARLAN, 163
HARMAN, 2 83 86 90 98 107
HARMON, 12 20 54 58 64
HARNER, 127
HARNEY, 52 109 114 138 179 185
HARPAN, 127
HARPER, 2 12 39 94 183
HARPOLE, 11
HARPOOL, 12
HARPOTT, 14
HARRAL, 118
HARREL, 95 148
HARRINGTON, 108
HARRIS, 5 13 16 17 28 31 36 44
    50 59 62 66 70 90 107 113 114
    132 134 138 145 146 147 149
    150 163 167 174 193 195
HARRISON, 11 29 62 69 97 107
    114 128 151 153 158 160 165
HARROD, 1
HARRY, 86
HARRYS, 46
HART, 14 24 56 58 59 92 114 161
    171 181 185
HARTLEY, 50
HARTWELL, 146
HARVEY, 5 11 18 60 67 90 99
    121 127 142 157 173

HARVY, 79
HARWELL, 22 114
HARWOOD, 72
HASSEL, 127 142
HASTING, 107
HASTINGS, 46 107 158
HATCHER, 14 36
HATCHET, 76
HATLEN, 81
HATTEN, 158
HATY, 76
HAUCK, 36 60
HAUDSBOROUGH, 85
HAUSE, 80
HAUSS, 135
HAVEY, 43
HAWK, 27
HAWKINS, 51 54 67 88
HAWKLEY, 46
HAY, 94
HAYNES, 38 39 55 146
HAYS, 11 14 29 33 43 54 100 120
    151 171
HAYSBOROUGH, 106
HAYWOOD, 6 33 104 147 162 169
HAZARD, 112
HAZEN, 40
HAZLET, 93
HEARELD, 41
HEART, 11
HEATH, 51 54
HEATON, 102 109
HEATSON, 16
HEBIER, 199
HECKNEY, 51
HELLUMS, 116 117
HELSHOURER, 130
HELTON, 51
HEMPHILL, 66 123 194
HENBY, 130
HENDERICKS, 176
HENDERSON, 1 18 29 31 38 39
    54 55 58 111 127 148 158 159
    164 165 169 192 195 198 199
HENDLEY, 71 85
HENDRICK, 38 173
HENDRIX, 11 116
HENFORD, 38
HENLEY, 8 92 116
HENLY, 38 44
HENNEN, 151

HENRY, 26 61 103 136 166 169
HERBET, 8
HERN, 79
HERNDON, 91 130 134
HERREY, 191
HERRIN, 38
HERRING, 17 64
HERROD, 27
HERRON, 47 175
HERTY, 2
HERVEY, 15 64 76
HESS, 24 26 101 154 161
HESSAN, 17
HEWELETT, 57
HEWITT, 156
HEWLETT, 22 57 84 146
HEYLAND, 145
HICKEY, 28 80 135
HICKMAN, 62 103 113 123 138
    166 168 169 175 185
HICKMON, 5
HICKORY, 80
HICKS, 21 90 105 112 127 164
HICKSON, 54
HICMA, 66
HIGGINBOTHAM, 15 134
HIGGINS, 46 181
HIGH, 95
HIGHTOUR, 138
HIGHTOWER, 138 154
HILL, 6 15 33 44 79 96 101 104
    107 127 129 130 132 136 138
    143 153 154 158 162 163 173
    178 180 188 189 194 200
HILLAMN, 46
HILLARD, 62
HINES, 33
HINKLEY, 46
HINNAT, 28
HINSON, 38 165
HINTON, 151
HIPPENSTALL, 47
HIPSHER, 9
HIROR, 100
HISE, 29
HITCH, 50
HITER, 124 157
HOAZRD, 185
HOBB, 104 147 169
HOBBS, 24 160 185
HODGE, 9 31 78 122

217

HODGES, 57
HODGIN, 41
HOFF, 46
HOFFMAN, 151
HOGAN, 77 95 116 118
HOGE, 37
HOGG, 5 10 21 68 134 161
HOGGAT, 192
HOGGATT, 161
HOGLIN, 28
HOGUN, 1 92
HOLAND, 101
HOLBERT, 170
HOLCOMBE, 45
HOLDEN, 165
HOLLAD, 135
HOLLADAY, 101
HOLLADY, 88
HOLLAND, 55 130 148
HOLLIDAY, 90
HOLLIMAN, 107 116
HOLLING, 12
HOLLINGSWORTH, 23 79
HOLLINGWORTH, 43
HOLLMAN, 116
HOLLOMAN, 90
HOLMES, 89 101 116
HOLT, 17 28 38 51 54 116
HOMAN, 45
HOND, 85
HONE, 44
HOOD, 161
HOOGGET, 156
HOOKER, 192 194
HOOKS, 180 194
HOOPER, 100 192 196
HOOVER, 182
HOPE, 44 195
HOPKINS, 16 18 41 53 56 72 82
  95 105 138 158 169
HOPTON, 54
HORD, 12 27 38 51 101
HORN, 146
HORNBACK, 38
HORTIS, 181
HORTON, 163 174
HOURS, 154
HOUSE, 32 63 148
HOUSTON, 18 44 45 51 82 138
  194

HOWARD, 11 16 17 26 70 91 92
  185
HOWE, 76
HOWELL, 13 38 43 44 79 122
  132 157 162 163
HUBBARD, 199
HUBBETT, 11
HUBBS, 160
HUCHESON, 44
HUCKABY, 44
HUDDLESTON, 17 64 67
HUDEBURK, 44
HUDSON, 88 167 172 175
HUDSPETH, 134 148
HUEINGSON, 148
HUEY, 80
HUFF, 10 17
HUFFAKER, 29
HUFFMAN, 17 118
HUFFTAKER, 35 40
HUGGENS, 67 68
HUGGINS, 32 176
HUGH, 190
HUGHES, 44 84 114 138 186
HUGHITT, 118
HUGHLET, 66 123
HUGHS, 49 50
HUGHTELL, 75
HUGININ, 24
HUGLET, 66
HULE, 9
HULERT, 10
HULL, 21 22 29 98 105 143 144
  188
HULLBELL, 47
HULME, 57 109 126 134 151 157
  159 161 175 190
HUMER, 142
HUMMEL, 38
HUMPHREY, 15 62
HUMPHREYS, 23 76 137 179
HUMPHRIES, 44 50 80
HUNESMAN, 11
HUNLEY, 11
HUNNEYCUTT, 148
HUNT, 12 15 33 39 47 79 96 116
  130 163 177 179
HUNTER, 19 36 49 96 138 144
  161 169 194
HUNTSMAN, 28 47

M'CRORY (continued)
157 158 195
M'CUESTION, 118 184
M'CULLEY, 198
M'CULLOCH, 33
M'CULLOCK, 159 170 175 179
M'CULLUM, 117
M'CULLY, 23 148
M'CURREY, 104
M'CUSTON, 31
M'CUTCHEN, 133 180
M'DANIEL, 16 74 79 93 101 157 199
M'DONALD, 14 40 44 65 74 75 77 116 146 169 196
M'DONNEL, 81
M'DONNOLD, 80 82 83 92 99 100
M'DOWELL, 127
M'DUFF, 130
M'DUGARD, 127
M'EACHRAN, 64
M'EWEN, 72 78 80 87 93 112 180
M'EWIN, 165 197
M'FARLEN, 105
M'FERRIN, 65 81 86
M'GAHEY, 127
M'GAUGH, 101
M'GAVOCK, 104 136 138 160 169
M'GEE, 31 82 101
M'GILL, 195
M'GILVEY, 141
M'GINSON, 64 74
M'GLOUGHLIN, 195
M'GRADY, 180
M'GUIRE, 27 106
M'GUNDY, 25
M'HOLLAND, 94
M'INTOSH, 162
M'INTRYRE, 141
M'IVER, 11 82 134 145 178 191
M'JIMSEY, 130
M'KABE, 11
M'KARAHAN, 175
M'KAY, 75
M'KEE, 6
M'KELVY, 139
M'KENDREE, 28
M'KENRIE, 163
M'KERAHAN, 146
M'KESICK, 117
M'KINNEY, 11 110

M'KINSEY, 42 127
M'KINSTREY, 47
M'KISSIC, 25
M'KISSICK, 69 107 122 143 150 173 188
M'KNIGHT, 44 88 132 134
M'LAIN, 127 146
M'LAUGHLIN, 130 158 182
M'LEMORE, 23 24 189
M'LEOD, 14 64
M'LIN, 44 132
M'LSKEY, 149
M'MAHAN, 3
M'MAHON, 117
M'MANN, 1
M'MECLAY, 107
M'MEEN, 154
M'MELLON, 133
M'MICKEN, 130
M'MILLAN, 25 28
M'MILLIAN, 84
M'MILLON, 107
M'MULLEN, 127 146
M'MURRY, 74 152
M'MURTEE, 143
M'MURTREE, 186
M'NAERY, 66
M'NAIR, 44
M'NAIRY, 31 92 104 113 123 156 161 178 185 187 188
M'NEALY, 118
M'NEELY, 93 157
M'NEES, 118
M'NEESE, 24
M'NIGHT, 1 182 196
M'NUTT, 10 13 14 28 67
M'PEAK, 127 134 195
M'PEKE, 107
M'PHAIL, 141
M'PHARLAND, 39
M'PHETERS, 51
M'PIKE, 181
M'QUEEN, 107
M'QUESTION, 134
M'QUIRE, 163
M'QUISTEN, 92 185
M'RAVIN, 1
M'RAY, 163
M'REYNOLDS, 101 107 132 158
M'RIERY, 107
M'RINNY, 25

MAYFIELD, 31 99 100 130
MAYHAM, 98
MAYS, 65
MAZE, 135
MCALL, 131
MCANDREW, 54
MCAULEY, 19
MCBEE, 48
MCCAMPBELL, 38
MCCANSE, 38
MCCARMACK, 38
MCCLELLAN, 36
MCCLENHAN, 58
MCCOWN, 38
MCCRAVENS, 52
MCCRAW, 38
MCCULLOUGH, 43 54 55
MCFALL, 111
MCFARLAND, 50
MCGEE, 59
MCGHEE, 40
MCGINNESS, 53
MCINTIRE, 50
MCIVER, 38
MCKIDDY, 50
MCKLERPY, 118
MCLAUGLIN, 44
MCLAURINE, 122
MCLEON, 200
MCLOMEN, 43
MCMAHON, 50
MCMILLAN, 50
MCMINN, 52
MCNAVIN, 1
MCNEAR, 38
MCNEIL, 58
MCNUTT, 1
MCORRY, 30
MCOTAY, 6
MCPETERS, 38
MCRARY, 18
MCUESTION, 113
MCUMMIN, 19
MCVAY, 43
MEAD, 24 28
MEADOR, 181
MEADOW, 91 146
MEANS, 79 107
MEARS, 116
MEASE, 17
MEAUX, 148

MEBANE, 122
MECRENY, 176
MEDEARIS, 117
MEDERAS, 138
MEDIARIS, 194
MEDLOCK, 134
MEDRICK, 149
MEEK, 160 177
MEEKER, 22
MEIGS, 48 69
MEKELL, 149
MELTON, 14 75
MENDINGEALL, 39
MENES, 38
MERCER, 19 77 98
MEREDITH, 54 136
MEREM, 5
MERHCT, 8
MERIDETH, 103 168
MERIDY, 160
MERIWEATHER, 28
MERONEY, 147
MERRICK, 17
MERRIT, 60 146
MERRITT, 60 154
MERRYMAN, 137
METCALF, 17 160
MEZZIAN, 199
MGEE, 17
MIAM, 161
MICHELL, 47
MIDISON, 181
MIDKISS, 29
MIDLEY, 28
MIETON, 1
MIGET, 16
MILES, 180
MILLEN, 16
MILLER, 5 8 12 22 27 36 38 39
    50 56 64 84 88 95 105 112 134
    146 149 163 171
MILLOGAN, 28
MILLS, 51 80 84 106 135 180 189
MILLWRIGHT, 149
MILTON, 114
MINOR, 28 150
MINSITS, 2
MITCHEL, 1 91
MITCHELL, 27 28 33 36 44 48 50
    60 62 72 76 77 91 107 117 118
    125 134 137 138 142 157 159

MITCHELL (continued)
161 166 184
MIXFIELD, 117
MIZELL, 183
MNEELY, 90
MOAD, 60
MOCRY, 31
MODGLIN, 11
MONDAY, 50
MONGLE, 90
MONROE, 1
MONTFLORENCE, 126 144
MONTFORD, 104 113 114 168
170 178
MONTGOMERY, 11 15 29 37 40
44 69 93 101 136 149 151 158
171 180 181 185 186
MOODY, 127
MOOR, 18 96
MOORE, 1 2 6 14 17 18 28 29 37
41 43-45 49-52 54 59 62 63 78
86 116 118 120 126-128, 134
136 138 139 149 150 158 160
166 172 174 176 180 181 184
189 193 195
MOORS, 2 16
MORDICA, 50
MORE, 64
MORELACK, 43
MORGAN, 6 141 167
MORGAN, 5 42 45 67 79 80 84 87
88 94 95 105 128 135 173
MORISSON, 136
MORLAIN, 165
MORR, 51
MORRAL, 31
MORRASON, 130
MORRAY, 1 28
MORRER, 181
MORRES, 146
MORRIS, 39 53 128 129 134 170
MORRISET, 51
MORRISETT, 43
MORRISON, 43 103
MORRISS, 26 143 189 197
MORROW, 174 186
MORSE, 33 64 67 77
MORTON, 38 44 50 163 179 196
MOSELY, 72
MOSER, 128
MOSES, 5

MOSLANDER, 174
MOSS, 3 15 64 92 109 116
MOSTANDER, 187
MOTHERAL, 127
MOTHERALL, 104 137 138
MOTT, 39 194
MOTTIS, 44
MOUNT, 107 118 195
MUCKETRATH, 83
MUCKLEROY, 107 169
MUGHES, 155
MUHERN, 31
MUIR, 22
MULKA, 171
MULKEY, 182
MULLEN, 160
MUNFORD, 33 36
MUNHELD, 162
MURFEE, 112 113 141
MURFREE, 19 91 184 194
MURFREY, 170
MURNEY, 54
MURPHEY, 85 88 163
MURPHREE, 104
MURPHRY, 101
MURPHY, 18 35 41 44 47 58 75
94 181
MURRAY, 144 187
MURRELL, 31 116
MURRY, 174 189
MURY, 173
MUSE, 127 138
MUSGROVE, 101 118
MUSICK, 15
MUSLANDER, 144
MUSREY, 11
MYERS, 51 54 110 118
NABOURS, 78
NAIL, 83 183
NALL, 163
NANCE, 50 131 165 181
NARIMOR, 28
NARK, 139
NARVILLE, 165
NASH, 23 75 89 98 104 151 161
165 195
NEAL, 7 87 141 146 160 163 192
NEALY, 105
NEEDHAM, 94
NEEL, 128 190
NEELEY, 67 180

227

PAINE, 10 12 21 90
PAIROTT, 46
PALLET, 181
PALMER, 11 15 17 92 114
PANE, 93
PANKEY, 64
PANKY, 181
PANS, 110
PARCE, 106
PARHAM, 162 181
PARISH, 166
PARK, 134 149 161 190
PARKE, 60
PARKER, 1 5 15 17 28 32 37 43
  56 59 75 84 107 117 140 149
  159 172 177 179 181 185
PARKES, 195
PARKISON, 30
PARKS, 134 156 191
PARLENA, 93
PARONS, 66
PARRISH, 101
PARROT, 10 63
PARRY, 117 161
PARSINS, 66
PARSON, 58 186 193
PARSONS, 37 38 50 59 60 114
  116 124 127 145 159 163
PARTEE, 149
PARTNER, 89
PATCH, 45
PATE, 7 64 84 163
PATIET, 75
PATRICK, 172 188 189
PATTEN, 136
PATTER, 163
PATTERSON, 11 32 38 39 55 74
  101 103 104 108 128 140 148
  165 168
PATTESON, 117
PATTON, 22 33 36 38 76 90 103
  107 113 118 135 140 146 162
  170 180 194
PATTY, 64 69
PAUL, 28 125 180
PAXTON, 22 117 130
PAYNE, 11 44 92 102 118 150
  163
PAYTON, 5 91 140 184 193
PEACCOCK, 134
PEACH, 145

PEACOCK, 158 165 182 187 195
PEADY, 103
PEARCE, 25 143
PEARSALL, 194
PEARSE, 38
PEARSON, 36 51 88 167 198
PEATZ, 22
PECK, 134 190
PEDDY, 136 155 168
PEEBLES, 127 146
PEERY, 130
PEETERS, 50
PENCOCK, 117
PENDARVIS, 17
PENDERGRASS, 11 193
PENKSTON, 68
PENNEY, 146
PEPPER, 124 181
PERKINS, 7 29 47 71 79 82 101
  102 113 116 142 146 159 170
  183 185 194
PERRIG, 195
PERRY, 11 25 105 106 110 116
  117 126 127 134 165 192
PERRYMAN, 127
PERSALL, 193
PERSON, 116 140
PERSONS, 170 196
PESSONS, 71
PESTALOZZI, 26
PETER, 52 159
PETERSON, 9 195
PETRO, 159
PETROE, 148
PETTAWAY, 194
PETTEGRUE, 82
PETTEY, 154
PETTIS, 127
PETTUS, 163
PETTWAY, 194
PETTY, 151
PEYTON, 38
PHAGAN, 40
PHAGEN, 30
PHARR, 11 107 167
PHEGAN, 37
PHELAN, 28 94
PHILIP, 14 28
PHILIPS, 26 43 74 101 181 194
PHILL, 41 196
PHILLIPS, 2 5 16 37 58 59 63 90

PHILLIPS (continued)
100 104 110 113 118 127 134
147 149 161 167 170 172 188
PHILPOTT, 15
PHURRISS, 117
PICKARD, 101 130 173 187
PICKERING, 26 127 128 182
PICKETT, 127
PIERCE, 46 109 181 182
PIGG, 182
PIKE, 26
PILLOW, 92 116 117 120 138 146
168 170 180 185
PINCKNEY, 117
PINDENGRASS, 42
PINKERTON, 154
PINKLEY, 109 151
PINKNEY, 40
PINKSTON, 180
PINN, 44
PINSON, 101
PIPER, 14 15 190
PIPKIN, 10 11
PIRKINS, 117
PISTOLE, 95
PITKINSON, 55
PITMAN, 107
PITT, 73 84
PITTMAN, 72
PITTS, 107
PITTWAY, 39
PLUMLY, 140
PLUMMER, 24 131 179
PLUMUR, 105
PLUNKET, 11
POE, 68
POGUE, 27
POINDEXTER, 51
POLK, 37 56 58 59 104 113 114
161 162 168 178 193
POOL, 17 76 79
POPE, 101 183
PORTER, 1 16 18 23 33 36 40 48
53 57 105 106 110 112 114-117
127 130 140 146 147 161 194
198
PORTERFIELD, 14 69 114 155
174 181 196
POSTON, 133
POTTER, 23
POTTERS, 50

POTTS, 154 163
POWEL, 66 90 95 132 163
POWELL, 11 14 124 130 149 159
POWER, 98
POWERS, 144
POYDRASS, 199
POYZER, 101 105 162
PRATT, 28 29 44 50
PRESS, 66
PRESTON, 60
PREWETT, 140 171
PREWITT, 91
PREWT, 98
PRICE, 17 38 56 77 80 163 165
171 174 187 195
PRICHETT, 29
PRIDE, 44
PRIEST, 184
PRIESTLY, 183
PRIMM, 180
PRINCE, 135 165 173 174
PRITCHARD, 47
PRITCHER, 90
PRITCHETT, 49 52
PROBART, 175
PROBERT, 117
PROPS, 123
PROVINCE, 43
PRUETT, 10 122
PRYOR, 6 25 131
PUCKKINGS, 184
PUGH, 16 29 76 101 117 127 163
PULUM, 180
PURDY, 146
PURKEN, 79 181
PURKEY, 42
PURKLE, 134
PURNEL, 165
PURNELL, 83 96 118
PURR, 117
PURRIS, 50 108
PURSELL, 5 118
PURSLY, 23
PURVES, 101
PUTERFIELD, 11
PUTTON, 117
QUARLES, 87
RABEY, 173
RABUCK, 158
RABY, 173 189
RACHAEL, 42 131

SIM, 156
SIMMERMAN, 43
SIMMON, 194
SIMMONS, 51 65 130 143 164 179
    180 194
SIMMS, 23 166
SIMPKINS, 175
SIMPSON, 6 25 47 52 88 108 134
    146 150 154 162 163 167 171
    179 187 189
SIMS, 43 50 84 117 130 145 149
SINCLAIR, 46
SINCLEAR, 39
SINDENBERGER, 158
SING, 98
SINGLETON, 158 181
SISSONS, 194
SITLER, 145
SITTON, 11
SITWEN, 107
SIXTON, 64
SKINNER, 141 144 173 187
SLATE, 137
SLATER, 155 167 168 199
SLATS, 176
SLINBOUGH, 28
SLOAN, 30 32 135 165
SLOANE, 17
SLODE, 141
SLOE, 16
SLOP, 141
SLOR, 102
SLOULALTT, 181
SLVESTER, 76
SMART, 17 90
SMEDLY, 51
SMELSOR, 100
SMILEY, 29 51
SMITH, 7 13 14 16 17 18 21 23
    25-28 32 33 36 37 41 44-51
    55-58 61 64 66 70 75-77 79 84
    85 87-89 95 96 101 103-105
    107 109-111 116 123 127 129
    130 134 140 141 143 146 157
    159 161 163 165 167 170 172
    176 179 180 187 193-195 197
SMITHFELL, 199
SMITHFIELD, 23 38
SMITTEN, 116
SMOTHERS, 97
SNAPP, 28 39 181

SNEED, 120 196
SNELL, 66 103
SNIDER, 50
SNODDY, 27
SNOW, 18 46 65 90 118 121 164
SNYDER, 7
SOAN, 73
SOINER, 77
SOLOMON, 101
SOMERVILLE, 109 151
SOPHY, 102
SORREL, 137 141
SPAFFORD, 70
SPAIN, 1 39 76
SPAKE, 148
SPARKS, 70 76
SPEAD, 130
SPEAKER, 134
SPEER, 149
SPELL, 162
SPENCE, 106 118 165 181 195
SPENCER, 25 112 133 147 180
SPICER, 126
SPINK, 37
SPIRES, 28
SPNCER, 114
SPOON, 163
SPRADBURG, 1
SPRAGGINS, 59
SPRATT, 175
SPREADLIN, 81
SPRENKLE, 116
SPRING, 127
SPYKER, 127 130
SQUIER, 101 115 127 163 180
SQUIRER, 145 154 194
STACEY, 152
STACY, 101 145
STAFFORD, 11 17 44
STAINBECK, 102 151
STAINS, 43
STALLIONS, 11 90
STAMPER, 103
STAMPS, 118
STANDEFER, 191
STANFORD, 15
STANLEY, 122 146
STAPLETON, 146
STATER, 121 149
STAURT, 62
STEADS, 45

TANNEHILL, 24 155
TANNER, 52 57 194
TAPLEY, 102
TARKINTON, 154
TARPLEY, 102 181
TARRANT, 146
TATE, 1 15 43 44 51 64 86 199
TATEM, 7
TATUM, 6 19 103 113 118 136
  173
TAUNT, 172
TAYLER, 116
TAYLOR, 1 5 7 14 40 45 49 53 57
  59 64 68 74 76 79 100 101 108
  117 124 127 129, 134 140 146
  149 150 157 161 164 179 183
  194 195
TEAL, 7
TEASLE, 181
TEEL, 63 75 85
TEEZEER, 55
TELFORD, 50
TELL, 19
TEMPLE, 44 55 139 180
TENNESON, 134
TENNESSON, 135
TENNISON, 180
TERMENT, 43
TERRELL, 10
TERREY, 149
TERRIL, 164
TERRILL, 108
TERRY, 74 75 145 155 171 191
TERVIN, 84
TESLEY, 170
THATCHER, 11
THAUGHTER, 39
THEBODEAUX, 198
THIGPEN, 181
THOMAS, 6 7 15 19 20 41 57 63
  68 76 79 85 102 122 127 134
  149 154 157 180
THOMPSON, 5 11 16 28 29 32 34
  36 39 44 51 76 78 92 95 101
  113 114 118 120 127 134 139
  143 145 150 154 164–166 175
  189 191 199
THORN, 179
THORNTON, 72 182
THORTON, 107
THRET, 158

THRIFT, 140 170 174
THROOP, 200
THRUSTON, 69.
THURMAN, 145
THURMOND, 162
THURSBY, 33
THURSTON, 39
THWEATT, 181
THYLMAN, 105 120 132
TIBS, 51
TILFORD, 124
TILL, 173
TILLEY, 125
TILMAN, 139 140 146 187
TILMON, 101 127 143 144 154
  172 188
TILSEY, 136
TIPTON, 49 135
TITSWORTH, 55
TOBER, 26
TODD, 28 165
TOLLEY, 95
TOM, 180
TOMLIN, 28
TOMLINSON, 130
TOMMERSON, 168
TOMPSON, 19
TONEY, 117
TOOLEY, 2
TOPP, 159
TORIAN, 1
TOTTEN, 9 14 18 64 67 68 73 81
  82 88 95
TOWNSEND, 2 94 119
TRANTHAM, 194
TRAVERS, 95 158
TRAVIS, 12
TRAYLOR, 144
TREDWAY, 50
TREDWELL, 1
TREMBLE, 180 194
TRIBBLE, 175
TRIGG, 10 25 36 66 83 85 87 96
  105 106 108–111 114 115 121
  124 125 127 133 150
TRIM, 102
TRIMBLE, 34 36 44 53 98 113
TRIVEAT, 107
TROTHER, 116
TROTTER, 155
TROUSDALE, 77 79 127

WILDER, 139
WILFORD, 118
WILKERSON, 78 96
WILKINS, 45 101 137
WILKINSON, 39 86
WILKISON, 66
WILKS, 28
WILLARD, 69
WILLET, 28
WILLETT, 52
WILLEY, 116
WILLIAM, 76
WILLIAMS, 1 5 7 9-11 15-17 23-
25 28-30 32 35 36 44 55 58 59
65 68 70 76 77 79 86 89 90 92
98 101-103 107 114 115 119
127 129-132 139 143 144 147
162 164 165 170-174 179 186-
190 193 195
WILLIAMSON, 21 76 98 109 127
130 151 156 164 180 181 183
195
WILLIE, 127
WILLIED, 107
WILLIMS, 179
WILLIS, 6 18 25 64 87 127 141
180
WILLOUGHBY, 67
WILLS, 130
WILMON, 76
WILSON, 1 2 5 7 11 16 23 27 30
32 39 40 43 44 51-55 61 62 66
77 84 86 90 91 101 103 105
107 117 118 123 131 134 135
144 146 154 157 158 167 170
178 180 181 183 195
WINCHESTER, 56 66 123 139
168 170
WINER, 98
WINFORD, 7
WINIELY, 92
WINKLE, 95
WINN, 11 24 96 107 122 165
WINSETT, 127
WINSTEAD, 179
WINSTON, 178
WINTAKER, 122
WINTER, 198
WIRBITTING, 99
WIRK, 107
WISEMAN, 15 80 95

WISENOR, 179
WISTLE, 87
WITCHER, 2 11 65 95
WITHERSPOON, 101 127 146 149
WITKERALD, 105
WITT, 30 39 75
WLLIAMS, 87
WLLIMS, 48
WOBACK, 64
WODKINS, 60
WODLEY, 195
WOLF, 39 110 117 164
WOLKMAN, 75
WOLSON, 107
WOOD, 11 24 25 39 81 92 93 107
116 130 148 154 180 195
WOODALE, 134
WOODARD, 102 116 164 178
WOODCOCK, 76
WOODLOW, 79
WOODS, 7 18 69 82 122 127 139
164 175
WOODSON, 72 181
WOODWORTH, 47
WOOLARD, 52
WOOLDRIDGE, 115
WOOLSEY, 29 128
WOOTEN, 94
WOOTON, 80
WORK, 62
WORLSEY, 24
WORMLEY, 180 195
WRIGHT, 7 8 14 16 28 34 44 51
64 65 89 114 130 138 139 151
154 164 165 173 177 188
WRITTEN, 167
WYAND, 159
WYATT, 139 153
WYGRAM, 129
WYLAND, 105
YAIS, 108
YANCEY, 29 39
YANDLE, 6
YARBOROUGH, 130 135 144 189
YARBURY, 92 185
YARNELL, 160
YATES, 114 119
YEARY, 158
YENT, 29 35
YEWELL, 130
YORK, 10 127

Our Ancestors of Albany County, New York, Volumes 1 and 2

Our Ancestors of Cuyahoga County, Ohio, Volume 1
(with Patricia P. Nelson)

Ralls County, Missouri Settlement Records, 1832-1853

Records of Randolph County, Missouri, 1833-1964

Ten Thousand Missouri Taxpayers

*The "Show-Me" Guide to Missouri: Sources for
Genealogical and Historical Research*

CD: Dickson County, Tennessee Marriage Records, 1817-1879

*CD: Index to the Arkansas General Land Office, 1820-1907
Volumes 1-10*

CD: Missouri, Volume 3

CD: Tennessee Genealogical Records

CD: Tennessee Genealogical Records, Volumes 1-3

23544233R00135

Made in the USA
Charleston, SC
25 October 2013